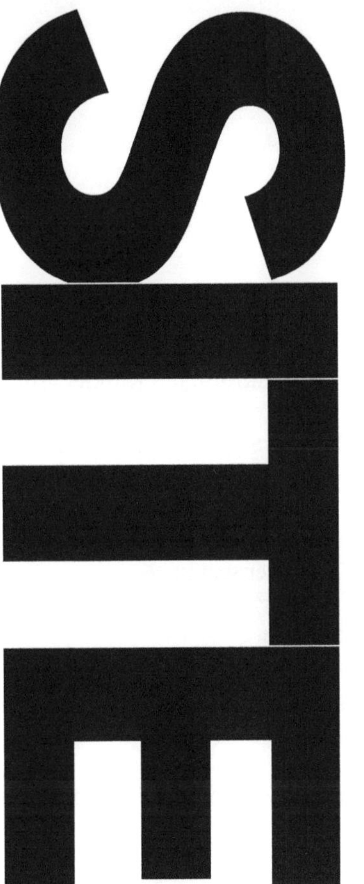
SITE

PUBLISHER & EDITOR: Sven-Olov Wallenstein
EDITORIAL BOARD: Brian Manning Delaney, Power Ekroth, Jeff Kinkle, Trond Lundemo, Staffan Lundgren, Karl Lydén, Helena Mattsson, Meike Schalk, Susan Schuppli, Kim West
GRAPHIC DESIGN: Konst & Teknik

SITE
Kungstensgatan 26
SE-113 57 Stockholm
Sweden

www.sitemagazine.net
info@sitemagazine.net

SUBMISSIONS: Text proposals to be sent to info@sitemagazine.net

ISSN 1650-7894
ISBN 978-91-86883-07-2

Distributed by Axl Books

31–32.2012

CONTENTS

Remake Remodel

This is the new version of SITE. Since the most recent issue, no. 29–30 (2010), we have had to cope with the difficult problem of having our funding from the Swedish Cultural Council reduced by two thirds. While for decades this government body has been a major and generous source for Swedish cultural journals, and has made it possible for a small country like Sweden to sustain a highly diverse publication ecology, recent shifts seem to introduce a different policy.

The drastic cuts were made for reasons that to us appeared obscure: the official explanation cannot be deemed as anything but intellectually vacuous — the funding was cut down because of the journal's "low quality," a judgment not accompanied by any further exemplifications or explanations.

Since then we have been forced to remake and remodel our way of working, which as such need not be a negative thing. Instead of publishing in a tabloid format, we have switched to a more book-like format that makes it possible to continue international distribution in a more efficient way, and in the end hopefully makes the journal easier to buy for readers inside, as well as outside, of Sweden. SITE will henceforth be available from most Internet booksellers, selected bookstores, and will be easy to order in those who will not keep us in stock.

The necessity of remaking and remodeling is however not restricted to journals. In recent years the European university system has been affected by major changes due to financial restrictions and policy changes that seem to directly target teaching and research in the humanities. This is no doubt a global trend, and the major thematic section, "Quality Education," with contributions by Karl Lydén, Kim West, Sara Farris, Hans Ruin, Stéphane Douailler, Danny Hayward, and Katja Diefenbach, addresses this problem as it has emerged in different national contexts.

In the UK, Italy, Austria, France, Germany, Greece, Spain, and in virtually every country in Europe, the Bologna Process seems to have produced a general quantification of higher learning along with restricted academic freedom and worsened labor conditions for professors, lecturers, and university employees at large. As was already presaged in Lyotard's classic analysis in the late '70s, the grand narratives of legitimation of education have lost their credibility in contemporary, post-industrial society: both the narrative of knowledge as a means of emancipation, and the German Idealist narrative of *Bildung*, have vanished, and legitimation seems to only reside in performativity, resulting in the mercantilization of higher learning. The question remains not only of how such a process may be resisted — for instance by a kind of passive resistance: minimize your attention, just send in the report — but also the question to what extent these transformations, deeply imbricated as they are in mutations of Capital itself, also open other possibilities.

A smaller thematic section is devoted to the idea of "late style," and presents texts by Sam Smiles, Bente Larsen, and Sven-Olov Wallenstein. Initially presented at a symposium at Moderna Museet in Stockholm, organized in conjunction with the exhibition "Turner Monet Twombly: Later Paintings," they examine the idea of late style, as it has been developed by, among others, Theodor W. Adorno and Edward Said, both in relation to the three artists, and as a general question of philosophy and aesthetic theory.

This issue also contains essays by Charlotte Bydler, Sinziana Ravini, Fredrika Spindler, Maurizio Lazzarato, Alex Costanzo, and Joel McKim. The topics addressed range from the Swedish artist Barbro Östlihn's work in New York in the 1960s, utopias in contemporary art, and the writing of the history of post-war French philosophy, to deployment of pastoral power technologies in French politics, the cinematic work of Wang Bing, and the debates surrounding the construction of an Islamic cultural center close to Ground Zero in lower Manhattan. •

THE EDITORS

French Philosophy Since 1945

Fredrika Spindler

French Philosophy: Insides and Outsides of Academia

Depending on one's inclination, one can choose to think of it as a miracle — or, for the more inquisitive, in can be put it in terms of a question: what soil, what events, what constellations made possible what might loosely be termed French postwar philosophy? Or, put differently: what are the points of coincidence, affinity, convergence, confrontation, displacement, and disagreement of such various thinkers and philosophers as Jean-Paul Sartre, Luce Irigaray, Jacques Lacan, Georges Canguilhem, Henri Maldiney, Jacques Derrida, Gilles Deleuze, Michel Foucault, Jean-Luc Nancy, Sarah Kofman, Louis Althusser and Jacques Rancière — to name but a few — who, with extraordinary productivity, both individually and collectively, managed to renew, invent, and recreate the philosophical landscape in the postwar period? At the intersection of these two questions, something both unusual and compelling can be outlined: a new (and much needed) segment of a history of ideas and philosophy, circumscribed in time and space yet pointing towards widespread and far-reaching roots, complicating its chronology by tracing lines of convergence and points of disjunctions in the form of specific themes or areas of problematization.

It is thus no trivial project that the editors Étienne Balibar and John Rajchman have undertaken with the 456-page anthology *French Philosophy Since 1945: Problems, Concepts, Inventions*,[1] the fourth and last volume in The New Press's Postwar French Thought Series. Few, however, would have been better equipped to construct such an ambitious anthology — Balibar being a part and co-creator of the winding process that the book maps out, Rajchman an excellent transmitter and interpreter of many of its main figures. The double perspective — the French horizon, which is the focus and point of departure, and the Anglo-American context, which is the presumed site of reception — also wields a double advantage: on the one hand, we get a profound presentation and thematization of a complex whole; on the other hand, a set of texts (complete or excerpts) that are

1 • Étienne Balibar and John Rajchman (eds), *French Philosophy Since 1945: Problems, Concepts, Inventions* (New York: The New Press, 2011).

published in revised translations, or for the first time, in English. This opportunity to partake of well-known texts by famous authors, as well as lesser known essays of either the same authors or others, indispensable for the French context while less well-known internationally, constitutes just one of the reasons why this book is a veritable goldmine.

But the book is more than just another anthology, regardless of how well it fulfills its role in that respect. What is presented is not just a certain set of key texts that all have constituted theoretical turning-points in their own time as well as today, but also a full and multiple thematic formulation of the questions at stake in the postwar reality from out of which new philosophical and theoretical movements such as structuralism and post-structuralism, the historically minded epistemology and new psychoanalytical theory would stem, as well as the New Novel, New Wave Cinema, and an increasingly unbounded aesthetic theory and practice. It is also from out of this scientific and cultural multiplicity that it becomes possible to understand the development of what Balibar and Rajchman, to be sure only on one occasion (presumably because of philosophical decency), call French "Continental philosophy", that is, its fundamentally cross-disciplinary character; its intimate grounding in the whole of humanities but also in the new natural sciences; its inevitable connections to political and social science as well as to arts and literature. From this commingling it becomes possible to understand why French postwar philosophy has had and continues to have such a transformative influence in most of these fields of culture today: as Balibar and Rajchman put it in their introduction, "no area would remain unaffected" (xvii). Yet, enlarging the analytical scope also renders possible a innovative way of historicizing from a specifically philosophical perspective: by widening the thematic inquiry to disciplines outside of strictly academic philosophy, and showing how analogous, though at every moment particular, questions are taken up, formulated, and discussed in divergent ways, the philosophical orientations also appear in a wider perspective than what previous presentations have achieved — for instance that of Vincent Descombes's *Modern French Philosophy,*[2] whose main focus is the Hegelian and phenomenological discussion. Not least, this is valuable for clarifying what might simply be termed the complexity of French philosophy: namely, that the invention of formations such as structuralism, new linguistics or social anthropology cannot be properly understood unless one makes evident their connection to contemporary re-readings and radical actualizations of

2 • Vincent Descombes, *Modern French Philosophy*, trans. L. Scott-Fox and J. M. Harding (New York: Cambridge University Press, 1980).

historical philosophers such as Spinoza, Kant, Nietzsche, Bergson and Marx, as well as the Stoics and ancient philosophy.

The Concept and the Subject

From what parameters, then, can French postwar philosophy, with its many different orientations, be understood? Balibar and Rajchman take their point of departure in a late text of Foucault, his introduction to Georges Canguilhem's *The Normal and the Pathological,*[3] where he discusses the development of modern or contemporary French philosophy in relation to German and English traditions, as well as their roots in Kant and the Kantian invention of critical philosophy. Central here is the very transformation of the idea of critique: the need to formulate a new critical thinking — what Foucault calls "the fourth critique" — departing from what in the historical development may be understood as the problem of finitude. What is at stake is how to formulate a critical thinking that no longer may be grounded in God or Man. This question, first put forth in the discussions in the 1930s of Husserl's *Cartesian Meditations*, enables Foucault to point out two diverging readings and developments: one championed by Cavaillès, which Foucault calls "a philosophy of the concept", the other proposed by Sartre, developing into a "philosophy of the subject". After the war, this initial divide was to be complicated and, in turn, generated a large number of new orientations, for example via Canguilhem's development of Cavaillès's philosophy of the concept in a historicizing perspective that draws on the life sciences, to Foucault himself, who would develop a conceptual analysis starting from a wider range of questions involving humanism and philosophical anthropologism from Heidegger and Marx, as well new methods in linguistics, critical theory, and social sciences. Hence, the question of the new formulation of critical thinking needs to be staged so as to encompass these parameters, and here, too, Balibar and Rajchman follow Foucault, in what he called bifurcations and their relating points of rupture, or "heretical points".

This tracing of lines and the localizing of breaking-points constitute a method that less proposes a history of individual philosophers, schools or movements, but rather pulls its strength from pinpointing those questions that emerged out of this originary divide between philosophies of concept and object. In short, the method here consists in defining "the clusters of discussion, or constellations of discourse, each with its points or lines of divergence" (xxi), as well as the inventions and concepts that stem from them. This is the basis for the seven principal clusters of discussion or areas of problems, which also make up

3 • Georges Canguilhem, *The Normal and the Pathological*, trans. Carolyn R. Fawcett (New York: Zone Books, 1991).

the book's seven parts — In Search of a New Critique, Histories of Truth, Questions of Difference, Event, The Subject, Institution and Insurrection and Thinking in Art — all of which are independent, but also overlapping. The problematizing rather than chronological set-up is completed at the very end of the book by a much needed, detailed and comprehensive chart that links individual works and persons to national and international major events. The result is a rare historical overview of a philosophy understood organically, moving by junctions and ruptures, growths, connections, and ramifications.

Critique, History, and Truth

Starting out with short and clarifying introductions, each part sketches a kaleidoscopic image of a multifaceted thought in movement. Part one, In Search for a New Critique, is rooted in the need to formulate a new critical thinking, a critical attitude that, in Foucault's words, is understood as "a kind of general cultural form, both a political and moral attitude, a way of thinking [...] the art of not being governed like that and at that cost" (38). This necessity is formulated from out of the different horizons opened up by Kant's philosophy, in whose aftermath the question of the finitude of man became the common denominator. That which was sought in different disciplines was an awakening from and a departing from the "anthropological slumber" bequeathed by Kant: Althusser develops an antihumanist Marx and analyzes humanism as an ideology, understood as a transcendental illusion; Ricoeur formulates the necessity of a new hermeneutics, grounded in what he calls the school of suspicion, whose key figures are Marx, Nietzsche and Freud, in contrast to a tradition of interpretation based in reminiscence and a phenomenology of the sacred. In "The Ends of Man", Derrida identifies the question of man's finitude as the key issue in French contemporary philosophy, but he also shows how it was already embedded in the metaphysical tradition culminating with readings of Hegel and Husserl. This question, which for Derrida just as for Levinas, albeit differently, calls for a thorough questioning of the idea of the Law, is then taken up in an almost opposite way by Deleuze, for whom the end of Man (as the end of God) constitutes a resolute liberation, making possible new ways of thinking and experiencing outside of the bonds of subjectivity.

A different perspective on these epistemological issues is then offered in the selection from Claude Imbert's *For a History of Logic*, which offers a brilliant and long overdue introduction to the French reception and interpretation of the divide between Husserl and Frege, via the mathematicians and philosophers Jean Cavaillès and Albert Lautmann, where later Merleau-Ponty and Wittgenstein would play major roles. Barthes and Blanchot are present here too, as front figures in the discussion of the new criticism's role in art and literature, while Althusser, Rancière and Bourdieu lay out the foundations for a new critical thinking concerning the political.

Part two, Histories of Truth, takes its point of departure in the postwar rethinking of the philosophy of mathematics, and the introduction of the role of history in mathematics. Derrida, translating and writing the introduction to Husserl's *The Origin of Geometry*, stresses the idea of a "history of truth" with far-reaching consequences for both the thinking of mathematics and for writing; Michel Serres develops Leibniz' mathematical models while Deleuze, starting out from studies of Bergson, traces a "minor" mathematical tradition, less focused on axioms and deductions than on problems and potentials, a tradition that after Bergson was developed further by Ilya Prigogine and Whitehead. The history of the natural sciences becomes plural, as Foucault shows in his highly pedagogical readings of Koyré, Bachelard, and Canguilhem, thereby making possible the development of the idea of a production of knowledge based on different, co-existing but also conflicting models.

In a critical history of systems of thought, it is thus the very notion of truth that undergoes a transformation from "demonstration" to "event", which is developed philosophically by Foucault and psychoanalytically by Lacan through the question of truth as fiction. For Badiou, truth as event calls for the question of fidelity, while, in Deleuze's view, it constitutes the possibility of transforming our understanding of the philosophical activity as such. If "truth" is understood as an emerging event, this means that its emergence as such is always dependent on the dramaturgy singular to the question or the problem itself: "dramatizations of ideas were always prior to relations of truth" (64); an ontological chronology which in turn calls for the necessity for every philosopher to understand how the drama in question is played out, who its actors are, and what constitutes its main target. The notion of truth is also discussed by Pierre-François Moreau through Spinoza's re-evaluation of the status of error, which can be related to Marx and Lenin, while Julia Kristeva addresses the relation of truth and plausibility in relation to "true-real". A consequence of this displacement of the notion of truth is the question of what cannot be contained by thinking, while still appearing as a constitutive part of it — thereby calling for a responsibility: the aporia, the question or the paradox, the incertitude or indetermination inherent to thinking.

Differences and Events

This question constitutes the bridge to part three, Questions of Difference — difference here understood as yet another decisive element for the new critical philosophy on all levels: ontological, political, linguistic, since it deals precisely with the ungraspable, slipping, and paradoxical, with the neither-nor. From Merleau-Ponty, in his "In Praise of Philosophy", to Lacan's idea of the "purloined letter", Lévi-Strauss's "floating signifier" and the linguist and philosopher Jean-Claude Milner's development of this in the form of "paradoxical sets" within all forms of identification, to Derrida's forming of the new concept *différance*, everything turns around the question of the conditions of questioning. For Deleuze, the notion of difference just as much concerns the conditions of thought, but its structure of ungraspability can only be understood in a radically positive or productive way that refuses all negative ontology. Liberated from its traditional subservience to logics of identity and contradiction, difference becomes the productive element within which all thinking can take place. The concept of difference is also central to political philosophy. Formulated in different ways by Rancière, Nancy, and Lyotard, it designates the empty space of positive identity and sense in relation to which all new forms of democracy must be formulated. The question is "what is the nature of wrongs for which there pre-exists no agreed means of settlement and which thus confronts us with questions and dissensus?" (120) Revolving around the same question, but in different ways, the fundamental and necessary groundlessness proper to philosophy here weaves its fabric through variations of difference: difference, *différance*, *différend*, disagreement.

Another aspect or variation on the same theme is developed in part four, now in terms of Event. If the philosophical and critical question ultimately concerns the conditions and the possibilities of thinking from out of a necessary perspective of finitude, itself characterized by a both inevitable and constitutive aporia or paradox, a central problem becomes how and in what forms *sense* appears. The event is thematized precisely as those critical moments when we are forced to think rather than reproduce *doxa* in its various forms. In Balibar and Rajchman's words, "it is the peculiar time of invention or creation in thought or philosophy" (149), critical turning-points that resist all programmatic prevision and mastering. The event, contrary to the "accident", necessarily generates sense, thereby forcing us into becoming-other (Deleuze), but in this also rendering necessary a larger reflection on what we, ourselves, were, are, and become: thus, the event is linked to questions of subjectivity and intersubjectivity, action and agency. The problem hence appears to have a large number of ramifications, and it demands analysis from various points of view. The event in relation to history is thematized by, among others, Foucault (actuality) and Althusser (the multiple structure of history), in Deleuze's understanding of Hamlet's "time out of joint", and in Derrida's post-Marxist reading of ghosts and messianic times, but also, from a very different perspective, by Sartre in his analysis of history as agency.

The link to the political is formulated in different interpretations of the revolution — as a possibility in the '60s, and as a failure in the '80s — but it also opens toward a multifaceted discussion in Foucault's understanding of "the time of the political". Yet another major discussion takes on the question of the event from the point of view of temporality. The roots of this can be found in Kant, Bergson, Husserl and Heidegger, and they are worked out in different ways, for example in Derrida's call for the future in terms of messianic time, which contrasts to Deleuze's analysis of the event as Aion, annulling the past as much as what is yet to come. The event understood as that which "happens to us" acquires a strong ethical sense in Victor Goldschmidt's analysis of Stoic temporality, which is also developed further by Deleuze via Spinoza and Nietzsche, where the ethical question becomes the question of how not to be unworthy of the event. With the explicit or implicit backdrop of World War Two, it also becomes possible to develop Freud's notion of the "traumatic event": in psychoanalytical theory, we find it in Lacan, in literature, in Blanchot and the idea of the literary event associated to "spaces of death", and also in history, in Pierre Nora's and Paul Ricoeur's discussions concerning memory and the Shoah.

The Subject Reconsidered

Part five traces a problem that is strongly intertwined with all the other themes: the Subject. Contrary to a certain number of received, simplistic representations of contemporary French philosophy's critique of, and even doing away with, the subject, a complex discussion is here advanced where the problem of subjectivity may be understood along two major axes: either in terms of the contrast between the idea of the "*constitution of* the subject in language, discourse and social formations", and or in terms of the idwea of the subject's "*constituting* role" in philosophies of consciousness (193). From the decentering of the subject and the discussions concerning the body and embodiment, critical readings are directed against the phenomenological ideas of the Flesh: Lacan talks of "the body in bits and pieces", Derrida of "the proper body" anchored in "hearing-oneself-speaking", while Deleuze, drawing on Artaud, develops the "body without organs" as well as the idea of an impersonal transcendental field from out of which "a life" can be understood in liberating contrast to the life of the individual.

In connection to the subject, the idea of alterity also requires rethinking, similarly to the idea of community, which is developed along different paths by Sartre, Levinas, and Derrida. In this part, there is a rich display of texts and excerpts: in addition to the expected texts by Deleuze (the luminous "Immanence: A Life"), Derrida, Blanchot, and Lacan, we also find Simone de Beauvoir, Georges Bataille, Luce Irigaray — who in a brilliantly tight excerpt discusses Hegel's view on the woman — and Levinas. Canguilhem's "What is Psychology?" retraces psychology's philosophical roots. The text — which ends with the famous warning that the road from the Sorbonne (that is, contemporary psychology's reluctance to relate to philosophy) indeed may in one direction lead to the Pantheon, but that the other direction leads to the local police station — should rightly be made compulsory reading by all theorists of cognitive behavioral therapy. In this section, we also find the analytically inspired philosopher Jacques Bouveresse's highly relevant reading of the understanding of the body in Descartes and Wittgenstein, as well as Foucault's own presentation of his philosophy (written under pseudonym), which focuses on processes of subjectivation. Finally, Derrida's critical dialogue with Jean-Luc Nancy is indispensable reading for anyone who has ever taken an interest in the question of the subject in contemporary philosophy, and its various developments from Heidegger to Foucault and Deleuze.

The Institution and the Political and the Aesthetic

The question of the subject inevitably leads to that of the political, which here, in an especially interesting way, is problematized under the heading Institution and Insurrection. Foucault's definition of the critical attitude — "we don't want to be governed like that anymore" — constitutes the point of departure for a formulation of the political as something that has to be thought outside of the given framework of the state and the institution; something that can be found in interstices, resistances, and alternative groups, outside of all predefined forms of identity and belonging. It is a political space defined in contrast to all forms of institutional power, indeed co-extensive with them, but never fully circumscribed, caught, colonized, or mastered by them. Hence, the question will also be about identifying not only what the institutional strategies are and how they are articulated, but also, what the counter-strategies are, which always appear within them. The political, in a time characterized by geo-political transformations and displacements of the forms of war and peace, needs to be understood as an-archic, groundless, without reference to any transcendent or historical ideas: it has "no other guarantee than its own activity, no necessity other than its own responsibility" (274). Therefore, the questions of the political must be reformulated and re-wrought: among the new conceptual constellations we find, for example, the relation between force and law, justice and violence, and, not least, the relation between war and politics. Foucault's famous reversal of Clausewitz's formulation that war is the continuing of politics with other means, Deleuze and Guattari's idea of the War Machine, Virilio's analyses of war and media, and also Derrida's discussion about violence and law, are here emblematic. With the challenge of thinking the common in terms of space and identities (Rancière, Nancy), the idea also appears of a necessary outside that determines both the political and the philosophical: Foucault's Group for Information on Prisons, the open university in Vincennes, and the Collège International de Philosophie, can all be seen as expressions of this movement. In this part of the book, the choice of texts is rich and multifaceted: Merleau-Ponty on Machiavelli, Sarah Kofman's analysis of Kant's idea of woman's dominion in the Anthropology, Jean-Claude Milner's study of identities in given and "indistinct names" from a logical, political and psychoanalytical perspective, and Lefort's brilliant essay on power based on an analysis of La Boétie's *Discourse on Voluntary Servitude*, are some of the examples.

From the political to the aesthetic, the path is short. The last part of the book, Thinking in Art, shows how French postwar philosophy cannot be thought outside of the transformation of literature and art that have occurred during the past five or six decades. In a movement that both returns to and transforms Kant's idea of the aesthetic, aesthetics in all forms — theoretical as well as practical — becomes a great laboratory for the inventions, problems, and movements of this time. New and far-reaching relations between philosophy, art, and literature can, as Balibar and Rajchman suggest, be said to have redefined the very history of philosophy understood as constructed on the basis of the philological and hermeneutic models of the nineteenth century, characterized by Hegel's and later Heidegger's theories of aesthetics and culminating with "the end of art". Instead, central concepts, both in art and philosophy, have migrated into transnationalism (rather than cosmopolitanism), heterotopias (rather than utopias), and "minor languages" (rather than great narratives). In this part, Merleau-Ponty writes on thinking in painting, Foucault on other spaces, Henri Maldiney on the relation between gaze, speech, and space, and Rancière on the politics of aesthetics and the idea of a distribution of the sensible.

A French Style?

Is it then possible, by way of Étienne Balibar and John Rajchman's anthology, to answer the question of what made French postwar philosophy possible, from which soil it developed, and why it, perhaps through what Pierre-François Moreau calls "a French style" (xx) in philosophy, were to spread and exercise a still undiminished influence, not only on the international philosophical scene, but also in many other disciplines, in the arts, and in political theory?

Answers can, no doubt, be outlined as the thematization and the collection of texts progress through the book: beyond the many — and sometimes irreconcilable — differences between the French theorists, thinkers and philosophers, which unfold in the space of two, at the most three, generations, there is, to start with, a common heritage in Classic and Modern philosophy — Kant, Nietzsche, Marx, but also Descartes, Spinoza, Leibniz and Bergson, without whom postwar French philosophies would have been literally unthinkable. Common to them also is the openness toward other disciplines and the will to reach beyond a strict and closed academic space. Last but not least, they have in common a vital capacity to actualize, renew, and transform the historical heritage, while a new historical moment was shaped around them. This, if anything, certainly meets the Nietzschean definition of philosophy's productive untimeliness. However, the question of common denominators to some extent becomes the one of less interest, since one of the strong points here is showing connections, clusters of discussion and diverging paths from shared contexts: at the center there are the questions and their prismatic multiplicity, never the answers in view of a desired consensus. Therefore neither the problematization nor the textual choice appear as polemic, on the contrary, it is open and rich, although without ever giving the impression of arbitrariness.

But despite the anthology's richness, questions can of course be raised. Beyond the impossibility of ever presenting a complex and living history in an all-encompassing way, the editorial choices always profile themselves both by inclusion and exclusion. That Balibar and Rajchman indeed trace royal paths, densely populated by major canonic names — Foucault, Derrida, Deleuze — represented by numerous texts does not constitute a problem in view of the rather absurdly minor place these philosophers tend to receive in the vast majority of contemporary philosophical dictionaries. The otherwise solid mobilization, reaching from Althusser to Sartre, Badiou to Bouveresse, Canguilhem to Milner, Gauchet to Goldschmidt, apostrophes, displaces and coexists with the famous texts. More problematic however, is the editorial choice concerning female representation: of 62 texts, only 5 have female authors, something that moreover has the unfortunate side-effect of making names as decisive for philosophy as de Beauvoir, Irigaray, Kristeva, Kofman, and Imbert appear as obligatory tokens. From a practical point of view, an index of names would have supplied extended possibilities of orientation in the developmental rhizome constituted by this presentation. These shortcomings — of which one cannot be considered minor — do not, however, obscure the fact that Balibar's and Rajchman's book constitutes an invaluable source — indeed, the very source-book they had the intention of creating — for anyone who wants to relate to contemporary philosophy. The bringing together of well and lesser known texts, the dissensual co-existence of so many fundamentally different philosophers within a shared milieu, the problematizing and thematizing framework that holds and knits them together, in itself constitutes a decisive and fundamental contribution to the ongoing (hi)story of philosophy. •

Fredrika Spindler is Associate Professor of Philosophy at Södertörn University.

Utopian Thinking in Past and Contemporary Times

Sinziana Ravini

At the beginning of this year, I started writing a text with the aim of deploring our disenchanted times, which I felt were suffering from a static world order and "there is no alternative" scenarios. But then the spring revolution arrived, with its domino effects on the London-riots, the Greek and Spanish uprisings, not to mention the occupations in New York and beyond — all signs of a world that is crumbling in front of our eyes, ready to break the chains of its slave mentality and find its way out. But "out" towards what? We still haven't found a new system of thought that can take us out of our current conflicts. I would like to suggest that we need to engage in utopian thinking, and by utopian I don't mean to retreat into escapist dreams of perfect societies deprived of antagonisms, but to use it as a progressive tool for aesthetico-political action — even if the relation between art and utopianism is a dangerous affair with a long history of failures on its checklist.

We've all seen how communist utopias were instrumentalised by the Soviet system, or how the microutopias of the 90s became a part of neo-liberal event industries. That doesn't mean we have to give up on utopian thinking. A utopia, even though doomed to failure, remains a promise of a better world to come. Utopian thinking can help us both imagine and realise a new world order. But before we jump into the future or start speculating into possible worlds to come, let's have a look at how utopian thinking came to life and try to figure out why "utopia" has such a bad reputation.

Utopias have often been connected to the idea of "non-place", coming from Greek *ou* ("not") and *topos* ("place"), and therefore rather an idealistic, irrational and highly unrealisable thing. But there is a second meaning that tends to be forgotten, namely "eutopia", derived from the Greek *eu* ("good" or "well") and *topos* ("place"), meaning "good place". These two meanings are often read together, so that the "good place" becomes "no place", giving utopian thinking the flavour of unrealisability. But does it have to be this way?

It all started with the Paradise, the place of absolute harmony. Eve's bite in the apple of knowledge led to the rupture from the sweet and friendly world of ignorance, and the "real world" became a space of regret and mourning of grandiose times. The idealisation of the past becomes a current theme in Hellenist times. Both the Greek poet Hesiod (8th century BC) and the Greek historian Plutarch (1st century) were caught up in mythologisations of the Golden Age where nymphs and shepherds lived in rustic innocence untarnished by the corruptions of civilisation. It all starts swell but ends up badly.

It's only with Plato's *Republic* that the utopian thinking is projected on a world to come who sees the past as wild and primitive and history as a means for the gradual improvement of man. Plato proposes an ideal state divided in a rigid class society containing the "golden", "silver", "bronze" and "iron" socio-economic classes. The "golden" citizens are trained in a 50-year long educational program for philosophic rulers. We are here a long way from the biblical equation: the perfect state as a state of blissful non-knowing, but we also get a aristocratic utopia, ruled by the merry few, where women and slaves are to have no input in government decision-making.

It's only with Thomas More and his famous *Utopia* (1516), the story of a fictional island in the Atlantic Ocean where peace and harmony rules between individuals, that a model of a more egalitarian world gets truly explored. Some readers have interpreted *Utopia* as a realistic blueprint for a realisable society, others see it more as a satire, aiming to expose and criticise the England of his time, yet fully aware of its idealism.

More's Utopia

But how utopian is More's *Utopia*? If we have a closer look at it, we soon discover that the notion of privacy doesn't exist. More's utopians are constantly supervised by the public eye. The utopians resist from committing crimes such as leaving the island without permission, stealing and murdering, out of fear of getting discovered. The utopians don't even have names. They function more like empty vessels waiting to be filled with collective material. Diversities are abolished in the name of the common. When it comes to free speech, Raphael Hythloday — the protagonist, whose first name refers to the Archangel Raphael who gives sight to the blind, and whose second name refers to the Greek word *Huthlos*, "nonsense" — declares: "Freedom of speech? Well that is about as absurd as taking a shit in a gold chamber pot!"

There are also a lot of unrealistic scenarios in More's *Utopia*. The utopians have clothes that serve for both warm and cold weather and the ability to tear up a forest with their own hands in order to transport it from one place to another. There are also some incongruities: the utopian leaders deliberately make gold seem undesirable in order to ensure that when it becomes convenient to have gold, like for example in the case of a war, the population of *Utopia* will be willing to hand it over to their government without being compensated in any way. In a truly ideal society individuals would have the possibility of choosing between several options and the knowledge they need in order to do so. Not in More's *Utopia*. Just as in the Biblical paradise, ignorance is the tool that holds More's *Utopia* together.

Another absurdity is how utopians look upon religion. All religions are tolerated but it's forbidden to believe that the soul dies with the body. When it comes to the belief in an after-life, religion becomes a justification for the prolongation of earthly pleasures: if you receive no compensation after death there would be no point in "struggling to be virtuous, denying yourself the pleasant things of life, and deliberately making yourself uncomfortable." This divulges the full extent of their greed, for clearly, the only motivation they have to be morally responsible is the promise of an afterlife.

The fear for the other is a constant trope in *Utopia*. Outsiders wearing jewellery are nothing but clowns, beggars are just lazy, and mentally ill "a source of entertainment, which is the only thing they're good for". When it comes to the sick "why go on feeding germs?" Perfection can thus only be achieved through exclusion and hard regulations.

Even the free time is highly regulated. As Nonsenso asserts: "everyone has his eye on you, so you're practically forced to get on with your job, and make some proper use of your spare time". The paradox of making "a proper use" of your "spare time" accentuates the hypocrisy of *Utopia*'s philosophy. You're free as long as you choose the right way to be free.

Still, More's *Utopia* is often depicted as an ideal state. Some time ago I stumbled over a very interesting essay written by Stephen Duncombe called "Politics as Art of the Impossible".[1] I was however truly surprised to read that More's *Utopia* "was everything his sixteenth-century European home was not: peaceful, prosperous and just". How come that *Utopia*, despite of its lack of freedom of speech, is seen as a "peaceful, prosperous and just" place? How come it's so easy to miss the obvious imperfections in More's *Utopia*? Perhaps we need an ideal model to hang on to, and this one is the best we have.

1 • Stephen Duncombe, "Politics as Art of the Impossible, The Case for a Dreampolitik in the USA", Open No. 20, *The Populist Imagination* (2010): 32.

Utopian thinking builds on a profound dissatisfaction with the present. Does it matter if this dissatisfaction can achieve a perfect state? Aren't these imperfections precisely there in order to give us the impression that we can imagine an even better order of things? A system of pleasant self-deceit that can fool us into the position of a potential utopist?

One of the strengths of More's *Utopia* is that we cannot really know where the satire ends and where the genuine political proposal begin. As Duncombe claims, the genius of More's *Utopia* is that it is both absurd and earnest: "It is through the combination of these seemingly opposite ways of presenting political ideals that a more fruitful way of thinking about dreampolitik can start to take shape. For it is the presentation of *Utopia* as no-place, and its narrator as nonsense, that opens up a space for the reader's imagination to wonder what an alternative someplace and a radically different sensibility might be like".[2]

More's *Utopia* is a production of pure imagination. Why did he refuse to provide a "realistic" alternative? Perhaps in order to keep the "what if" thinking going on through centuries. Perhaps *Utopia* can only be a work in progress. At least if we believe Duncombe who claims that "impossible solutions — are means to dream of better ones". He concludes his essay by saying: "Bismarck might have insisted that 'politics is the art of the possible', but a much more powerful case can be made today that politics is the art of the impossible".[3] This might be true. A lot of political scenarios insist on their possibility, on their immediate realisation, on promises that are seldom kept and dream scenarios that are easily forgotten. Where does that leave art? Should artists confine in coming with impossible solutions? Or should they look for the possible? The question is perhaps falsely put. If Utopia is the search of a place that never arrives, or the realisation of a world that can never be perfect, then Utopia is not a place, but a tool for political imagination and action.

One shouldn't forget that Marx and Engels were highly sceptical towards utopian thinking, claiming that the new social order could only be obtained through a revolution of production relations that have to be anchored in the real and not in the imaginary realm. Yet, the utopian dimension is dominating the east-European art scene, from the radical avant-garde movements and the Stalinist social realism to the ironic or post-ironic interpretations of utopian ideas in our times. If we look at how artists have worked with the notion of utopia in the last decades, one can see four clear tendencies: a) a nostalgic mourning of lost utopias b) an ironic play with the same, and c) a wish to create new utopian scenarios that could either be realisable here and now, or d) in times to come. Sometimes these four tendencies can be found in one in the same art practice, but let's

2 • Ibid, 37.
3 • Ibid, 38.

try to keep things apart for some time, before we jump to any more conclusions.

From "Post-" and "Retro Utopias" to "Micro Utopias"
Needless to say, the notion of utopia has often been a subject of ridiculisation. Take for example Ilya Kabakov's famous installation: *The Man Who Flew into Space from His Apartment* (1968–2000) who strives toward socialism's cosmic utopias with a formal universe made out of poor components from socialist everyday life. This post-utopic work is presented like a grandiose dream in ruins. The allegory of a decayed social utopia is also present in Oleg Kulik's "The Red Room" (2009), where Kulik is standing naked in the snow waving a red flag with two dogs masturbating against his legs while he is pointing into the future. The post-utopianism of the 80s was replaced by the new-utopianism of the 90s, which often directed a brutal critique towards the romantic dimension in utopian thinking, while at the same time trying to recuperate its more totalitarian aspects. In the 80s there was also a new branch of retro-avant-gardists like Irwin/NSK, but according to the historian Inke Arns, "the fixation on totalitarian tendencies inscribed upon the avant-garde were lost when openly repressive political systems became democracies".[4]

Another interesting phenomenon is the retro-utopianism in former Yugoslavia. The members of the artist group Cosmo Kinetic Cabinet Noordung are for example not orienting themselves towards the future like the neo-utopists, nor do they stage utopias as a ruin, but rather use the past as a vehicle into the future. The big challenge is to try to catch avant-gardian utopian ideas "before the catastrophe", and realise them here and now.[5]

According to Boris Groys the most utopic aspect of utopian art after the dissolution of communism, is its ideological reconciliation with capitalist forces. He writes: "One could say that it is an extension of real-socialist paradise, which now accepts everything it once refused to include; in other words, it represents a utopian radicalization of the Communist demand for the total salvation offered for all, including those usually considered dictators, tyrants, and terrorists or capitalists, militarists and profiteers of globalization".[6] This radicalised utopian inclusiveness is often mistaken for being ironic, but it's nothing but a post-historical idyll looking for reconciliation.

If the internationalist-Communist utopia from "the East" had universalistic approaches, the "western"

4 • Inke Arns "Avant-Garde in the Rear-View Mirror: From Utopia under General Suspicion to a New Notion of the Utopian," in 7 *Sins Ljubljana — Moscow*, Moderna Galerija, Museum of Modern Art, Ljubljana, 2005, 17.
5 • Ibid, 19.
6 • Boris Groys, "Privatisations, or Post-Communism's Artificial Privatisation(s)," in 7 *Sins Ljubljana — Moscow*, Moderna Galerija, Museum of Modern Art, Ljubljana, 2005, 24.

Micro-Utopias of the 90s have had more “glocal” ambitions. The social turn of the 90s had a more pragmatic approach to the notion of Utopia. If you can’t save the world, try at least to save your neighbourhood. Working in small scales, with the reorganisation of modes of production, and the social relation as the telos of all artistic practices, these microutopias, whether they consisted in eating (Rirkrit Tiravanija), massaging (Suraci Kuzelwong), redistributing our sources (Superflex), travelling (Pierre Huyghe) or just living together (Carsten Höller), had one thing in common: the reenchantement of the everyday life, which immediately connected the practices to a preoccupation with the here and now.

The post and retro-utopian aesthetics has had a true renaissance with the fall of the wall and the arrival of new generations that have lived both in communist and new capitalist times, having the opportunity to compare the two systems with each other. Few can have missed David Maljkovic’s romantic recuperations of architectonic leftovers of utopian times. *The Scene for New Heritage Trilogy* displays a futuristic world that has lost contact with its cultural heritage. The first film, set in the year 2045, features a group of travellers that are visiting a memorial park for victims of the Second World War, and a silver sci-fi tower that no longer seems to have any meaning to them. The second film, set 20 years later, depicts a young boy’s spiritual pilgrimage to the tower of the deserted monument from which he can contemplate a snow-filled landscape. The third and final film shows some youngsters erring and playing around the tower. These three ways of visiting or interacting with a historical place relate to the artist’s own memories of obligatory visits under the Communist regime. In difference from the futuristic attempts of utopian modernism that wanted to realise everything here and now, Maljkovic’s work has an anticipating aspect that suspends the time and the subject, gradually transporting the protagonists to a dimension outside of time.

Subjective Utopias

If we return to More’s *Utopia*, we would have to admit that it’s the creation of a single man with a single vision, despite of all the philosophies and attitudes throughout the novel. In a way, perhaps we all have our personal utopias. But what happens when an artist creates a utopia by and for himself? Does the notion cease to have any relevance?

Pavel Pepperstein has always worked with individualised utopias. In an interview recently he claimed: “Everyone should have a future entirely of their own”. Through colourful and narrative watercolour drawings, he is taking utopia into an entirely imaginary scenario, projected on distant futures. On one

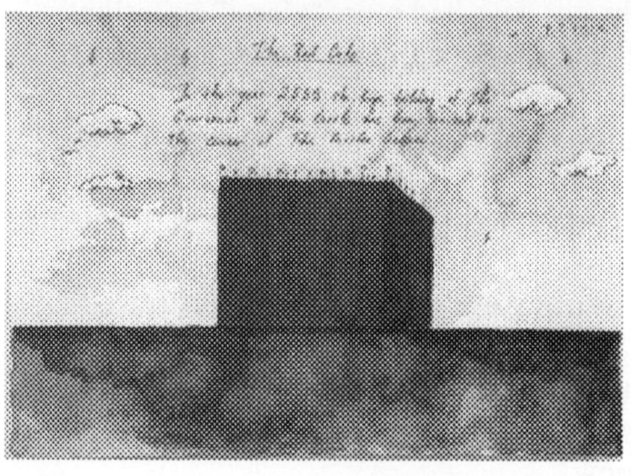

▲ **Pavel Pepperstein, *The Red Cube*, 2009.**

drawing one can see a gigantic red cube in the middle of the ocean, crowned with hundreds of flags, entitled "The red cube" with a text underneath saying: "In the year 2555 the huge building of the government of the earth has been erected in The Centre of The Pacific Ocean". Another drawing displays "The Antenna for Communication with those who died, Construction in the year of 2999". Socialist dreams are being mixed up with capitalist ones in an overglobalised, post-cultural future. Black and red squares become bricks and playing cards in a politico-surrealist children's dream. There is also a layer of dark nihilism in Pepperstein's drawings that doesn't always manifest itself. In the beginning of the 90s, with the fall of the Soviet empire, Pavel Pepperstein, Yuri Leidermann and Sergei Anufriev started to call themselves "inspectors" doing "medicinal hermeneutics", identifying the Soviet Union as a semiotic construction that could be endlessly reinterpreted. This new form of Moscow Conceptualism was inspired by the world of children's books, Pepperstein's own father, Pavel Pivovarov, being a famous book illustrator.

Another subjective utopist is Pierre Huyghe who recently transformed the abandoned National Museum of Arts and Popular Traditions in Paris into a multinarrative, imaginary space where actors enacted something that could be described as a mixture between a dream, a black mass, a psychoanalytic session, a talent show and a laboratory of fictions. Only a few were initiated in the Eleusinian mysteries of Huyghe's practice.

"The Host and the Cloud" experiment (2009–2010) was a situation, recorded and witnessed by a specially invited audience, on three different occasions that celebrated: Halloween, Valentine's Day and May Day. The role-playing and the fragmented narratives looked like the journey through the mind of an absent subject, who later on manifests itself in a film as a somnolent rabbit wandering through a rainforest. Why travel through space, when you can travel through fictions? The artist's mind becomes the ultimate utopian sphere, a space of pure subjectivity that can be experienced, interpreted and eventually turned into an intersubjective space where the beholder becomes the supreme protagonist.

Intersubjective Utopias

What about utopia as a space for immediate action? The micro-utopic embellishment of the everyday that was so fashionable in the 90s is still a current gesture, but there are also other tendencies, with artists that are more interested in the creation of discursive, imaginary utopias like for example the MFK — Malmös Fria Kvinnouniversitet (Malmö's Free Women University) led by the members Johanna Gustavsson and Lisa from the Swedish feminist YES Association! In 2009, they arranged a collective staging of a feminist utopia at the artist run gallery 16 Beaver Group called: "We won! A feminist utopia". In the invitation one could read:

> Let's treat ourselves to a temporary amnesia about the practical aspects of the here and now and instead try to visualize an intense, ecstatic future together...We concentrate on the room we are occupying and within the surrounding walls we imagine no longer being in opposition — no more defences, no longer the feeling of being two steps behind. We imagine the world as it will be when we have won, the day after the revolution, when patriarchy, capitalism, racism, sexism and their brothers have fallen, and a new world rises from the ashes. We allow ourselves no compromises, going all the way, to the extreme. And from that glorious point in the future we recount our steps back to where we are today, mapping out our path to success.

This year MFK organised a series of workshops at Konsthall C called "Insisting to be a part of this moment / movement", where they decided to transform all the theory and practice into a collective mode of action. Their newly published manual "Do the Right Thing" could be interpreted in any form and made public (or not) by a couple of agents in the Swedish art world that were specifically chosen by MFK.

MFK image from workshop at Konsthall C 2011.
▾

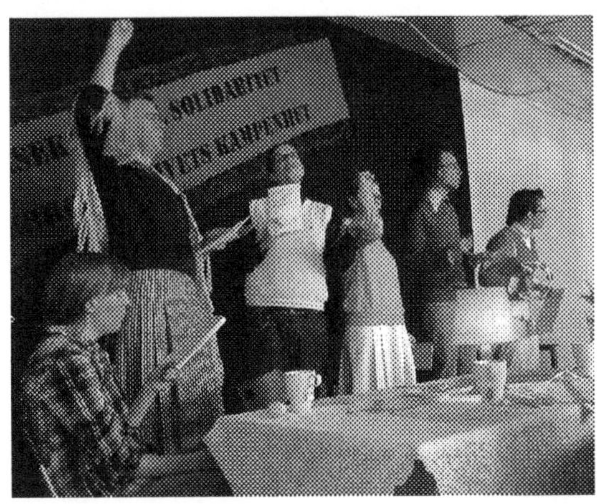

When it comes to methodology, MFK has always applied the form of pragmatic and playful workshops where people can interact both physically and intellectually. "Use of the body is obligatory, a hands-on, mapping of the future. If you are not ready to get down and dirty — don't bother knocking". MFK's strength lies in the fact that they never get stuck in a confrontational thinking where the critique of the system is affirming the very thing they are criticising. Instead, their affirmative and imaginary practice is in constant development, seeking collective visions for the future. The big question here is how do you maintain individuality within the collective? And how are conflicts resolved within such a collective? In MFK's case, it's more about creating a collective interdependence with people from different generations and backgrounds, where conflicts can both occur and persist, since only fascist utopias are applying a politics of exclusion.

Godard famously claimed that "democracy is giving 15 minutes to the Jewish people and 15 minutes to Hitler". On my question whether MFK could imagine sitting and dreaming together with people like Jimmy Åkesson — the chairman of the right-wing party Sweden Democrats, the answer was "no", since "one has better chances in coming far if the positions of the participants are not too remote from each other". When it comes to the content of the utopian scenarios that have been imagined, one suggestion that has been collectively agreed upon is the vision of a society where the suggestions of minorities would come first on the agenda, and where criminals would not be punished by being left alone or isolated, but taken care of and integrated, with a consideration of all the factors that have contributed to the crime they committed. MFK's utopia is a discursive one that has to undergo constant re-evaluations.

There are many artist groups and communities that try to create autonomous zones that act out the dream of an ideal community: The Romantic Geographic Society, Hägerstens Botaniska Trädgård (Hägersten's Botanic Garden), Spells, Kultivator, The Pirate Bay and Gelitin. Some more spectacle-oriented one than others.

The Brooklyn based street artist Swoon (also known as Caledonia Dance Curry) creates floating artist communities built out of New York City trash and sails around the world, inviting all kind of artists and activists to join her journey. The rafts look like a mixture between Christiania and the Waterworld, with tins and towers, colourful steps and platforms, flags and all kind of bizarre materials. In 2009 Swoon and 30 artists arrived at the Venice Biennial with "the Swimming Cities of Serenissima," a cityscape of surrealistic rafts made of both American and Slovenian garbage. They stopped at various points on the way to meet the locals, collect found objects for their "cabinet of curiosities" on board and to organize the final performance entitled, "The Clutchess of Cuckoo." Once in the Venice Lagoon, the rafts and their company performed throughout Venice nightly and docked at Certosa Island. Swoon's work hovers in an interspace between art and anarchy, never quite escaping the society of the spectacle, while at the same time never having to do any bigger

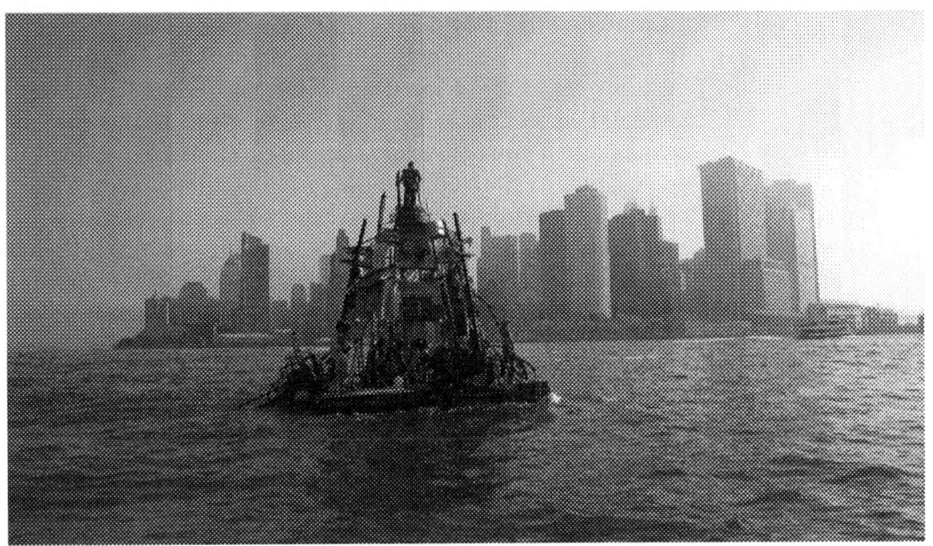

▲
Swoon, *The Swimming Cities of Serenissima*, 2008.

compromises with her anarchic philosophy, since most of the people that get to take part in this floating dream world seem to share the same ideological horizon. Yet, Swoon's creation is not entirely hers but the result of an artistic community with different kinds of skills and aesthetics, that finally merge in an eclectic symphony of forms. The positive thing with nomadic utopias is that they tend to be more welcoming and less dogmatic than static ones.[7] On the other hand, one can ask oneself how radical these autonomous spaces are when they choose to visit big social events like the Venice Biennial. At the same time, the politics of total withdrawal, the exodus à la Negri and Hardt give space to neoliberal forces to govern our visual economies.

Minnesministeriet (The Ministry of Memories), an anonymous group of Swedish artists and activists, is an example of a community that has chosen to connect the "withdrawal from" (Negri and Hardt) with "an engagement with" (Chantal Mouffe). On the night of June 15, 2011, the Ministry of Memories chose to bury a commemoration plate with a text that refers to the events during the EU summit in Gothenburg, which usually go under the name "the Gothenburg riots." The plate was fixed to the ground through a mass of cement that filled up a 1 meter deep hole. On the plate one could read a text describing the horror of the police shooting at the demonstrators. But how do you dig a pit in Gothenburg's most central park without being detected? It is said that the Ministry of Memory pretended to be involved in a film set with a bunch of cameras and lights, thus hiding behind the most common tools of visualisation. The following day, the Ministry of Memories held a ceremony

7 • Renée Scherer, *Utopies Nomades*, Les presses du Réel, Paris 2009.

surrounding the monument while reading out a collective manifesto and handing out roses to the attending audience. The gesture referred to the Social Democrats that offered flowers to the police in 2001, "rewarding" them for their efforts in relation to the Gothenburg events. In a time where monuments are only erected to "official victims", the memorial erected to those who risked their lives in a society that sees itself as a democracy is more important than ever. This utopian space is perhaps as far away as an angelic paradise. But who says that utopias can't be spaces of both sad and hopeful negations of the given? In the manifesto of the Ministry of Memories one can read:

> We are the ones who remember, who will always remember. We are the ones whose lives depend on not forgetting. Our political task is to manage the memories that the regime has denied ... We know that when we remember the story we create another now, a different order. We know that when we remember another world is possible.

Utopian politics is exactly about this: imagining another world order. We are far from a point where we can have collective dreams. We are also far from a point where we can say "we". I mean, can we ever engage in a discursive, intellectual battleground in search of a common utopia with a right-wing politician, an islamic fundamentalist or an anarchist? We've for a long time now envisioned utopias as happy, harmonious spaces voided of conflicts and differencies. But this is equal to the end of thinking. This is why utopia has such a bad reputation. The utopian spaces of our time are far from being utopian, there are even far from being democratic, discursive or inclusive. No wonder that our world is so divided. Does it have to be this way? Can art make a difference?

Utopian artists will always oscillate between subjectivity and intersubjectivity, action and interaction, closed and opened fields. At the end of the day, it's not so important how we do it, but what we produce when we do it. And when it comes to the imaginative power of utopian thinking, we're only at the beginning of a long and marvellous journey that can both re-enchant our world and give us the material for the construction of future ones. •

Sinziana Ravini is an art critic and writer living in Paris, and a co-editor of Paletten.

Universal Modernism, Swedish Art Heroine

Charlotte Bydler

According to Ruth Noack and Roger Buergel, chief curators of *Documenta 12* (2007), modernism is our time's antiquity. Modernism or some local version of it has indeed been "our" universal history for a long time. Regardless of whether this is entirely true or not, I would like to follow the unpacking of the neo-avantgarde art scene in New York as set out by Annika Öhrner, especially when the lead role is played by a white woman (mother of two, even if that is no big deal in the text) from middle-class Stockholm. What kind of entity is this art scene? What is the place of a woman from the Stockholm semi-periphery, who has migrated to Manhattan? What is the Manhattan art scene to a Stockholm counterpart? And last but not least, what is to be gained by undertaking once again an analysis of the art historical investment in vanguard modernism today?

This project opens on a visual note. Annika Öhrner enlists the aid of a coffee table book, *New York: The New Art Scene* (1967), by the Italian photographer Ugo Mulas. This is, as it were, an updated version of the classic format — *the lives of the artists*. However, this *new* art scene of the sixties is not inhabited by lonely genius artists but by people, parties, and happenings. In this scene we find Barbro Östlihn (b. 1930 in Stockholm, d. 1995 in Paris). The bottom line is clear: artists' positions in the New York neo-avantgarde are being hammered out in a social universe. In a parallel universe, other people are writing the history of modernist Swedish art. Making sense of art is world-making, an activity that takes place — literally — somewhere. Just like the photo in Mulas's book that depicts Barbro Östlihn's small painting *Subway Lock* (1963) hanging on the wall in Roy Lichtenstein's studio: the artist herself on the outskirts of the centre.

Annika Öhrner's dissertation on Barbro Östlihn is a rich and long needed introduction to the artist. Today, Östlihn's work has a strong presence both in Sweden and the US — albeit shown less frequently than that of her ex-husband and collaborator Öyvind Fahlström. Some of Östlihn's current recognition must certainly be credited to Annika Öhrner herself, in her capacity as curator and scholar. The author knew the artist intimately through their personal relations as well as through her work. However this is not a hagiographic project, nor is it a biographic attempt to situate the person-as-the-work. The investigation's primary brief is to examine the apparent contradiction between the fact that this female artist was recognised in New York, but is absent from or lacks a deeper context within Swedish art history textbooks on the 1960s. This fate is certainly shared by several artists who are marked by stains like gender, sexuality, or skin colour.[1] However this merely underlines the urgency of the basic question: what makes (Swedish) art history such a hostile environment for difference?

Rephrased for the present book, the broader provocation that the author sets out is this: *What is it that made Barbro Östlihn's position possible in the USA during the early 1960s, but impossible within Swedish traditions of the avantgarde?*[2] No less than seven subsequent questions contribute to making the problem more manageable, ranging from the personal to the more textual. These include understanding the artist's painterly project in the 1960s, and identifying concepts used for describing Östlihn in a number of 1963 New York art reviews; grasping Östlihn's position within the Manhattan art world; effects of Manhattan urbanity and art life; studio work practices in relation to both Östlihn's and Fahlström's work; understanding the Swedish field of art through case studies of exhibitions championing a transnational avantgarde; and finally the construction of a uniform art-historical narrative of the 1960s in Swedish textbooks.

In 1961 Barbro Östlihn left Stockholm for Manhattan. With Öyvind Fahlström, her husband at the time, she immersed herself in this new environment. The couple ended up taking over Robert Rauschenberg's apartment at 128 Front Street, before moving to East Village in 1967. The addresses given in the book are not mere biographical information but tied to Östlihn's canvases from the period, which have strikingly descriptive titles that refer to actual locations or houses that the artist painted. Öhrner makes interesting connections with a large body of photo studies and notes by Östlihn, and elegantly highlights how a documentary element complicates the standard formalist frame for her paintings as discussed by a number of Swedish art history textbooks. The physical environment that Östlihn painted also signals her sense of belonging — her social and cultural capital in the art field; her social network and meeting spots in lower Manhattan.

1 • Similar feminist art history projects are Linda Fagerström, *Randi Fisher — svensk modernist* (diss.) (Lund: Ellerströms, 2005); and Eva Zetterman, *Frida Kahlos bildspråk: Ansikte, kropp & landskap: Representation av nationell identitet* (diss.) (Gothenburg: Acta Universitatis Gothoburgensis, 2003).
2 • *"Vad gjorde Barbro Östlihns position och måleri möjliga i USA vid tidigt 1960-tal men omöjliga i den traderade svenska berättelsen om avantgardet?"* (italics in original). Annika Öhrner, *Barbro Östlihn & New York. Konstens rum och möjligheter* (Stockholm: Makadam, 2010), 12.

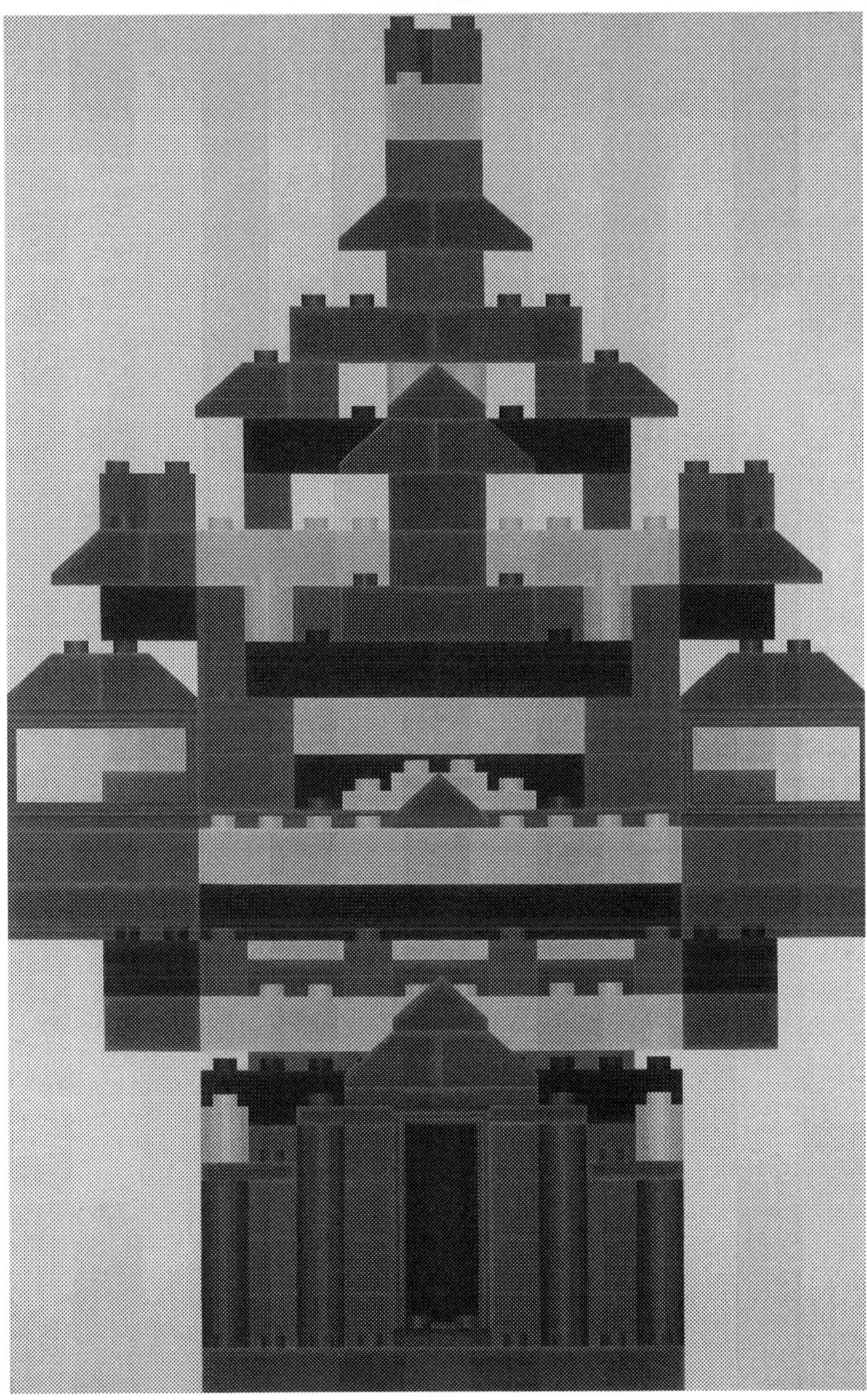

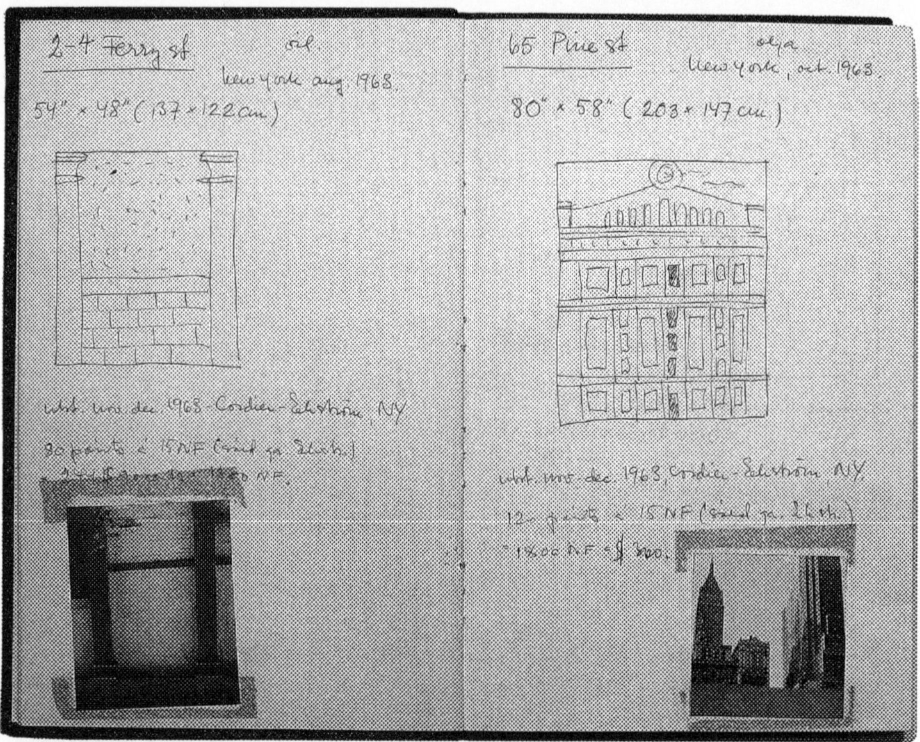

▴
Barbro Östlihn, Notebook.

According to Pierre Bourdieu a social field is autonomous in several important ways. Struggles for dominance in the art field are conditioned by each agent's habitus, and the *possible* positions existing in the field. Artistic relations in the avant-garde emerge here as positions in the struggle within the art field, rather than as stylistic traditions. Bourdieu distinguishes between fields of production and consumption, and the ways in which they create positions that are subject to power and capital flows. The aim of understanding Barbro Östlihn's artistic position within this social field of art, along with the idea of the "art scene" that frames the writer's argument, can certainly be said to have been well attended to. This individual focus is a paradoxical benefit of the field study format. The subtitle, "konstens rum och möjligheter" literally means "the rooms (or space, or places) and possibilities of art".

Öhrner demonstrates how Östlihn's social and cultural capital grows through her encounters with Fahlström in Stockholm, then with Rauschenberg and Jasper Johns, Arman, Lichtenstein, Billy Klüver, Jean Tinguely, and others in New York. She also develops a discussion of the gendered division of labour and power in Östlihn's and Fahlström's collaborations. Barbro Fahlström's (Östlihn's) initials on the Fahlström-attributed

◂
Barbro Östlihn, *Erik's House*, 1965.

painting *Dr. Livingstone, I Presume* (1960–61, Centre Georges Pompidou) have, for instance, been covered by the frame. Öhrner caustically concludes that the rough understanding between the artists seems to be that Östlihn produced works for Fahlström and he gave her a male collegial network.

But even though "the" field of art constantly churns out new actors and practices, it is hard to envision a position that could be described as an autonomous and separate sphere of action. Some parts are market driven, other aspects more local or bound up in multiple registers and hierarchies. However as a specific locality and set of opportunities or lack thereof in a given situation, an art scene on the other hand might appear to be more concrete than that of a field — socially, discursively, and geographically. Alan R. Solomon, US pavilion commissioner to the Venice Biennale in 1964, lent his voice to this idea by showing how the conception of an "art scene" was operationalised at the time. The same year, Arthur C. Danto published his seminal article "The Artworld" (1964). Such interesting cross-references show how grounded and widespread this theoretical understanding of an "art scene" was. Öhrner places Östlihn's career in between America and Europe. This is a more distinctive situation that should be distinguished from other aspects of the "international" avantgarde. Consider the difference between the Swede Östlihn working with the support of national cultural policies and grants (which to an even greater extent applies to Fahlström) and US citizens on the New York art scene. Their relative dependence on market or state institutions like the Moderna Museet in Stockholm makes a difference. The spatial-material perspective zooms between the concrete studio-home in Stockholm and New York and the more abstract spaces of the Manhattan Urban Renewal project, or even the social space that is the art world, which includes artists' labour and the positions that are produced in the studio space. Included in this social space we find exhibitions, the cross-section between artworks, public, and art institutions.[3] But in looking for avantgarde positions, the art field fractures into national and gendered — not to speak of racialized — art scenes with sometimes slim chances of linkage.

3 • Annika Öhrner, *Barbro Östlihn*, 18.
4 • Öyvind Fahlström, "The Ecstatic House." *Konstrevy* (471966): 152–55, 191–92, and "Barbro Ostlihn." *Art International* (Feb. 1968): 46–48, in Annika Öhrner, *Barbro Östlihn*, 36.
5 • "By discussing the way in which photography points out or designates, I have here showed that the indexical function of the photograph can be interpreted as performative. The photograph designates the fact that someone has turned the camera towards the motif and taken the picture. In other words, the photograph implies the one who has made a selection from reality." Annika Öhrner, *Barbro Östlihn*, 59. However, I understand Green and Lowry's views on the performativity of photography on page 57 otherwise. If the photographic act is part of a performative statement it is also tied to a specific time and place. The inverse does not necessarily follow.

The 1963 reviews of a solo show at Cordier & Ekstrom provide material for a discursive analysis of Östlihn's painterly project. Öhrner also turns to Fahlström's articles "The Ecstatic House" (1966) and "Barbro Ostlihn" (1968) that locate her paintings within a context of the "new abstract painters in New York: Stella, Reinhardt, Kelly, et al."[4] Öhrner thus demonstrates how Östlihn's paintings are located within the New York avantgarde. However, topical issues and connections in the Manhattan 1960s avantgarde cannot be readily assumed as valid on the Stockholm art scene, and even less in current art history, in Sweden or elsewhere.

Similar discursive limits apply to textbooks in art history. They may represent some sort of abstract doxa, but it is very difficult to identify practitioners who would endorse the kind of statements given in these introductory surveys. These books promote an institutionalised discourse: the institution of the art history textbook with strict limits set by comparable coffee table books on the small Swedish market. There is a gap between discourse surrounding Östlihn's one-person gallery show at Cordier & Ekstrom in 1963 and that of today's art history textbooks. What do 1960s New York reviews signify to Swedish art history textbook writers, and inversely what do positions in textbook art history tell about Östlihn's position in the 1960s? According to my experience (with its typical limitations) neither art historians nor artists rely on textbooks as valid sources to historical oeuvres; the survey genre is tied more closely to a consumerist position within the field.

The way the idea of performativity is used in the study also calls for a comment.[5] The descriptive titles of Östlihn's paintings have been mentioned, as well as her habit of collecting photos and notes on physical environments for future work. If I understand correctly, the author suggests that there is a performative gesture in Östlihn's titles and photo materials that unmoors the formal meaning of the paintings and orients their interpretation towards the painter-author. But why are these neighbourhood photo studies performative gestures beyond the fact that they produce an author effect? The referents of symbolic titles, and indexical-iconic photographic pictures could be said to anchor the meaning of the paintings when brought together. A performative effect however implies a specific situation, someone who can realise a potential such as recognizing Barbro Östlihn's range of motifs as a strategic proof of her membership in the Lower Manhattan avantgarde. If so, this presupposes familiarity with both locations and those who frequent them.

Although published in Swedish Öhrner's book will, no doubt, be followed by several articles in international forums.

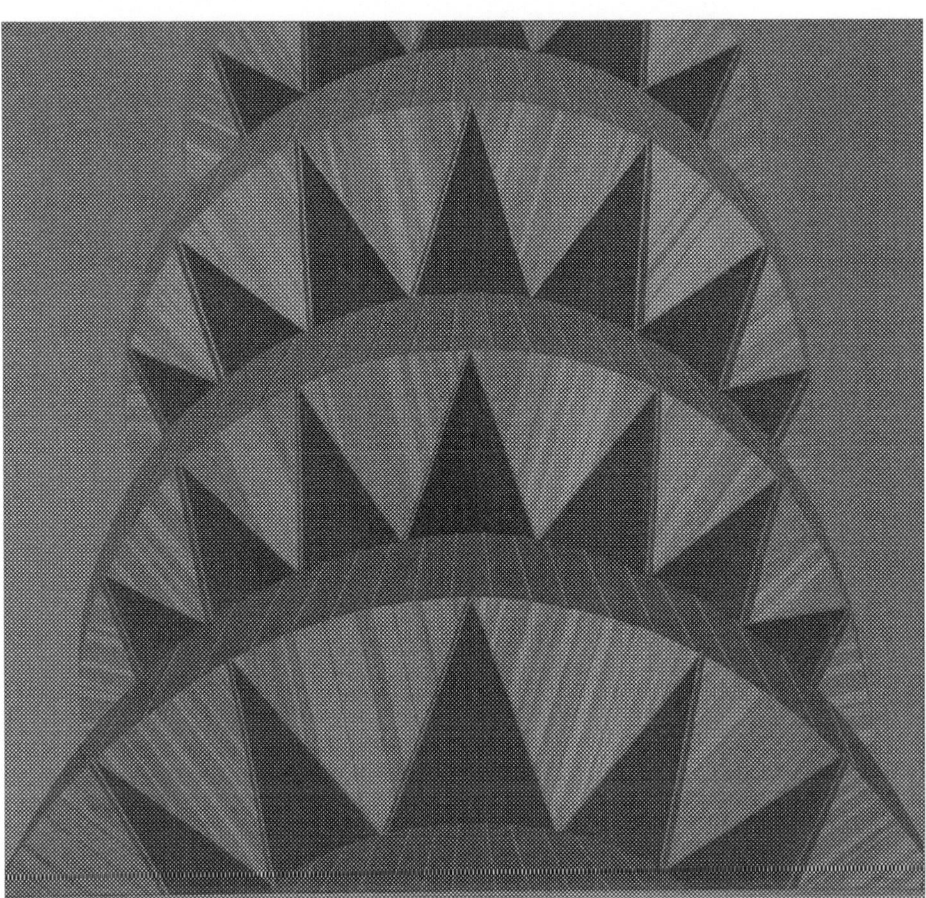

▲ **Barbro Östlihn, *Chrysler Building*, 1962.**

However the choice of language puts more at stake than simply the size of the audience. Implied readers always give the narrative a certain optic in advance. There is no universal way to relate Barbro Östlihn's participation in a 1960s New York art scene vis-à-vis present day Swedish art history. The art field may be more or less autonomous from other fields such as those of economy and religion, but within the social field of art several scenes coexist that also undergo aesthetic and institutional reconstitution. If the book had been written in English, universal identification with New York motives and discourse might well be expected. Öhrner does show us how well Östlihn connected to New York through the incorporation of street names and iconic buildings into her paintings, but that does not immediately translate into an advantage in the Stockholm art scene.

Social capital is consumed and must be replenished. This explanation is as good as any for the absence of certain artists in art history, Swedish or otherwise. Publishers may like to think that some male masters are too dear to survey-book readers to be replaced by women. However, a curator and writer of Annika Öhrner's calibre shows us that history is not written once and for all. In fact, her curatorial practice undermines the claim that art history is the privileged domain for authors and readers. It is a performative field of potentialities, but only in proportion to its relevance to in-group agents. •

Annika Öhrner, *Barbro Östlihn & New York. Konstens rum och möjligheter*, diss., (Dept. of Art History, Uppsala University / Gothenburg & Stockholm: Makadam, 2010).

Charlotte Bydler is Lecturer in Art History at Södertörn University, Stockholm.

"Pastoral Power" and the Techniques for Controlling the Poor and Unemployed

Maurizio Lazzarato

In the course of my research into job insecurity, I discovered the richness of Foucault's toolbox when it comes to an analysis of techniques for governing the unemployed and the poor (the "RMIs") in France.[1] First I would like to present his theory of pastoral power and confront it with the control of job insecurity as a mass phenomenon in our societies, and then, via the literature of Kafka, which Deleuze and Guattari relate directly to the theory of power in Foucault, analyze the production of culpability carried out by welfare bureaucracy.

In the labor market, different *dispositifs* are at work, and heterogeneous power relations exist. Apart from these general laws, passed by the parliament, and which define, for example, the minimum working hours, and apart from the roles and norms negotiated by the social parties — employer and labor unions — which may relate to the agreements between enterprises, as well as to the modes of financing and distributing unemployment benefits, there is a whole "archipelago" of factual power relations that are neither global nor general, but local, molecular, and singular.

Individual monitoring of the unemployed, techniques for making RMIs "enter" into the labor market, management of companies, coaching of employees as if they were "unemployed,"

1 • *Revenu minimum d'insertion,* the minimal wage stipulated to ensure that the unemployed can make their "entry" (*insertion*) into the labor market. *Trans.*

generalized continual training and education, the means for accessing credit and repaying one's debts — all of these install processes of subjection that are different from being subjected to a law, a contract, or a democratic institution.

These techniques of differentiation, individualization, and molecular subjection, which are sketched out or prefigured in what Michel Foucault calls "pastoral power," have been inflected, modified, enriched, and augmented, first by the "police" of the *raison d'Etat* in the 16th and 17th centuries, and then by the welfare or "providence" state, *l'État-providence* (where the word "providence" points to its religious origin) at the end of the 19th and the beginning of the 20th centuries, in a process that has transformed the techniques for "governing souls" into techniques for "political governing of men." This genealogy permits us to specify the molecular nature of the effects of power produced by a liberal governmentality.

Christianity, the only religion that has organized itself into a church, "gave rise to an art of conducting, directing, leading, guiding, taking in hand, and manipulating men, an art of monitoring them and urging them on step by step, an art with the function of taking charge of men collectively and individually throughout their life and at every moment of their existence."[2]

This art of governing is, as it were, completely unknown to political philosophy and to the theories of law. This form of power, "the strangest form of power, the form of power that is most typical of the West, and that will also have the greatest and most durable fortune," this form of power, which is "unique [...] in the entire history of civilizations,"[3] has, unlike the majority of modern and contemporary political models, no relation to the Greek and Roman political tradition.[4]

The pastoral power and its modern sequels should not be confounded with the procedures utilized to subject people to a law, to a sovereign, or to democratic institutions. Governing, Foucault says, is not the same as "ruling," it is not the same as "making law." All the theories and practices of sovereignty (of the king, the prince, the people), the theories and practices of the *arche*, i.e. a political organization founded on the question of who is entitled to command and who is entitled to obey (which is the fundamental question in the political analyses of Hannah Arendt and Jacques Rancière), all the theories of juridical-democratic practices, and not to forget

2 • Michel Foucault, *Sécurité, territoire, population* (Paris: Seuil, 2004), 168; *Security, Territory, Population*, trans. Graham Burchell (London: Palgrave Macmillan, 2007), 165. Henceforth: *STP* (page references to the French edition).
3 • *STP*, 134.
4 • Foucault would be astonished in two respects by the analysis of biopower proposed by Giorgio Agamben. First, because Agamben makes Foucault's theory of power into a metaphysics, and second, because its genealogy would lead us back to the Roman political tradition. This is categorically excluded by Foucault.

most currents of Marxism — all of them overlook the procedures of governing conducts, which, in fact, are what is essential in the power relations within capitalism, and particularly in contemporary capitalism.

Foucault enumerates the characteristics of this "micro"-power, and in each case he underlines that which distinguishes them from the modern and ancient practices of "macro"-power. Pastoral power establishes between human beings a series of complex, continuous, and paradoxical relations, which are not political in the sense in which this is understood by democratic institutions, by political philosophy, and by almost all revolutionary and critical theories. Pastoral power is a "a strange technology of power treating the vast majority of men as a flock with a few as shepherds."[5]

Unlike sovereignty, this power is not exerted over a territory (city, kingdom, principality, republic), but on a "multiplicity in movement" (the herd in the practices of the church, and "population" in governmentality).[6] Instead of relating to individuals as legal subjects "capable of voluntary actions," of transferring their rights and delegating their power to representatives, and of assuming public offices of the *polis*, pastoral power focuses on "living subjects", on their everyday behavior, their subjectivity and consciousness.

The pastor, Foucault remarks, is fundamentally not a judge, a man of the law, or a citizen, but a doctor. Pastoral power is a "benevolent" power; it attends at once to the herd and the sheep of the herd, taking charge of them one by one. Unlike sovereignty (or the law), which is exercised in a collective manner, pastoral power is exercised in a "distributive" fashion (its action takes place "from individual to individual", in intimate relations, and it communicates via singularities). It is preoccupied with every soul, with every situation in its particularity, rather than with a superior unity formed by the totality. Its actions are local

5 • Michel Foucault, "Omnes et singulatim: Toward a Critique of Political Reason," in *Essential Works of Foucault*, ed. James M. Faubion (London: Penguin, 2002), vol. 3, 303. Henceforth: *EW*.

6 • The space in which pastoral power is exercised does not have the same nature as the space of sovereignty and its disciplines. If sovereignty "capitalizes a territory" and discipline is exercised over a closed space by a hierarchical and functional distribution of elements, pastoral power, just as the police and then later the welfare state, is exercised over a multiplicity in movement and over its "milieu." Pastoral power, transformed from a government of souls into a political government of men, will "plan a milieu in terms of events or series of events or possible elements, of series that will have to be regulated within a multivalent and transformable framework." The "specific space" of this type of power thus relates to the "temporal and the aleatory" (*STP*, 22).

7 • The political government of men does not first of all aim at the "common good." Already in the 16th century government is defined as a manner of disposing and conducting men and things, not toward a collective whole, a "common good" (kingdom, city, republic, democracy), but toward "convenient ends." This implies a plurality of particular ends (to produce the largest possible amount of wealth, increase the population, etc.), whose convergence, coordination, and synthesis are problematic.

and infinitesimal, instead of global and general.[7] Pastoral power, like its heirs, the "police"[8] of the *raison d'État* and the welfare state, is occupied with details: it intervenes into the infinitesimal, into the molecular aspects of a situation and a subjectivity. It is a continuous and permanent power. It is not exerted in an intermittent way, like the power founded on rights, sovereignty, or citizenship (transference of rights by contract, delegation of power by vote, exercise of magistracy), but throughout the day, and throughout one's life.

Pastoral power is individualizing. The techniques of pastoral individualization do not pass through the statutes of birth and wealth, but through a "subtle economy" that combines merits and faults, their trajectories and circuits. This economy of souls installs a complete dependence, a relation of subjection and absolute and unconditional obedience, not with respect to the law or to "reasonable" principles, but to the will of another individual. "To obey because it is absurd" is the motto of Christian subjection, the culmination of which is the rules of monastic life, whereas the Greek citizen does not allow himself to be led by anything but the law and the rhetoric of men, to the effect, Foucault claims, that "the general category of obedience" did not exist among the Greeks.

The pastor is also a doctor of the soul, who teaches forms of existence. The pastor should not limit himself to teaching the truth, but also and above all he has to guide consciousnesses, by way of a mode of acting that is "non-global and non-general," always specific and singular. Saint Gregory enumerated up to thirty-six different ways to teach, varying in relation to the individuals that are to be addressed (rich, poor, married, sick, happy or sad, etc.). This teaching does not occur through the laying down of general principles, but by way of "an observation, a supervision, a direction exercised at every moment and with the least discontinuity possible over the sheep's whole, total conduct." Pastoral knowledge thus produces "a never-ending knowledge of the behavior and the conduct of the members of the flock he supervises."[9]

The techniques of confession, examination of consciousness, etc., form a series of instruments for the investigation and examination of the relation to oneself and to others, which makes it possible to act on the affects and sensibilities of each subjectivity. The pastor must "account for every act of each of his sheep, for everything that may have happened between them, and everything good and evil they may have done at the time."[10]

8 • Police means to further both the life of the citizens and the vigor of the state. "In seeing to health and to supplies, it deals with the preservation of life; concerning health, factories, workers, the poor, and public order — it deals with conveniencies of life. In seeing to the theater, literature, entertainment, its object is life's pleasures." (*EW*, 321)
9 • *STP*, 184.

The guiding of consciousness in pastoral power does not, as in ancient societies, have as its goal self-mastery, autonomy, and freedom (from the dependency on passions), but, on the contrary, aspires to a renunciation of all will, to humility, and to the neutralizing of all individual, personal, and egotistic activity.

Furthermore, pastoral power is not a power that installs and constitutes a community of equals and peers ruled by the principles of equity and liberty. It does not promote and support actions by citizens according to the modalities of the republican and democratic tradition, but a system of reciprocal and generalized dependencies. The techniques of pastoral power aim at the fabrication of a subject that is "subjected" to networks that imply everyone's general servitude to everyone.

The assimilation and transformation of these techniques of individualization by the police of the *raison d'État* in the 16th and 17th centuries will not fundamentally alter its nature. The police guarantees "a set of controls, decisions, and constraints brought to bear on men themselves, not insofar as they have a status or are something in the order, hierarchy, and social structure, but insofar as they do something, are able to do it, and undertake to do it throughout their life."[11]

The economy of merits and faults, the guiding of conducts in everyday life, and subjection, are still today the driving force behind practices that are supposed to individualize, control, regulate, and order the behavior of those that are governed, in work, unemployment, health, consumption, communication, etc.

The techniques of management that expand from the corporate sphere out into "social security" (individualizing regulation of unemployed, RMIs, poor) and into society at large (schools, hospitals, communication, consumption) are always inspired by those molecular practices that distribute merits and faults, and produce dependency and subjection, even when dependency and subjection, as in the case of the individual entrepreneur, occurs through activation and mobilization of the individual's own initiative, freedom, and capacity to act.

Pastoral power is not exercised in the open, in the transparency and visibility of public space, but in the opacity of micro-relations (from individual to individual, from institution to individual), in the dimly lit everyday activities in the factory, the school, the hospital, the social service institution. It is these molecular power relations — which produce fractal and multiple divisions and hierarchies, more subtle and mobile than the traditional oligarchies of wealth and birth — that will undergo a constant extension and an exponential growth in capitalism.

10 • *STP*, 173.
11 • *EW*, 416.

The Individual Monitoring of the Unemployed and RMIs as a Technique of Pastoral Control

Now I will cite a few extracts from interviews with RMIs that we are in the process of conducting, and which relate to the individual tracking to which they are subjected by institutions for the control of the poor.

The relation set up in individual monitoring consists in the action (of the agent) on the action (of the beneficiary), and it aims to structure that latter's capacity for acting. It thus constitutes a "strategic" relation between two subjects, in the sense that while the relation remains non-symmetric, both the agent and the beneficiary are "free," as Foucault would say, i.e., they have the capacity to act differently. It is expressed in techniques that aim to conduct the conduct of the beneficiaries, control their behavior, to activate, motivate, and make them embark upon a pre-set track (*project* is the most frequent word) and attain a corresponding identity. The techniques used in the monitoring relate to life, to intimacy, to that which is most subjective in the RMI beneficiary. They incite the poor person to question himself, his "lifestyle," and his "projects." They oblige him to undertake work on himself.

But in this individual monitoring, techniques and strategies of resistance also emerge, opposed to those mobilized by the institutions, where the individual aims not to be governed, or to govern oneself otherwise, to govern oneself. Should we, with respect to individual monitoring, speak of a production of subjection? Should we speak of a construction of competences that correspond to what economists call "human capital," i.e. to an autonomous individual, responsible for his employability?

D: For instance, the competence checks, they propose them all the time and you had better know what this means, there's always a dimension which becomes very intimate. I know people who have made extended checks, and even though they are super-oriented towards employment and their potential to change their life, it's also an exercise that you don't propose to everyone, that you're not necessarily used to doing, a kind of life-check where you stop to reflect on yourself, a kind of intrusion of a really disgusting vocabulary, but which gives you an opportunity to reflect.

F: Since I look young, and indeed I was young, the relation often becomes one between an adult and a teen — and on top of that, it was a woman — ; I will find my way, she's there to give me advice. For the moment it's not very alarming that I don't have a steady job yet... Sometimes it's easier to play the game, to give them what they want to hear, instead of being "really sincere."

D: One time she asked me questions about my interests or what I wanted to do with my life or why I had chosen to do what I had done, and I turned the question back to her, "and you, why are you working in the social sector?" Because I felt it was going too far, that I didn't have to tell her my whole life (...) I thought that if she insisted, it's because of the image she has of me, how she interprets the situation: that I'm someone who hasn't yet found his line of work, his way, that I must be helped so that I better understand what happens, because I have potential, but I have to find my way.

U: I couldn't stand that type of relation, where I had to justify myself, tell the story of my life, and I told her absolutely nothing — she must have taken me for an idiot.

E: (...) I'm playing a game even if it sometimes can be at the limit of what interests me, for instance being confronted with the responsibility for a project that would be possible and realistic. Sometimes this comes close to the question: what makes you get up in the morning and do things? This sort of monitoring also forces you to think about "projects" that you would like to do, but that you haven't started yet — or that you will never start, since you don't know, since it's difficult and it poses questions about what you're getting into, about your life and "what projects" — this word is there all the time — you're doing. But this is not what they think, in the sense that it could touch me, they just use these words. It's like speaking about different things using the same words.

Now I would like to cite some brief extracts from a round table that we organized with the agents from the unemployment benefit society, who are in charge of the RMI, and who intervene in the control of the unemployed and the poor. These extracts will serve as an introduction to the last part, which deals with the production of responsibility and culpability in the recipients of unemployment benefits and RMI via techniques of pastoral power, which I, however, will analyze through the literature of Kafka. The references to Foucault are direct and stimulating, as Deleuze and Guattari suggest, since they interrogate, in a different fashion, the new relations of power and subjection in which we are caught.

M: In my work, what the logic of "entry" amounts to, particularly in relation to the logic of integration, is that it acts on the person. In other words, it's the person who must re-qualify and enter into a process in order to meet the standards. This is the basic problem of structural unemployment, since the responsibility is handed over to the individual: they are the ones who are unable to get a job, and social work will consist in acting directly on these people. And when the work of the APNE encounters the work of the educator out in society, it's within this logic. This contributes considerably to orienting what we do: one thinks a priori that it is the individuals who must improve their capacities.

A: At the local employment office, this is what we bring about, to make the "client" responsible for his situation. This is really it. And on the opposite end this produces a general sense of complicity, which is either hard to accept or is completely accepted, and it maintains a form of everyday impotence, which gives rise to resistances, although in individual ways. This is because the counselor on the opposite side is also rendered responsible for his capacity or incapacity to make the "client" employable or not.

Kafka and the Production of Culpability

> Social security was born out of the labor movement, and it ought to be inhabited by a luminous spirit of progress. But what do we see? This institution is nothing but an obscure nest of bureaucrats, among which I serve as the unique and representative Jew.

The production of culpability — a strategic effect of neo-liberalism treated at length by Nietzsche, who was the great inspiration for Foucault's theory of power relations — can also be analyzed via the literature of Kafka.

Kafka was way ahead of his time, since his characters speak of a reality, of an organization of work and administration (the welfare state), which seems closer to us than to the interwar period.

Bürgel, the secretary of communication in *The Castle*, says something that has become familiar to us: "We make no distinction between time, time as such, and the time of work. These distinctions are foreign to us." And K., the land surveyor in *The Castle*, experiences a relation to power that we, following Foucault, could qualify as biopolitical, in the sense that it encompasses his life in its totality: "Nowhere else had K. seen administration and life entangled to such an extent, so entangled that one sometimes felt that each had taken the place of the other."

The institutions of *administration*, like the RMI, unemployment benefits, etc., say something before they articulate a discourse of any kind. They posit that there is a problem (such as unemployment, employability, etc.), and that it will no longer be society that is called upon to ensure the *individual monitoring*, but... *you*, "Joseph K.!" There is a sliding from "there is a social problem" to "you are the problem!" This sliding is contained in the institutions themselves, in their practices and procedures, before it exists in the heads of social workers and beneficiaries.

Just as in *The Trial*, the accusation is never clearly formulated (one attempts to incite the following thought: unemployment, that's your fault! — but that's difficult, because the fact of unemployment has vague, undefined, and imprecise contours. The only possible definition is a political one, which is not without posing certain problems!).

But it is soon forgotten that the accusation is more than muddled. Gradually it produces the sensation that you are guilty of something, that you are *defective*, since a paper has indeed been received, you have indeed been summoned and/or arrested, and you must indeed present yourself at a certain address, at a certain hour, in a certain office. The *arrest* of Joseph K. does not in any way change his life, he continues working and living as he did before. He is thus at once free and under arrest. No matter if you're guilty or innocent, there will be a dossier on *you*, "Joseph K!" There is a dossier somewhere, there are functionaries occupying themselves with it, but *you will never see* anything but the servants of the institution, never the grand procurators. And furthermore, is there a vertical institution of offices, with bosses and underlings, or does everything occur horizontally, between *subalterns*? In fact both are true, but in any circumstance, the useful piece of information is always to be found in the adjacent office, you must always knock at the next door, ad infinitum.

3949 is a telephone platform that takes the place of the face-to-face encounter with the agents of the institution. It is the contemporary version of the office. One must dial 3949 several times in order to arrive at different functionaries and verify whether the same law applies, since they all interpret it differently. Often they are ignorant of it, and anyway they hang up within six minutes. Then you have to knock at the adjacent door, etc. 3949 is a deterritorialization of the office and the functionary.

The "tribunals" of *The Trial*, just like the accusation, have no clearly defined limits (the barriers that delimit the bureau of administration are "mobile, and one must not see them as precise demarcations," Barnabas says in *The Castle*). They are dispersed in the city, and it is unclear of whom they consist.

I contend that the *law* in Kafka is more akin to social laws, to the regulations of social security, etc., than to the penal law, since the former is relatively malleable, it proliferates continually and expands permanently. It has margins that the beneficiaries as well as the functionaries can exploit, depending on the institution in question.

Of the three types of acquittal — real acquittal (*which has never been heard of*), apparent acquittal (which *calls for a violent and momentary effort*), and indefinite postponement (*a small and constant effort*) — it is the last that interests us the most.

Real acquittal exists only theoretically. Apparent acquittal stems from disciplinary societies, where one passed from one enclosure to another, from one culpability to another: from the family to the school, from the school to the army, from the army to the factory, etc. And each passage is marked by a judgment or an evaluation: you are no longer a child, you are no longer at school, etc., which leads to another process that gives rise to another dossier: you are a soldier, you are a worker, you are retired, etc.

Indefinite postponement, on the other hand, maintains the process indefinitely in its first phase, i.e., in a situation where one is presumed to be at once innocent and guilty (you are caught up in a process: you have been summoned, and there is a dossier). In indefinite postponement, the verdict that declares you guilty or not guilty never comes. The state of being suspended between innocence and guilt obliges you to be constantly mobilized, accessible, and to stay sharp.

Indefinite postponement demands even more attention, "a small but constant effort," the painter Tintoretti says, i.e., a more intense subjective implication.

The law has no interiority, the law is empty (the law is *pure form*), since it is *you*, "Joseph K.," who must, if everything works well, contribute to its construction, and *construct your sentence by working on your dossier and keeping track of when you are summoned.*

In the monitoring relation, woven by culpability and trial/process, you must play the game while still remaining aloof from it. You must anticipate the developments, the turns, the bumps, without really believing in them (there is a *cynicism* of the functionaries and the beneficiaries).

In all respects *your subjectivity* is summoned, and it implicates itself. It works, thinks, hesitates, poses questions to itself, even against *your* will.

The indefinite prolongation of the first phase of the process implies a monitoring without end. The time spent by the accused and the time spent by the monitoring are adjusted to one another.

The interrogations are very brief; if you don't have the time to go, or don't feel like going, you may be excused a couple of times; with certain judges one can even regulate the schedule in advance for a whole period; in the end it's about presenting yourself from time to time to the magistrate in order to fulfill your duty as an accused.

Just as in *The Trial*, to be accused does not mean to be at rest. It's work, you must follow your dossier, spend a lot of time on it (whoever is *industrious* spends all of his time and money on his defense).

For the intermittent, the task of following their trial and dossier becomes a second job. One must be updated on the development of the law, on its transformations. One must probe its subtleties. One must rise to the same level of knowledge as the functionaries, even surpass them. The RMIs prepare for their meetings, for their face-to-face encounter with the institution, and they elaborate a tactics of their own. They perfect more or less fantastic "projects." They are all engaged in delivering, directly or indirectly, indications and information, caught up in a feedback loop with the institution.

In the disciplinary societies the penal law was justified by the struggle against illegalities and by the promise of a peaceful society, but in reality, instead of eliminating illegalities, it produced and differentiated *crimes* and criminals. In the same way, in the societies of control, the social law is justified by the struggle against unemployment and the promise of full employment, but it does nothing but invent, multiply, and differentiate thousands of ways of employing all of your time being unemployed. Just like the penal law, the social law has not failed, but fully succeeded. •

Translation: Sven-Olov Wallenstein

Maurizio Lazzarato is a sociologist living and working in Paris. His most recent book is *La fabrique de l'homme endetté : Essai sur la condition néolibérale* (Editions Amsterdam, 2011).

Inventing a Silence

Alexandre Costanzo

The most wonderful thing about my burrow is the silence. — Franz Kafka

A man exits from a hole, a cavity in the rocks facing an abandoned village in the deserted landscape, and starts walking. Later on, we see him crossing the vast, snowy and desolate country, carrying heavy bags. And the camera follows him all along his enigmatic journey in a curious companionship *(Man with No Name)*. Somewhere else, two workers start a game of chess in the break room of a factory, while another one is about to get dressed. The camera takes in the whole scene, then centers on the game, and finally shifts to the undressed man. He departs and the camera rapidly sets off in pursuit, following him through the corridors, all the way to the door through which the man hurries. The cameraman opens the door, which leads to a shower room where the workers are washing off *(Tie Xi Qu: West of the Tracks)*. All these scenes form a very singular cinematic grammar. In fact, there is a lot of moving along in the films of Wang Bing: when there is walking, he catches people on their way, bringing us along to experience the real in some kind, raw. It is fair to say that what characterizes this work is first of all the walking, the march. And the obvious question is: where are these steps taking us?

In accordance with this grammar, the chronicle of a woman, *Fengming,* begins with the only outdoor scene of the film. We see the back of an old woman dressed in black, walking through the alleyways of a city on a clear winter's day, slowly avoiding the icy patches of the street. The camera follows her for some minutes, tracking her footsteps all the way to her apartment. It halts at the ending point of the woman's path, leading to the threshold of a dimly lit door. Inside the apartment, we find her filmed from a slight angle, sitting in a big armchair where she starts to talk. From this moment, the story will go on for almost four hours, filmed by Wang Bing without any cuts, principally in one medium shot. In this living room, she recounts her memories, speaking in one single stream of words. From the young woman she was at seventeen, enthusiastic about the revolution after the Second World War, to the accusations of right-wing sympathies that fell on her and her husband in 1957, leading to the couple's deportation to a labor camp and the death of her husband. This agonizing story told by Fengming thus comprises the death of her beloved, years of hunger

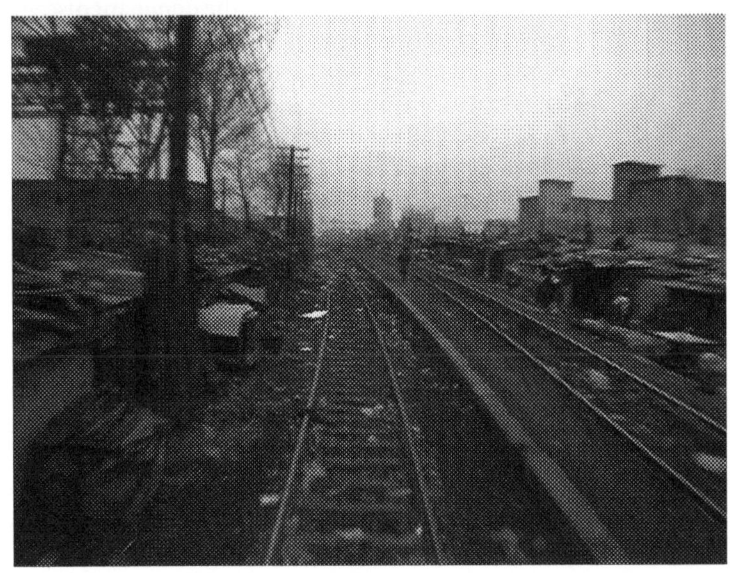

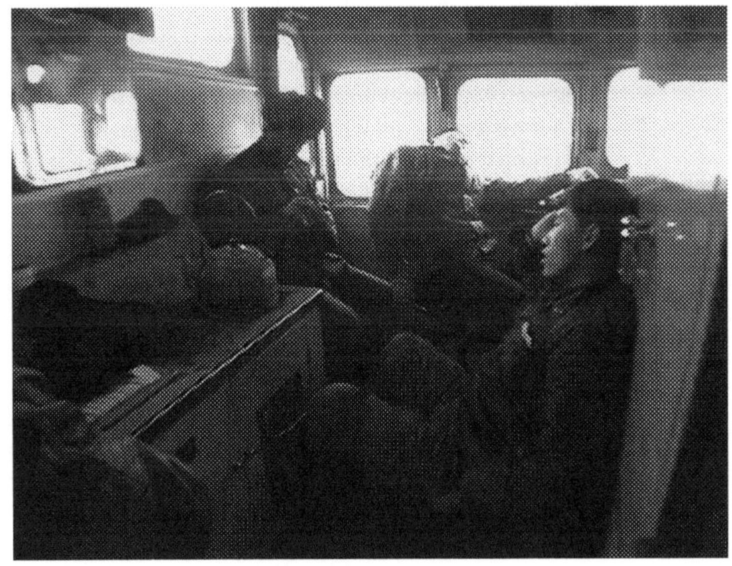

◂
Stills from Wang Bing, *West of the Tracks*, 2003.

in the camps, broken dreams, and a destroyed existence. She recovers the word that was taken from her during the political accusations, in the camps, and in the dominant discourse. And she speaks simply to say that she never was a traitor, to vindicate this man and the 500,000 other internally exiled, and to say what is real about an existence that is reduced to a "one must go on". Because one had to survive, by swallowing cottonseed or stealing pinches of flour. One had to go on. In this old lady, at once frail and alert, there is something like a force, life plain and simple, a courage that continually pushes her further. But what is striking is the precision of her remarks, reminiscent of meticulous paintings, full of details in its scenes: scenes of battle, her declining eyesight, the flour balls, her horrible time at the camp with her husband, the return to daily life, two kids to bring up, and then the cultural revolution and renewed suspicions against her, which would once more lead to expulsion to the Chinese countryside, lasting until her late rehabilitation...

And the camera of Wang Bing doesn't cut once, but adopts itself to the singularity of the place and the story. As she is telling this tragic story, shadows creep slowly across the room. After an hour, he interrupts her to ask if she could turn on the light, which she does before mechanically resuming her account. There is the patience of the scene, the recording camera, the strong affect that keeps growing as the words continue, the passing of time, as well as the tiredness growing as time passes; yet one listens, one imagines the things she says, and one observes this woman and her living room, the low table, the seaside painting, the knick-knack, before returning to her testimony. Between what she tells us — by acquainting us in the phantoms of her history — and what we see, there is a gap of an intimate distance, created by the recording camera making its film.

So Wang Bing is filming people, a woman in this case. He is filming people, but he is also filming time, by unfolding — as the words and scenes progress — a continuous present. In this sense, the film does nothing more than double the world as a continuous imprint of reality. It records this world in one single medium shot, like an erased and attentive presence, a companion to what takes place. And he leaves to Fengming to care for the mise en scène: from her small steps on the street leading to her apartment, to the surrounding daylight, the location, the small events that occur and finally the duration of the interview. The document is almost uncut, and the fixed camera shows the empty armchair while patiently waiting for the woman in those brief moments when she goes to the bathroom, or unplugs the phone that rings in the middle of her testimony. Thus there is no mise en scène: there is only what unfolds for a few hours. This is the art of Wang Bing: he constructs this subtracted presence as the fiction of a companionship to things, people and the present. The filmmaker is first of all a spectator of a situation, committing himself to what happens. In this fashion a world unfolds, a continuous present: the history of a frail woman, the triviality of things and the intimate unfolding of time. What Wang Bing suggests is nothing less than to live in the time and situation of the present, where he offers us to engage with the words of this woman.

Between what she says, what we see, and what we hear, there are moments and spaces constructed in the very intervals, when our gaze moves over the objects, the gestures, or a face, and then returns to what is being said. In doing so, these faint intervals open up to a scene of emancipation. The filmmaker and the old lady are really at the suitable distance for an "egalitarian" relation, just like the spectator who from this must create his or her own trajectory: there is nothing more to it than seeing or hearing, and this is the only intensity/power. There are no effects, nor any comments; there is just the empty space between them, which confronts us with what we see and hear in the patience of the shot. And this is perhaps the invention of the film: it opens up a time which is about listening and watching, and by doing so it invents a sort of void of dead angles, to be inhabited by the curious trajectories of our eyes and ears.

"I have no hesitation in stating that cinema has rarely gone such a long way toward making us aware of what it is to be a man. (And also, for that matter, of what it is to be a dog.)" These were the words by which André Bazin characterized *Umberto D.*, the famous film by Vittorio de Sica, and we could readily state that these words equally well define the work of Wang Bing, which also aims to give a bewildering and irrefutable report on the human condition. In *Man With No Name*, Wang Bing offers us another portrait, but this time without any words, presenting us with a lonely man, whose life is reduced to the most banal and minimal functions. He lives alone, does not talk to anybody, eats, sleeps, and passes his day working and watching over the land where his life takes place. In this manner we spend almost an hour and half in his company, getting familiar with his presence and his gestures, while he is walking or fertilizing his land, while he is preparing the fruits of his labor or smoking a cigarette, only to find him out on the fields again the next day...

The cinematic grammar of Wang Bing is as always one of a curious companionship, sharing a mutual light, mutual spaces and a mutual time, as well as the cold and the silence. The camera follows the man from behind and moves in lockstep with him as the scenes unravel, it stops to see its subject depart far away, follows him through a landscape or, most

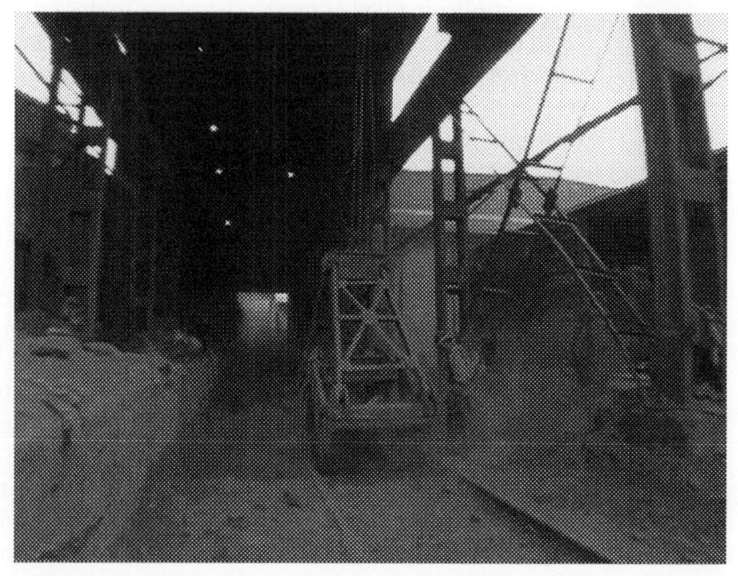

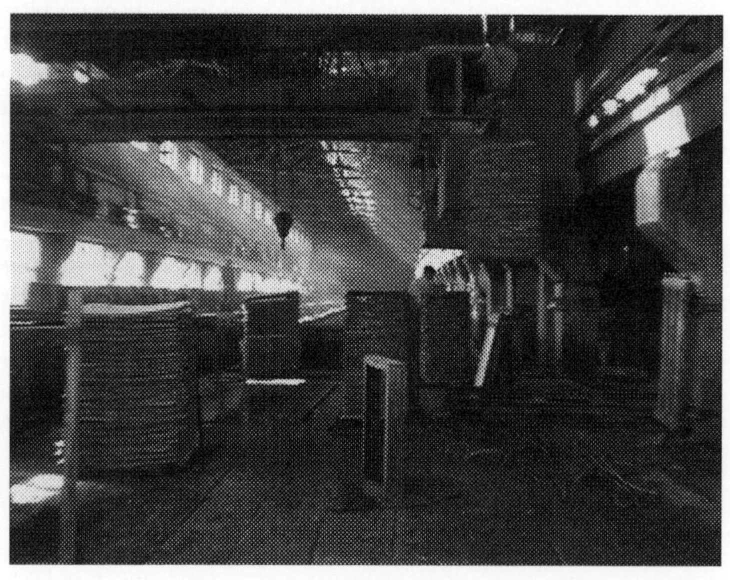

◂
Stills from Wang Bing, *West of the Tracks*, 2003.

often, it approaches him, fixes its gaze upon him and accompanies him patiently. It is always these curious figures of style and always these long sequence shots, whether the camera is still or in movement. Cinema has rarely gone such a long way towards making us aware of what it is to be a man — or for that matter, of what it is to be a dog. But here as well, as in the case of Fengming, there is an identical "one must go on". Thus he walks with his bags and fertilizes the land to secure his survival, according to a principle of determination and hard work. And following its traces, the camera pursues the beautiful and obscene real that overflows, exceeds or escapes the patience of the shots. It is the reality of a man who in fact collects dung from the fields to survive and winds his way through the countryside, but leads his life independently in his own kingdom. There is only one world. Doubtlessly, this is what we feel when we encounter this man with no name, and this is also what he tells us with his silence: I am a man, here is the place that I have made my own, here where I collect dung from the roads with my bare hands, and, above all, here where I keep going on. So in a sense one could say that the work of Wang Bing meets that of Samuel Beckett, when the latter recounts how a larva creeping in the dark with its bag extorts from another, met by chance, the anonymous story which is life. Here is also a man with his bag, crossing beautiful and terrible territories, and he meets someone else. The work of Wang Bing is always about the same thing: he meets men and women, and every time, by following them step by step, he extorts from them the silent or talkative story of what it is to live.

Of this grammar we can immediately say that it enables one to film the crudeness of a reality that we accompany and pursue. However, there is something more striking that characterizes the art of Wang Bing, and it is what the silence tells us: for example, the silence of the cameraman who watches and listens while Fengming talks, or the silence of the series of pictures of people, of scenes or landscapes that succeed one another in *Tie Xi Qu: West of the Tracks*. And with *Man With No Name*, this is all the more refined since its protagonist doesn't say a word, but simply goes on with his day. The method of Wang Bing is still the same: he accompanies people and situations according to a protocol that establishes a principle of equality between every character that takes part of it. There is a kind of care in the filming that induces this distance. In a clinical manner, he demonstrates the reality of the people by accompanying them, but his gaze is distant from the misery in the foreground. Because it is not about displaying somebody's suffering, or about helping whoever it might be. It is not about displaying a crude and miserable reality — it is present here as well as elsewhere — but he actually devotes himself as much to the beauty of people, landscapes, and situations. A beauty of shots permeates the whole film, a beauty that first of all tells us that we share it with the protagonist, and that there is only one single world. Thus we see him doing what he can to arrange the place where he lives, fertilizing the earth with rigor and care, crossing the vast plains while pursuing his dreams with a rare determination, which is exactly what makes this miserable character appear to us more like a sort of king lost in his own kingdom, a sublime wanderer from a one of Sophocles's tragedies, a man who creates his own path — while the camera registers the riches of his experience.

That being said, this mathematics of equality yet again opens the temporality of a merged continuous present, where anything that happens is defined and carried out by the other, the one being filmed. We remain spectators of a world through this camera that listens and watches, and it will be the other who gives to it its sense, that is, its direction in the shots and movement. And we discover trivial things in the works of Wang Bing: a man is irritated and complains, another worries about losing his job, and a third is angry. A woman talks in a living room, and somewhere else a man is out on a march... But across the intimate distance and the silence, a space is always accorded to the void in which our attention, as well as our eyes and ears, can wander. In *Fengming,* this distance is manifested through the patience of the shot, and in the actual distance in the space between the woman and the director. This distance is sharpened in *Man With No Name* by means of the silence, which is a silence to be populated. So the question will be: what does the silence say? Or even: what is this peculiar time, or this kind of void that structures a "rapport" to the things and to the worlds? What Wang Bing does is to construct a time that comprises a vacant space. And this "void" is nothing but a territory for emancipation. It gives time to the eyes to see and the ears to hear, it opens up a space and a time for the "body" of the spectator, a sort of intimate distance. And this is what it means to populate a silence. The eyes and ears go elsewhere, in the patience of the shot, but also with the direction of the steps as soon as the camera is summoned by a situation — there is someone to follow or there is a single shot of a scene, a landscape, or a face. And this is how the spectator makes his own film: the eyes and ears make their own way in the gap created by the distance, the experience of a time, and the void suggested by this kind of silence. We stated above that Wang Bing films people, but he also films time. And it is an emancipated time, some holes, spaces in the interval of certain trajectories, experiences, and lives.

Seeing, hearing, walking: these are the abstract passions of Wang Bing. There is a lot of moving along in the films of Wang Bing, and he catches people on their way. However, it is not about getting a grip of a lost sense; it is about following someone step by step. To Wang Bing, sense is never anything else than what is given by chance in confrontations and scenes: so he walks. To put it in another way, sense cannot simply be reduced to the signification of things and the world; here, we are dealing with direction. This is why he follows the trace, falls in behind somebody, and drags the anonymous accounts out of people he meets. He walks, he follows and pursues, but most of all he watches and listens, demonstrating for us the beauty of a miserable world. Perhaps this beauty amounts to the lost joy which Fengming is looking for in her history, while evoking the sky of her youth that "became blue anew" when she encountered communism, or while talking about the "moment of joy in plain dreariness" of a night with her husband when experimenting with the intensity of love. And there is the quote from Tolstoy that she retained from her beloved: "As long as there is life, there can be happiness". Surely, there are no longer the carefree joys of a blue sky, but life is still there, and life has a determined desire to fight and to live, as seen in the man with no name or the workers and the people from *Tie Xi Qu: West of the Tracks*. But the beauty is also what is constructed by the camera. It rushes in pursuit of people, but it also searches for something in the steps of the people that it follows. Reality is raw, life is miserable, and yet the world is beautiful, as is the rust, dust, and steam from the factories, or the men and women who break the ice on the water to take a bath in the scarcely lit washrooms. All this constitutes a grand poetics of matter, light, noise, sensations of cold or heat, or even hunger, in the curious synesthesia of *Tie Xi Qu: West of the Tracks.*

Certainly it is the walking that gives meaning and direction to the steps of the people. But there is another thing that the camera captures while accompanying these wanderings: it proves the "sensuality" of a temporality, the viod of a silence, and the intimacy of a distance. And it is in these "spaces" where a people can exist. And doubtlessly, between this absent people and the dead angles of the perception and determination of the steps of men and women, one glimpses the horizon of an improbable encounter. Because this is where the steps of Wang Bing lead us, in this curious territory where paths cross. So what remains with us after the film is the sequence shot of which you never know the end, following in somebody's footsteps, watching and listening to a woman talking while time passes by in her company, or going along the railroad tracks leading who knows where, traversing the landscapes like the aisles of factory halls or the detours through back alleys or homes. We do not know where we are, where we are going, nor what exactly happens; instead we discover this more or less through the detour of confrontations, before going somewhere else or following somebody new. The recurring theme is that of strolling through the life of people to discover whatever you may find there, the level of reality, of existence or of what it means to be a man. And all this occurs according to a principle of moving along, where the quotidian, errant or busy wanderings harmonize with those of the camera, which advances by its own care in time and space. Perhaps this care amounts to negotiating the improbable equation of beauty and the real through the lives of people, but first of all it would imply the injunction of openness. And then our eyes and ears can decide on their routes through the patience of the shot, which is where one — in its determination to move along, following the steps of people — stumbles on emancipated spaces and times. •

Translation: Karl Lydén

Alexandre Costanzo is a philosoper and writer living in Paris.

The Ground Zero Mosque that Wasn't One: Media and Architecture in America

Joel McKim

On December 9th, 2009, the *New York Times* ran a front-page article revealing that a five-story building in Lower Manhattan, located some two blocks north of the Ground Zero site, had been earmarked for the construction of an Islamic cultural centre. The building, at 45 Park Place, was formerly home to the Burlington Coat Factory, but had stood vacant for nearly eight years after sustaining considerable damage to its upper floors from falling airplane debris during the 9/11 attacks. At the time the newspaper feature was published the building had already been in use for several months as a Muslim prayer space, accommodating an overflow of worshippers from a crowded mosque located a little further north in the Tribeca neighbourhood. Feisal Abdul Rauf, the imam leading the $150 million project, envisioned the cultural centre as a means to challenge religious extremism and promote inter-faith dialogue between the moderate Muslim community of Manhattan and other New Yorkers. The structure would house cultural and recreational facilities open to all (including a fitness centre, a swimming pool, childcare facilities and a culinary school) in the mold of the 92nd Street Y or the Jewish Community Center. I recall my initial amazement upon reading the story, not because Muslim worshippers had been practicing their faith so close to the most scrutinized and emotionally charged building site in America or that a far more ambitious Islamic centre was being proposed at the location, but because there seemed to be relatively little opposition to either of these developments. The New York Times article listed Mayor Michael Bloomberg and Joy Levitt, the executive director of the Jewish Community Center, amongst those already voicing their support for the project. Levitt is quoted as saying, "For the J.C.C. to have partners in the

Muslim community that share our vision of pluralism and tolerance would be great." More astonishing still, the staunchly conservative Fox News Channel also seemed unfazed by the prospect of an Islamic cultural centre in Lower Manhattan. When the imam's wife, Daisy Khan, appeared on the Bill O'Reilly show on December 21st to discuss the project, guest-host Laura Ingraham concluded the amicable interview proclaiming, "I like what you're trying to do."

The general acceptance of the proposal appeared to be an indication that the psychic wounds inflicted on September 11th had finally begun to heal and an encouraging sign that the U.S. may be far more open to its Muslim citizens than many had presumed. But perhaps the lack of controversy should not have been cause for surprise. After all, Lower Manhattan has been home to two mosques for decades. The congregation of Masjid Manhattan has been worshipping peacefully on Warren Street, only four blocks from Ground Zero, since 1970. Masjid al-Farrah, a mosque in the Sufi tradition of Islamic mysticism where Imam Rauf has been leading prayer services since the mid-eighties, is located eight blocks further north on West Broadway. Although a now largely forgotten episode of New York's history, Lower Manhattan's close connection to the Arab world actually extends back even further in time. From the late nineteenth century until the 1940s, the section of Washington Street directly south of Ground Zero was commonly known as Little Syria. A 1939 WPA Guide to New York describes the rich sights and smells of the neighbourhood, with shops selling (along with shish kebabs, knafe and baclava), "graceful earthen water jars," "tables inlaid with mother of pearl," and "Syrian silks of rainbow hues."[1] While the majority of the Syrian and Lebanese immigrants who populated the area were Arab Christians, the period is a reminder of Lower Manhattan's long history of accommodating cultural difference within its boundaries.

And yet, from our current vantage point, the initial ease with which the city of New York embraced the idea of an Islamic community centre in Lower Manhattan also seems like quite a distant memory. During the summer and autumn of 2010 the project (officially named Park51) became the subject of an unrelenting media storm in both the traditional and online press. Referred to almost exclusively as the "Ground Zero mosque," the proposed centre was regularly characterised in these reports as a defiant symbol of Islamic victory on September 11th, an affront to the memory of the victims and a potential breeding ground for jihadi movements. Although certainly not alone in their indictment of the project, Fox News pursued the story with

1 • In Andrew Ross's "The Odor of Publicity." *After the World Trade Center: Rethinking New York City,* ed. Michael Sorkin and Sharon Zukin (New York: Routledge, 2002), 123.

particular verve and at the height of the controversy hosted commentators who oppose the centre on a nearly daily basis. The list of potentially misleading statements that circulated frequently within mainstream news coverage is too long to recount, but amongst them were recurring claims that Park51 would constitute a thirteen-story "mega-mosque" looking down on Ground Zero (the location of the center is not actually within sight of Ground Zero and only the two basement floors of the structure are to be devoted to prayer space) and that the opening of the "mosque" would provocatively coincide with the tenth anniversary of 9/11. Conservative commentators have persistently cast doubts on Feisal Abdul Rauf's ideological position and organizational affiliations, dismissing the well-respected imam's thirty-year track record of promoting inter-faith dialogue in New York and the numerous calls within his published writings for the development of democratic ideals in the Islamic world.[2] After months of sustained negative coverage within the conservative press, polls reported as many as seven out of ten Americans opposed the construction of the centre.

How might we begin to explain this rapid media transformation of an Islamic cultural centre into a dangerous and triumphalist "Ground Zero mosque"? Apart from exposing a national undercurrent of mistrust, the Park51 situation also reveals some troubling changes to the way communication technologies, politics and urban development converge in a post-9/11 America. In the aftermath of the 2001 World Trade Center attacks we witnessed two very different examples of media intersecting with issues of architecture that are worth recalling. The first was a remarkable public response to the challenge of rebuilding at Ground Zero in which New Yorkers, unsatisfied with a lack of transparency and lack of vision in the official development process, employed media technologies as a tool for intervention. Using the internet as a means to organize, pool knowledge and spread information, community coalitions formed under such names as the "Civic Alliance to Rebuild Downtown New York", "Rebuild Downtown Our Town" and "New York New Visions." These voluntary groups of architects, urban planners and Lower Manhattan residents produced thoughtful and substantive guidelines for redeveloping the area, stressing the need for diversity and mixed-use planning, and pushed city officials, at least temporarily, to change their level of public accountability. While these groups worked to alter the process of urban development in New York, another set of

2 • If a more legitimate critique were to be leveled at Imam Rauf it would be that he is often overly admiring of the contemporary American political and economic example. Post financial crisis, the unadulterated praise he bestows, in his 2004 book entitled *What's Right with Islam: A New Vision for Muslims and the West,* on "capitalist democracy's" traditions of unrestricted usury and the rights of the corporation appears somewhat misplaced.

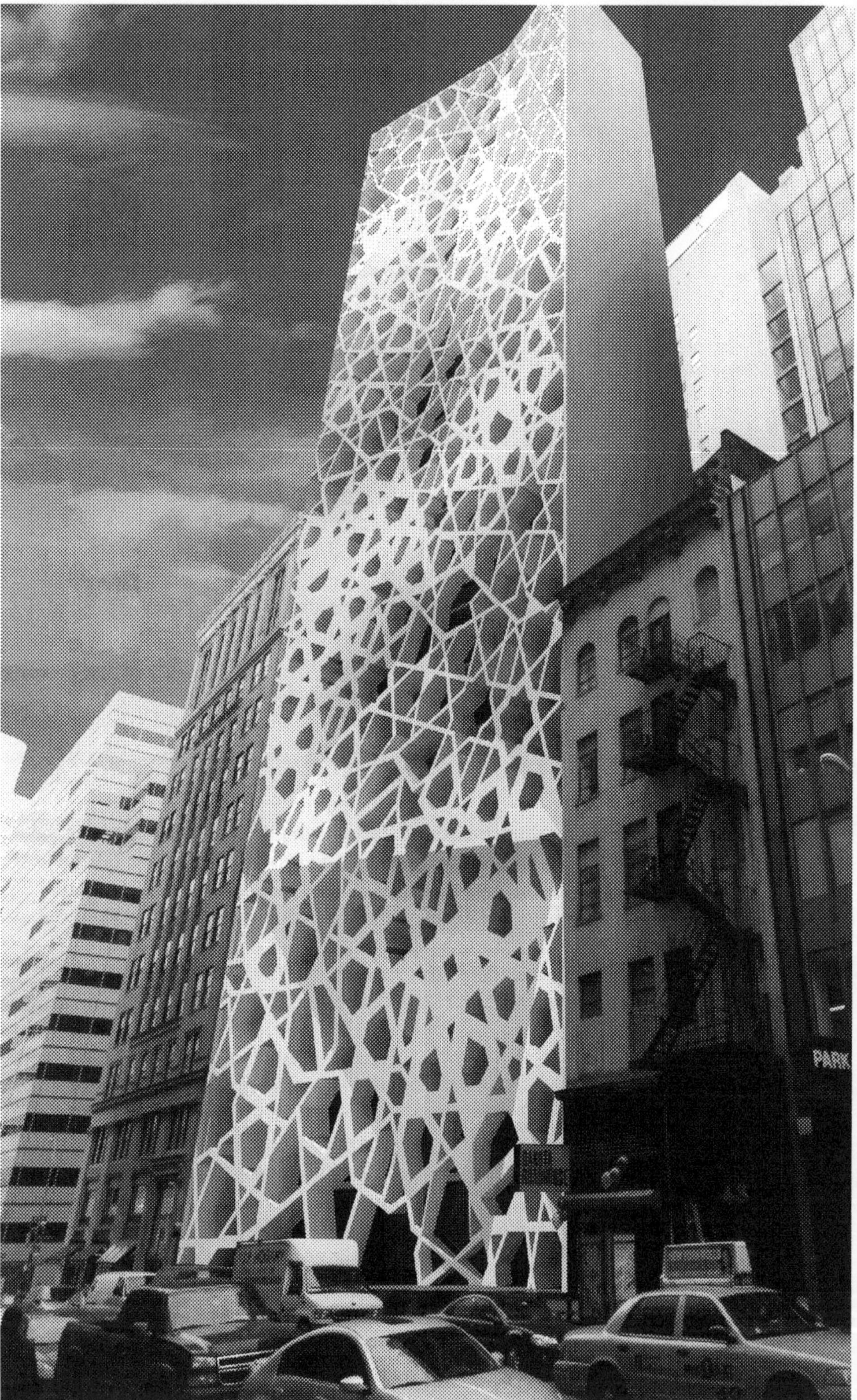
PARK

Design Sketches, Park51, © Soma Architects, New York, 2010.

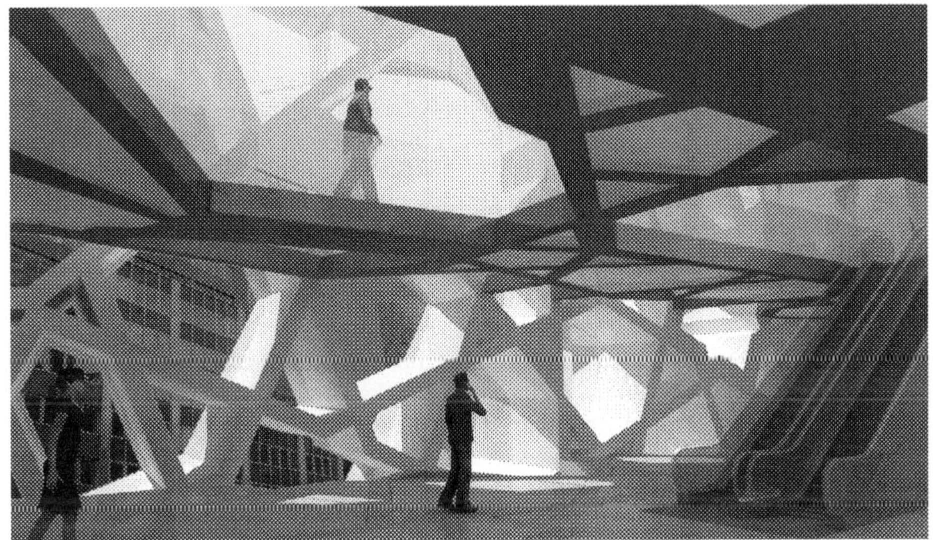

grass-roots organizations were also establishing a prominent presence online. The 9/11 conspiracy or "Truth movement," a loose organization of protest voices ranging from victim's family members to esoteric millenarians, has also called for a form of political transparency. At its most reasonable the movement questions officially sanctioned reports of 9/11 and makes demands for greater government accountability, but its members often descend into paranoiac and frequently xenophobic explanations of the "inside job" variety. Architecture is a primary obsession of the movement. Its members scrutinize the buildings involved in the attacks, studying the physics of load bearing columns, controlled demolition techniques and material melting points for signs of an even more sinister truth behind the event. Examining the movement is an object lesson in how information, or in this case misinformation, spreads online. But while 9/11 conspiracy claims continue to circulate within informal channels, the mainstream news media, taking seriously its role as an evaluator of credibility, has granted the "Truth movement" little access to its broadcast stream.

As all news providers move online to a greater extent, distinguishing between verifiable and questionable information becomes increasingly difficult — editorial content blends with user-generated commentary and mainstream news is always but a link away from a personal blog or an interest group-produced video. In the online environment, all sources of information reverberate against each other ceaselessly. Traditional and new media no longer run parallel to one another, they are interwoven. But in the case of the Park51 discussion, the tenuous, yet crucial, demarcation line between credible and incendiary sources of information has eroded considerably. One indication of this change in media attitudes is the space provided by the mainstream news to conservative blogger Pamela Geller, co-founder of the "Stop Islamization of America" organization and a leader of the protest movement to prevent what she terms the "Islamic Supremacist Mega Mosque at Ground Zero." The entries in Geller's "Atlas Shrugs" weblog are often virulently anti-Muslim, with posts ranging from the inflammatory (bearing such titles as "There Is No Moderate Islam" and "Extremist Imam Rauf's Totalitarian Khomeinism") to the almost comically paranoid (including an article insisting that the planned Flight 93 memorial in Shanksville, Pennsylvania is actually an Islamic crescent pointing to Mecca). During the Park51 controversy Geller was a fixture on Fox News, but she also made several appearances on CNN, ABC World News and MSNBC, becoming, despite her extreme views, the de facto spokesperson for the "Stop the Mosque" campaign. There is certainly room for debate concerning the Islamic cultural centre — some 9/11 families and other New Yorkers have sought to highlight the sensitive nature of the location without resorting to a demonization of the city's Muslim population — but the mainstream media must remain cognizant of the impact their validation of speakers has on the discourse surrounding the project.

On May 25th, 2010, Manhattan Community Board 1 voted twenty-nine to one in favour of the Islamic center's construction, arguing that it would bring much needed social and cultural services to the downtown area. Reportage of the Park51 debate is growing the disparity between national opinions and the wishes of the community where the center would reside. It would be unfortunate if a project that has the potential to help revitalize a Lower Manhattan neighbourhood still slow to recover from the devastation of 9/11 is needlessly scuppered as a result. •

Joel McKim is a post-doctoral fellow in the Department of the History of Art and Architecture at the University of Pittsburgh. He is currently completing a book entitled *Memory Complex: Competing Visions for a Post-9/11 New York*.

Late Style

The following texts are all based on talks given at the symposium "Late Style," at Moderna Museet in Stockholm, November 18, 2011. The symposium was co-organized by Moderna Museet and the Department of Culture and Communication at Södertörn University, in connection with the exhibition "Turner Monet Twombly: Later Paintings."

The aim of the symposium was to examine the idea of late style, as is has been developed by, among others, Theodor W. Adorno and Edward Said, in relation to the works of Turner, Monet and Twombly, but also as a general question of philosophy and aesthetic theory.

Late Style

Who's afraid of Red, Blue and Yellow?

Sam Smiles

The title of this paper sounds as though I was referring (inaccurately) to the late work of Barnett Newman. *Who's Afraid of Red, Yellow and Blue?* was the name given to a series of paintings produced in the 1960s, the last decade of Newman's life. He produced these works at a time when he felt that the cause of abstraction still required defence and his provocative title set down a clear challenge to those who questioned the purpose of the kind of art he made. *Who's Afraid of Red, Yellow and Blue?* may be regarded as a defiant manifesto for Newman's aesthetic and the group tendency to which his art belonged. It asserts the artist's integrity and his refusal to let hostile criticism deflect him from the route he has decided to follow. Its title might be considered as Newman's condensed restatement of something that lay at the heart of his painting: the possibility that primary colours when properly understood provided the means for making significant art. But the title's use of the word "afraid" also hints at Newman's continuing preoccupation with the sublime, where fear is one of the responses triggered in the beholder when confronted by experiences that lie beyond the rational mind's comprehension.

Now, all of this — the defiance of the critics, the reliance on colour as the basis for painting and the importance of the sublime — may equally be said of Turner. Of course, the art world of the middle of the nineteenth century was so different to the art world of the middle of the twentieth century that we must be wary of pushing these affinities too far. However, as Jeremy Lewison's brilliant exhibition in this museum has made clear, when treated with sensitivity, a variety of perspectives open up precisely because transhistorical comparisons help us to think new thoughts.

My talk today is not going to make a case for any deeper links between Turner and Monet or Twombly, or Barnett Newman for that matter. Instead, what I hope to show you is the nature of Turner's practice as an artist in the 1840s, to see whether we can draw some further conclusions about the work he produced in his old age, what his intentions for it were and, crucially, what this says about Turner's own reckoning of what he had achieved as an artist. The title for my paper comes from something that John Ruskin recorded in his diary after visiting Turner's studio on the 29th of April, 1844. Ruskin had first met Turner in 1840 and quickly became known as Turner's most loyal defender. The first volume of *Modern Painters* was published in 1843 and in that book Ruskin had taken on Turner's critical enemies, arguing that Turner was the greatest landscape painter who had ever lived. The meeting in April 1844 went well, with Turner talking freely to Ruskin about the works on display in the gallery attached to his studio. On reaching the painting Ruskin calls in his Diary "Moses writing Genesis" Turner lifted the curtain covering it and said merely "red, blue and yellow." Ruskin makes no further comment about this remark in his Diary except to note that Turner said it in a good humour.[1] This picture is, of course, one of the exhibits in this exhibition, and I want to use it as a point of entry into Turner's work of the 1840s.

The painting had been completed by Turner in time for its exhibition at the Royal Academy, in 1843. The title under which it was exhibited then, explains why Ruskin knew it as "Moses writing Genesis", but its length and complexity indicates clearly that this was much more than the illustration of a Bible story. The full title is: *Light and Colour (Goethe's Theory) — The Morning after the Deluge — Moses Writing the Book of Genesis.* The painting was exhibited in an octagonal frame and there are reasons to think that Turner had originally thought of using a circular composition. Both arrangements concentrate the design, such that we feel the power of light radiating out from the centre. We see Moses seated, seemingly airborne with a book on his lap, holding a pen or perhaps a stylus. Immediately below him is a serpent on a pole, alluding to the biblical story, in the *Book*

1 • Joan Evans and John Howard Whitehouse, eds., *The Diaries of John Ruskin* (Oxford: Clarendon Press, [3 vols 1956, 1957, 1959]), vol. 1: 1835–1847, 273.

of Numbers, of Moses making a bronze serpent and lifting it up on a pole to cure those Israelites who had been bitten by snakes. This episode was seen by John the Evangelist as foreshadowing Christ being lifted up on the Cross for the benefit of all humanity. Below the serpent we see the drowned remains of those overwhelmed by the Flood, while emerging from that watery world are human forms which ascend into the air. The prismatic colour, seen as though reflected on one enormous bubble, reminds us of the rainbow God placed in the sky after the Flood as a symbol of hope.

As you will have noted, there is a chronological difficulty here. The story of the Flood comes in the *Book of Genesis*, the story of Moses in the *Book of Exodus* and the three subsequent books of the *Pentateuch*. Traditionally, Moses was believed to be the author of most of the *Pentateuch*, so Turner has some justification for showing him writing the *Book of Genesis*, but he cannot have actually witnessed the Flood which is presumed to have taken place many centuries earlier. Turner therefore seems to be saying something about the nature of historical narration — that it is a record of events but not a witness of them. Moses' position in mid-air registers the fact that he is not physically present and is detached from what he is writing about. What Turner presents us with here is, perhaps, not so much a picture of the receding flood, but Moses' creative act in imagining the flood.

Late Style

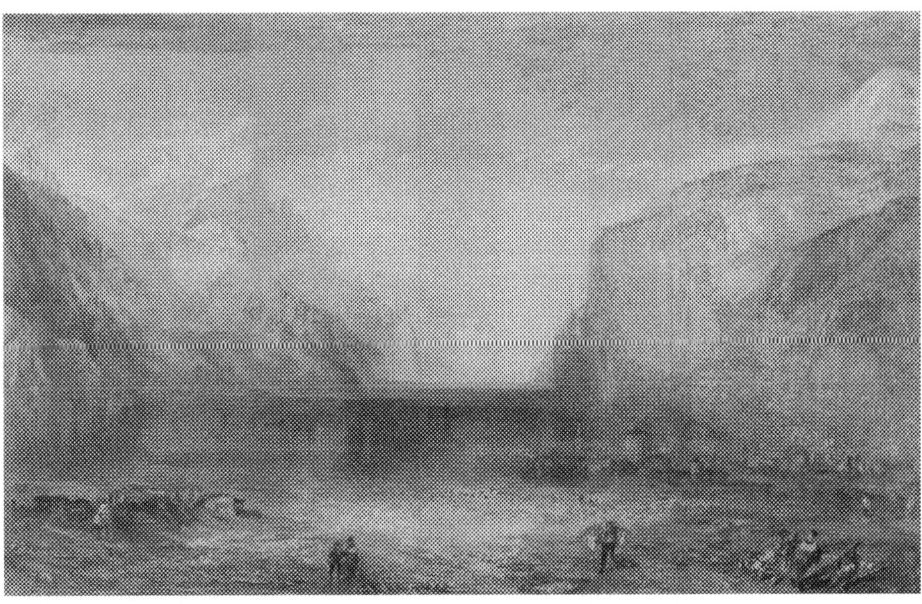

▲
Joseph Mallord William Turner, 1775-1851, British, *Fluelen: Morning (looking towards the lake)*, 1845, Watercolor, gouache and scratching out on paper, Yale Center for British Art, Paul Mellon Collection.

There is an additional difficulty of interpretation. Iconographically, the picture is symbolic of optimism and hope and Turner's reference to Goethe's theory underlines this, for Goethe's *Zur Farbenlehre* associates the colours Turner has used here with positive values. And indeed, in this picture's companion, *Shade and Darkness — the Evening of the Deluge*, also exhibited in 1843, Turner used a palette Goethe associated with negative values. But the verses Turner supplied to the Royal Academy exhibition catalogue for *The Morning after the Deluge* point in an unexpected direction. Part of his *Fallacies of Hope* poem, the lines read as follows:

> The ark stood firm on Ararat; th'returning sun
> Exhaled earth's humid bubbles, and emulous of light,
> Reflected her lost forms, each in prismatic guise
> Hope's harbinger, ephemeral as the summer fly
> Which rises, flits, expands, and dies.

By itemising bubbles and short-lived May flies Turner indicates that whatever hope seems to be expressed in the picture, through its iconography and colour symbolism, will be very short-lived.

I have looked at this picture at some length to demonstrate something of its complexity. It is a disturbing picture not only for its technical radicalism but also because of its conceptual difficulties. It is multifaceted, self-contradictory even, and it frustrates our desire to give a satisfactory account of its meaning. Yet, all Turner would say to Ruskin about it was "red, blue and yellow." What are we to make of this remark?

I would like to suggest three possibilities. First, that Turner was deliberately frustrating Ruskin by refusing to let him have an account of the picture's meaning that would emphasise factual details rather than visual experience. Aware of Ruskin's tendency to present his work as founded on the understanding of natural phenomena and so make him primarily a communicator of truths of observation, Turner's remark insists that Ruskin pays attention to painting as painting, directing his gaze to formal and technical qualities, looking at it rather than through it. As Ruskin himself admitted, he asked Turner repeatedly to explain to him the meaning of an earlier painting of the 1840s, *War. The exile and the rock limpet* (1842). But Turner was prepared to do no more than hint at its meaning.[2] Judging from remarks made at other times in his career, it seems to have been a cardinal belief with him that the meaning of a work of art could not be reduced to a description.

2 • John Ruskin *Modern Painters V*, 435n; quoted in Walter Thornbury, *The Life and Correspondence of JMW Turner*, second edition, 1877, 304.

The second possibility is that Turner's remark was not merely designed to improve Ruskin's critical habits, but was a declaration of what Turner believed his art to be, its essential achievement laying in the liberation of colour as a formal language.

The third possibility brings us back to the title's direction to Goethe's theory of colour. Turner had read this book in the translation of his friend and colleague Charles Eastlake, published in 1840, and had annotated his copy freely. From his notes we can see that he engaged closely with the text. In the context of Goethe's theory and Goethe's disagreement with Newton on the relationship of colour to light, "red, blue and yellow" was much more than a phrase simply describing pigments or Turner's use of them in colour orchestration within this composition. It was an invitation to consider the theoretical debate about one of the most fundamental attributes of vision itself. In one sense all three of these possibilities can co-exist and reinforce one another. But as with the complexity of the painting's title, what this points to is that the paintings of Turner's final years were every bit as rich in meanings as what had come before.

Late Style

The reason I want to stress the complexity of Turner's work is that it bears on a major concern with respect to late style as an idea. Since the early 1900s the terms "old age style" "late style", and "late work" have become a familiar part of the critic's vocabulary. Turner is regularly placed among those artists whose final works can be described as examples of "late style". In 2003 Martin Lindauer, published the results of a questionnaire distributed to art historians in the USA, who tended to agree on 38 artists possessing a distinctive late style. In rank order the first half of that list comprised: Titian, Cézanne, Constable, Degas, De Kooning, Goya, Matisse, Michelangelo, Mondrian, Monet, Picasso, Rembrandt, Braque, Corot, David, Kandinsky, Kokoschka, Renoir and Turner.[3] So there is an orthodoxy here. What is meant by "late style" is not so easy to pin down, but a general consensus has emerged about its major features. The late work is presumed to be distinctive in more than the chronological sense of distinguishing an artist's last works from his earlier ones. We pay special regard to the late works of great artists, expecting to encounter formal challenges and an intensity of vision of a very special kind. These are, after all, the artist's culminating work in which the experience of a lifetime is distilled into its final statements. As normally employed today, late style shares with the romantic notion of genius a restriction to a small group of

3 • Martin S. Lindauer, *Aging, Creativity, and Art: A Positive Perspective on Late-Life Development*, (New York: Kluwer Academic/Plenum Publishers, 2003), 175.
4 • Theodor Adorno *Aesthetic Theory*, trans. Robert Hullot-Kentor (London and New York: Continuum, 2004), 51.

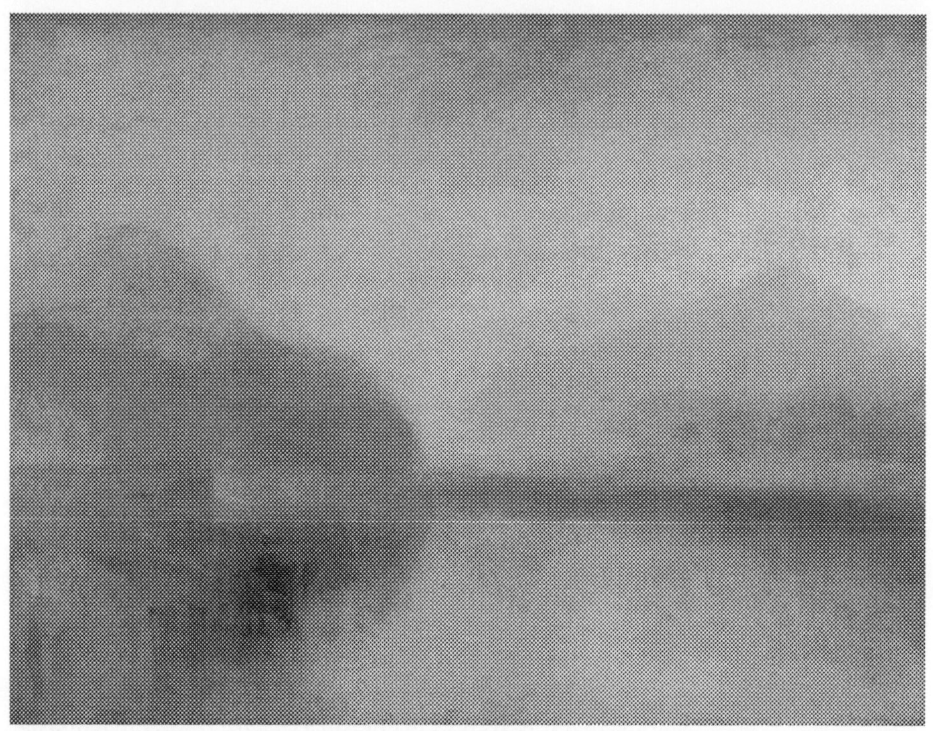

▲
Joseph Mallord William Turner, 1775-1851, British, *Inverary Pier, Loch Fyne: Morning*, ca. 1845, Oil on canvas, Yale Center for British Art, Paul Mellon Collection.

exceptional (predominately male) talents, but unlike genius, which is characteristically associated with the young artist's brilliance, it proposes that certain sublime geniuses can maintain that pitch of intense creativity throughout their careers and in their final years produce work of exceptional intensity, exploring new worlds of form. I would also like to suggest here that the twentieth century's fascination with Turner's unfinished work may be partially explained by one other characteristic feature of late style description: the idea that the aged artist is primarily working for himself alone, no longer required to subject his vision to public scrutiny or so beyond caring that he is indifferent to criticism. If so, work left in the studio is not incomplete but an authentic record of the artist's uncompromised creativity. For some, indeed, it is the late style at its purest.

This is how Turner appears in the writings of Adorno. Adorno's references to Turner are few, but he makes a brief appearance in *Aesthetic Theory* in a particularly suggestive passage about authentic art and its qualities. Turner is included in a group of creative talents — the others being Gesualdo, El Greco and Büchner — whose modern rediscovery backs up Adorno's general proposition that "Only the most advanced art of any period has any chance against the decay wrought by time."[4] Such an art can be reactivated posthumously when the historical conditions that obscured its truth are replaced by new circumstances that permit its truth to be revealed. It is unfortunate that Adorno doesn't specify what truth Turner's art articulates, but we may assume, I think, that he valued the integrity of the paintings that Turner exhibited towards the close of his life as working the material of painting without giving ground to the expectations of a bourgeois audience. Just before mentioning Turner, Adorno offers three reflections on significant art, talking about the power of the art work to annihilate the second-rate, to disintegrate contemporary values and to take risks.[5] And this is why, I believe, he was drawn to Turner's work. And while it was Adorno's meditation on Beethoven that prompted his remark "In the history of art late works are the catastrophes," some of the more general elements in his characterisation of late work in Beethoven's case would apply to Turner's example, too. Here I'm thinking particularly of the idea that the material in late works is superabundant, the conventions are left to stand unmastered by subjectivity.

Adorno's idea of catastrophe in late work brings me to the valorisation of catastrophe in Deleuze and Guattari's approach to Turner, whose most extensive statement on the artist occurs in their *Anti-Oedipus*. But Turner's final paintings are cited in a number of their writings, of which this statement from 1991 is the most immediately applicable to this conference:

> There are cases in which old age gives, not eternal youth, but on the contrary a sovereign liberty, a pure detachment in which one enjoys a moment of grace between life and death, and in which all elements of the machine combine to launch into the future a figure that cuts through time: Titian, Turner, Monet.[6]

For Deleuze and Guattari Turner is an exemplary artist insofar as his oeuvre includes pictures which they refer to as "the series Turner does not exhibit, but keeps secret." It is these works, the unfinished oil paintings, they find intriguing. For them, there is a politics of representation whose normal operation is bound up with a repressive ideology of identity and subjectivity. But these unfinished works refuse to signify. As Deleuze said of Turner in 1981: "The artist's hand has stepped in to exercise its independence and to smash a sovereign optical organization: nothing more is seen, as in catastrophe or chaos."[7] So Turner begins his career as the painter of natural catastrophes — avalanches, storms and the like — but by the end of

5 • Adorno *Aesthetic Theory*, 43–44.
6 • Gilles Deleuze and Félix Guattari, *What is philosophy?*, trans. Graham Burchell and Hugh Tomlinson (London and New York: Verso, 1994), 1–2.
7 • Gilles Deleuze, *Francis Bacon: Logique de la sensation* (Paris: Editions de la Différence, 1981), 66.

his life has made painting itself catastrophic. Any artist working at the extreme limits of intelligibility runs the risk of complete incoherence. But Deleuze and Guattari's conclusion for late Turner is positive — this is a breakthrough, not a breakdown. In their reading, Turner's unfinished paintings are catastrophic because they abandon the normal conventions of representation. In place of a fixed and ordered world, what we are presented with is a dynamic flux, where identities are provisional and everything exists as potentially subject to change.

For me, however, the question that hovers over all of this is one of interpretation. I have no doubts at all that Turner's last paintings are worthy of the admiration they have received in the modern period. But how should we examine Tuner's work in the 1840s from a historical point of view? Did Turner see his production as breaking new ground? Are these paintings distinctive when compared to his work of previous decades and if they are distinctive what explanations can we provide that help to make sense of them? If these works are examples of Turner's late style what do we mean by that? Is this simply a modern critical convenience or is it something that Turner and his contemporaries would have understood? Most crucially, is it true that the late works of an artist are characteristically turned "inwards", as it were, to concentrate on formal concerns or to offer philosophical meditations on life, as opposed to their former outward-turned engagement with social and cultural agendas? In the rest of this paper I will do my best to answer these questions.

At the time of Turner's death in 1851, the standard view of artistic production took decline in old age for granted, with an almost inevitable weakening of physical capabilities and a slackening of mental strength. With respect to Turner's work of the 1840s, although some patrons of his watercolours stayed loyal to the end, the general public's understanding of Turner's output came from seeing his oil paintings at the Royal Academy. Here the balance of opinion was negative overall. Even Ruskin saw evidence of decline in Turner's closing years. For Ruskin Turner's Third Period was the decade 1835–45 which, although he described it as "the crowning period of Turner's genius," he also said that it contained serious evidence of decline: loss of distinctness, compositional weakness and increasing feebleness of hand. After 1845 there was nothing of any quality. As Ruskin said: "In 1845, his health gave way, and his mind and sight partially failed. The pictures painted in the last five years of his life are of wholly inferior value."[8] Writing after Turner's death about some of the later exhibited works, for example, the *Angel standing in the Sun* of 1846,

8 • John Ruskin, "Notes on the Turner Gallery" in E.T. Cooke and Alexander Wedderburn (eds), *The Works of John Ruskin* (London: George Allen, 1903–12), vol. xiii, 99.

Ruskin declared that he would "take no notice of ...pictures painted in the period of decline. It was ill-judged to exhibit them." Their only value lay in their biographical evidence, with some features of their handling revealing the mental disease which, for Ruskin, set in towards the close of 1845.

For all Ruskin's belief in Turner's decline, the artist died just as a more positive idea of creativity in old age began to emerge. In 1854 Jacob Burckhardt pointed out in his *Cicerone* that great art could be produced after one had turned 50, citing Leonardo, Giovanni Bellini and Michelangelo who produced "their most wonderful works when they were old men...".[9] Burckhardt may well have been responding to recent critical approaches to Beethoven, who had died in 1827 and Goethe who had died in 1832. Conventionally, what Beethoven and Goethe produced at the end of their careers fitted the expected pattern of decline; when compared to the works of their maturity the late string quartets and the second part of *Faust* (to take the two most obvious examples) seemed mannered, self-indulgent and erratically composed. But it had become clear to some critics that Beethoven and Goethe's last works needed to be judged by other criteria and this idea gradually became intellectually respectable. In the latter part of the nineteenth century critics began to champion these final creative statements. And this idea had repercussions for the visual arts. For example, in 1878, Ruskin's friend, the Rev. William Kingsley, aware that the battle for Beethoven's late style had been won, defended Turner's last watercolours in precisely these terms: "These late Swiss Drawings bear the same relation to his early work that Beethoven's Choral Symphony does to one of the simple movements of his early Piano Forte Sonatas."[10]

Late Style

These critical perceptions of Turner's work are important and I have no quarrel with new interpretations of Turner's art. But I am concerned that we don't lose sight of the historical situation of the 1840s, which was, after all, the environment in which Turner was working. So let me talk about Turner's work in the 1840s without the benefit of hindsight, seeing the works as current — a professional artist still at work — rather than as late — a great artist's final statements. In the rest of this talk I will look in detail at some of Turner's paintings from the 1840s and will propose that Turner's last works can be understood as still very much engaged with the art world of Victorian England.

In 1840 Turner was 65; he exhibited his last four oil paintings at the Royal Academy in 1850 and he died in 1851 aged 76. By the medical standards of

9 • Jacob Burckhardt, *The Cicerone: An Art Guide to Painting in Italy* [1854], trans. Mrs. A.H. Clough (London: T. Werner Laurie, 1918), 55. Burckhardt extends these remarks to Fra Angelico.
10 • "Rev. W. Kingsley on the Turner Drawings" in E.T. Cooke and Alexander Wedderburn (eds) in *The Works of John Ruskin* vol. xiii, 535.

the day he would have considered himself old at 65. Indeed, Turner's own physician Sir John Carlisle had written a popular guide to health in old age and in that book accepted the normal definition of senility beginning at the age of 60. Turner's physical health deteriorated as he aged. This is not to say that he quickly became infirm, for he remained remarkably active up until the mid-1840s, but the evidence that survives shows that he suffered some acute illnesses and was also affected by more chronic conditions typical of a man of his age: he needed reading glasses, he had digestive problems, arthritis restricted his mobility and he eventually lost his teeth. Nevertheless, he carried on producing work and the paintings that particularly concern me today are a group of unfinished paintings that Turner was working on in the middle of the 1840s.

One of these pictures is known today as *Norham Castle, Sunrise.* It was one of nine paintings Turner based on compositions from his *Liber Studiorum*, an engraved part-work originally published twenty years earlier. Left unfinished on his death, this picture was not exhibited until 1906, when the Tate Gallery mounted a new display of Turner's later work. In its drastically abbreviated handling and chromatic daring *Norham Castle, Sunrise* has become for many an icon of Turner's modernity, the artist's late style of the 1840s apparently anticipating not only the sorts of visual effects later associated with Monet and Whistler but also looking forward to twentieth-century abstract art.

Paintings like these seem ideally suited for inclusion within the late work paradigm: they recapitulate earlier work, they are radical in appearance, their commitment to a final and uncompromising vision implies an indifference to criticism, they seem to point to the future. But the trouble with this way of writing about late style is that it positions the artist out of place and out of time. So I'm going to offer some thoughts about a possible contemporary context for Turner's reworking of the *Liber Studiorum* in the 1840s. In so doing I mean to maintain a notion of the radicalism of Turner's later paintings but to understand that radicalism as occurring in very particular circumstances.

There is no doubt that the original *Liber Studiorum* was a project that Turner had taken very seriously. It was first offered to the public in 1807 as a part-work on a subscription basis, each issue containing five plates, ranging across the varieties of landscape in Turner's art. Publication stopped prematurely in 1819 after 14 parts had been issued, amounting to a frontispiece and 70 engravings. As stated in the Prospectus, the *Liber Studiorum* was intended "to attempt a classification of the various styles of landscape, viz., the historic, mountainous, pastoral, marine, and architectural." Turner also added a sixth category identified by the initials EP, probably to be understood as Epic or Elevated Pastoral. When he produced his nine oil paintings of *Liber Studiorum* designs in the 1840s, six of them were EP subjects, which suggests that he placed a special value on this category.

The intentions and meaning of the *Liber Studiorum* have been much debated. In part it is obviously a response to Turner's hero Claude Lorraine's *Liber Veritatis*, but there is an important difference. The *Liber Veritatis* was designed to offer an authentic record of Claude's works. Turner's series was not primarily a record of his own works to that date, but was instead largely devoted to engravings of new subjects. As such, it is something of a propaganda piece for the importance of landscape painting in the early nineteenth century, especially the ability of landscape painting to engage with all the phenomena of the visible world. In this context, we need to remember that in the early 1800s, with contemporary art theory still promoting history painting as the most important branch of the profession, landscape painting had to fight its corner. The publication of the *Liber Studiorum* may be viewed as a strategic manoeuvre in that campaign.

The *Liber Studiorum* was originally issued during Turner's early maturity; he was 32 when it began publication and 44 when it stopped. In his old age his interest in it was revitalised. In the summer of 1845, shortly after he turned 70, he had the publishers McQueen's run off fifteen new sets. At approximately the same time he had begun work on a group of oil paintings based on *Liber Studiorum* compositions. Nine of these are known to exist today and most Turner scholars suggest they were produced at some point between 1840 and 1848. None of these nine paintings was exhibited in Turner's lifetime, nor were they displayed in his home or studio. They are normally regarded, therefore, as unfinished works, although the dispersal of six of them outside the Turner Bequest (the work left in his studio at his death and acquired by the nation in 1856) suggests that Turner may have considered them finished enough to dispose of before he died.

To remind you of the difference between Turner's original *Liber Studiorum* of 1807–19 and its transformation into oil paintings in the 1840s I will quickly show six more of its subjects to compare the engraved plates with the oil paintings of the 1840s.[11] Clearly, what we have here is a transposition of the *Liber Studiorum* into another key, but this begs two questions. Why did Turner feel it necessary to go back over an established series and reformulate it? And why did these new works remain unfinished and unexhibited?

11 • The paintings are catalogued in Martin Butlin and Evelyn Joll *The Paintings of J.M.W. Turner* (New Haven and London: Yale University Press, 1984), 298–304.

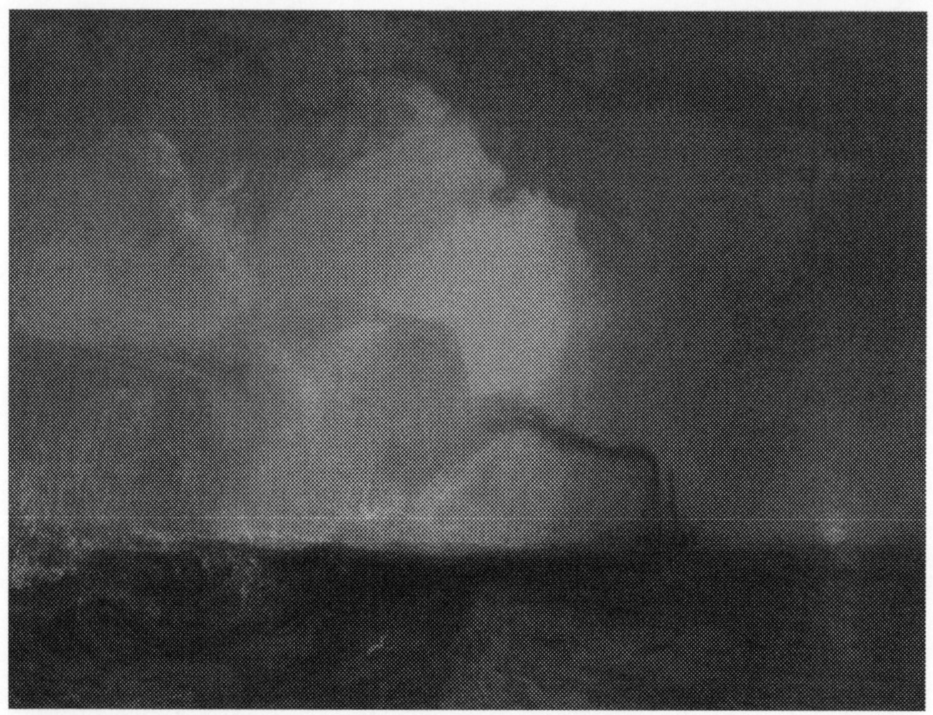

▲
Joseph Mallord William Turner, 1775-1851, British, *Staffa, Fingal's Cave,* 1831 to 1832, Oil on canvas, Yale Center for British Art, Paul Mellon Collection.

Advocates of late style propose that the work of elderly artists becomes idiosyncratic because they are finally beyond the reach of criticism and can work for themselves alone. So in this case the late *Liber Studiorum* paintings could be seen simply as an elderly artist's indulgence. A letter of November 1842 Turner wrote to his namesake, the banker and art collector Dawson Turner, would seem to confirm this; asked what he was doing, Turner replies that he was "endeavouring to please myself in my own way if I can."[12] Yet despite this comment, in the early 1840s Turner was not withdrawing from a professional artist's life; he was still active in the Royal Academy, he maintained contacts with patrons and he sought new commissions. So instead I suggest we understand "pleasing myself in my own way" as an indication that by his mid-sixties Turner had come to a settled view about what now distinguished his art.

12 • John Gage (ed.) *Collected Correspondence of J.M.W. Turner* (Oxford: Oxford University Press, 1980) 190.

As evidence we can turn to the series of Swiss sketches and finished watercolours he produced in the 1840s. These are very different in character to the finished watercolours he had produced earlier in his career. Conscious of their novelty, early in 1842 Turner approached Thomas Griffith, his dealer, with a proposal that potential purchasers should be shown fifteen sketches or "samples" and four "specimens" of what the finished watercolours derived from them would look like. Ruskin reported the conversation that took place about the possibility of sales of the finished works. Turner was disappointed that Griffith valued them only at 80 guineas, including commission, because as Griffith told him "They're a little different from your usual style."[13] Two years later, on a visit to Turner's gallery, Ruskin talked to Turner directly about these Swiss watercolours which he and others patrons were now buying. "I alluded to the peculiar atmosphere of his recent drawings. 'Yes,' he said 'atmosphere is my style.'"[14]

Late Style

The following year, 1845, Turner made an allied remark about an oil painting, *Staffa, Fingal's Cave*. Exhibited at the Royal Academy in 1832 it had failed to find a buyer until 1845 when the New York collector James Lenox commissioned the painter C.R. Leslie to buy something of Turner's on his behalf. On the picture's arrival in New York Lenox complained it was indistinct. Leslie reported this to Turner, who replied "You should tell him that indistinctness is my fault."[15]

We also need to remember that Turner's activities at the Royal Academy's varnishing days had become a thing of legend by the 1840s. These days were set aside to allow artists to put finishing touches to their pictures in the exhibition space, but Turner famously used the opportunity to provide a virtuoso display of bringing to completion what was little more than a lay-in when first submitted to the hanging committee. From at least the mid 1830s, when he turned sixty, we have eyewitness accounts of his extraordinary technical procedures on these occasions.

One last piece of information from the 1840s: in an undated draft for a codicil to his will, probably written between 1846 and 1849, Turner's arrangements for the pictures he wanted to leave to the nation, included a rotating exhibition on a five-year cycle, with unfinished drawings and sketches exhibited for one year, unfinished oils for one year, and finished pictures for the remaining three. It would seem, therefore, that Turner's last creative decade witnessed not only a self-acknowledged change in style but also a

13 • John Ruskin, "Notes on the Turner Gallery" 477.
14 • Joan Evans and John Howard Whitehouse (eds) *The Diaries of John Ruskin*, 273.
15 • Letter from Charles Robert Leslie to James Lenox, 4 November 1845, New York Public Library, Manuscripts and Archives Division, MssCol. 1732: James Lenox correspondence 1837–78, 2.37–38.

willingness to show sketches, something that ran counter to the academic precepts he had inherited
in the 1790s.

The reason I have detailed this evidence is because it alludes to Turner's self-consciousness about his practice. And what I want to go on to say is that this self-consciousness need not be understood merely as Turner ignoring the critics to paint for himself. What if, instead, the varnishing day demonstrations, the new style of his watercolours, the talk of atmosphere and indistinctness, the celebration of the sketch were strategic positions adopted by Turner in response to the art world of the 1840s? His practice had always been combative; throughout his career he had promoted his position by taking on all comers, rivalling the great artists of the past as well as his professional colleagues in the present. Likewise, as I have already suggested, while the *Liber Studiorum's* original appearance may be seen as a treatise on landscape, in its ambitions for landscape painting it can also be read as a manifesto for landscape, as the best response to the complexities of the world. To reissue the engravings of the *Liber Studiorum* in 1845 may simply have reminded a new audience of those claims, but the sequence of oil paintings on *Liber Studiorum* subjects goes beyond that. It takes the idea of the *Liber Studiorum* and reworks it radically.

Now we have to be careful here; these oil paintings are not conventionally finished and what looks extreme in terms of handling may have been modified when they were exhibited, rather like the way the sample studies of Swiss scenes were turned into finished watercolours. But Griffith, you may recall, in declaring that those drawings were not in Turner's usual style was referring to the worked-up watercolours, not the sample studies. I propose that the *Liber Studiorum* paintings of the 1840s, even had they been exhibited, would also have remained relatively loose in handling and atmospheric in effect, just as some of his finished paintings did. At a time when Turner regularly ran the critical gauntlet, they would have exaggerated the very elements of his style that so inflamed his opponents.

Why do this? As I have already said, proponents of late style would say simply that Turner in his old age had no one he needed to please, indeed was "pleasing himself in his own way" and so was free to articulate his final vision of nature, a vision that most of his Victorian contemporaries could not share and only we moderns are capable of understanding. Turner, on this analysis, stepped back from society to concentrate on some final personal vision. It's a compelling argument, but as you'll appreciate it's not one I share. Instead, I will suggest that had Turner's health remained good this series

16 • John Gage (ed.), *Collected Correspondence of J.M.W. Turner*, (Oxford: Oxford University Press, 1980), 198–99.

would have engaged in cultural debate just as much as Turner's earlier production. He was, I believe, holding out for a type of art practice under increasing assault.

Let's consider the circumstances. Here the correspondence with Dawson Turner may hold a clue. In 1844 he sent Turner a copy of his book *Outlines in Lithography* and in his reply Turner thanked him, on behalf of all British artists, for how well Dawson Turner had defended them against hostile criticism.[16] Turner was quite explicit about the nature of this criticism, mentioning by name the German connoisseur and museum director Gustav Waagen who had published his survey of *Works of Art and Artists in England* in 1838. In this book Waagen attacked the 'flimsiness and negligence' of the British school in the forty years following the death of Sir Joshua Reynolds — the period that coincides exactly with Turner's professional career — and had singled out Turner's later work for hostile criticism. I have already quoted from the letter of 1842 when Turner reported to Dawson Turner that he was "endeavouring to please myself in my own way if I can" but if we read on we find that he immediately qualifies that remark by saying "after all my determination to be quiet some fresh follery comes across me and I begin what most probably [is] never to be finish'd." Of course, this may be nothing more than Turner's realisation that he had too much work on his hands, but I think it plausible that what he was planning in 1842 was something that we might consider an "answer" to Waagen, using the *Liber Studiorum's* demonstration of varieties of landscape to insist on not only the importance of landscape painting, but also the significance of an "atmospheric" or "indistinct" approach as a means of engaging with visual phenomena in all their complexity. From Turner's point of view, what Waagen called "flimsiness and negligence," should be defended as a sophisticated mode of intellectual understanding.

Turner may well have felt an obligation on him to do this, for in the 1840s his position was increasingly isolated. Some of the most significant artists who had worked alongside him in the field of landscape were already dead — Girtin prematurely in 1802, Bonington likewise in 1828, Constable in 1837, Cotman in 1842, Callcott in 1844 — and although landscape painting remained a very popular genre, ambitious younger artists were drawn increasingly to domestic and historical subjects. The idea of landscape as a morally serious engagement with contemporary culture, which had been Turner's doctrine throughout his professional life, was not widely shared in Victorian Britain.

And beyond landscape Turner would have been very aware of the new orientation towards precision of execution in contemporary painting. Here a whole tendency in British aesthetics was changing. In 1835, the family of Jacques-Louis David put on an exhibition in London of sketches, drawings and four paintings: *Andromache lamenting over the body of Hector*, *Marat murdered in his bath, Bonaparte crossing the Alps* and *Mars disarmed by Venus and the Graces* — "the last work of the painter at the age of seventy-five." As had traditionally been the case, British critics found nothing to admire in the "cold precision and mechanical labour" of David's art, which was seen as mere ultra-elaboration, sacrificing pictorial harmony for effects of realism.[17] This attack on David was, in effect, a defence of the British school where atmosphere and colour were given a much higher priority than drawing. But although this hostility to David was traditional, by the middle of the 1830s it was also clear that a new orientation in painting was emerging that had much more time for precision in drawing and that British artists and critics were prepared to find value in it.

Paintings by the German Nazarenes, for example, had begun to have a profound influence on a number of British artists, William Dyce being one of the first major talents to respond to their clarity of design. Likewise, the popularity in England of the French artist Delaroche, who exhibited occasionally at the Royal Academy, is also part of this tendency towards a practice very different from the kind of painting Turner had developed. The growing taste for hard outlines, smooth surfaces and enamel-like colour owed something to the new appreciation of fifteenth-century art, as witnessed by the enthusiastic reactions of critics and connoisseurs to the exhibition of Van Eyck's *Arnolfini Portrait* at the British Institution in 1841 and its purchase by the National Gallery the following year. The primitivising aesthetic seen especially in painters like Dyce and in the acquisition of the Van Eyck speak to a reorientation of British taste towards painting before Raphael. The importance of the Nazarenes and 'Germanic' taste in painting was further promoted by Prince Albert, following his marriage to Queen Victoria in 1840. When a Select Committee debated in the early 1840s how the new Houses of Parliament were to be decorated, the critic who had attacked the English School in the 1830s, Gustav Waagen, was called to give evidence and German expertise was recommended. Indeed, so widespread was the popular interest in the new art from Germany that when Ruskin approached the publisher John Murray in 1842 to propose that Murray publish the first volume of *Modern Painters*, his defence of Turner, Murray declined it on the grounds that Turner wasn't a promising subject for the market — a book on the Nazarenes would do much better.

Now, we know that Turner was drafting and redrafting his will in the

17 • *The Spectator* 30 May, 1835, 518.

1840s, intending to leave a collection of paintings to the nation, housed in their own gallery. If, on the walls of the Royal Academy and the new Parliament building, the "flimsiness and negligence" of the British school was to give way to the new "Germanic" aesthetic, in Turner's own gallery the visitor would have been exposed to a very different experience. Is it possible that Turner envisaged the creation of a painted version of the *Liber Studiorum* as a programmatic challenge to the view of art that was winning critical acceptance and that would shortly be displayed at Westminster?

Of course, we will never know, for neither this series nor the gallery were ever realised. Looking at Turner's exhibition record, it is clear that his production of pictures for exhibition at the Royal Academy did not diminish in the early 1840s, showing his usual quota of half a dozen paintings every year from 1840 to 1846. There would have been little enough time to develop all of the *Liber Studiorum* pictures in addition to these. So it is reasonable to suppose that Turner allowed this sequence of paintings to develop slowly over the early 1840s, working each of them up to the unfinished state we see now, ready for completion to exhibition standard when the full number had been produced. He had some grounds for optimism with respect to that; he was in reasonable health for a man in his later sixties and was physically robust. In the second half of the 1840s all this changed. His last foreign tour was in 1845 and after 1846 he showed very little at the Royal Academy: in 1847 he showed one work only, *The Hero of a Hundred Fights,* a canvas of the early 1800s onto which he superimposed in his current style an image of the new Duke of Wellington monument emerging from the foundry. In the following year, 1848, he showed nothing, in 1849 two works, another reworked painting and an old painting from 1803 which he exhibited unaltered. Only in 1850, with a final quartet of Carthaginian paintings, a theme he had first treated in the 1810s, did he show entirely new work. Turner's watercolour production also fell off, making a total of about sixteen finished works over the last five years of his life. In these circumstances of severely reduced activity there was little prospect of completing the *Liber Studiorum* series.

To conclude. What I have suggested is that Turner's example can certainly be read off against a check-list of attributes commonly associated with the late style paradigm: the works of the 1840s are difficult, some of them recapitulate earlier work in a more radical style, they seem to anticipate later approaches to painting. And for that reason it has been tempting to regard Turner's later work as giving him entry to that exclusive club of male geniuses whose late styles are considered to be similarly profound and forward-looking. But Turner's work of the 1840s demonstrates what art historians have also found to be the case with the so-called late work of other artists: that their last works are not in fact merely self-expressive gestures but are context-driven and just as open to historical analysis as the artist's earlier works. In both cases a proper understanding of the artist's cultural situation, is essential for any engagement with the work. •

Sam Smiles is Emeritus Professor of Art History at the University of Plymouth. He is currently completing a book entitled *Turner's Last Paintings: A Study of His Production c.1835–51*.

Late Style

Water Lilies and the Gesture of Melancholy: On Monet's Late Works

Bente Larsen

A predominant motif in the late works of Monet is water lilies. It is a motif that he got from his garden in Giverny, where he lived until his death in 1926. He constructed the garden himself, "for the pleasure of the eye and also for motifs to paint."[1] Covering approximately 1,000 square meters, a water pond was ringed by an artful arrangement of flowers, trees, and bushes, crossed by a Japanese-style wooden bridge, and filled with water lilies. Except for short trips to London and Venice in 1908, this aquatic wonderland and flower garden became his principal preoccupations for the last twenty-six years of his life. During his final twenty years, Monet painted more than 500 paintings of his garden in Giverny, and most of them had water lilies as a motif.

It is the motif of water lilies that will form the primary focus of this essay. I will look into how Monet's depiction of them gradually changes during the last 20 years of his life, from the predominantly idyllic use of palette and pencil to a liberation of both. It is in these paintings I see the late style of Monet, not in the earlier serial paintings, as it is often done. To make this point clearer I shall discuss what I view as the characteristics of the three periods of Monet's oeuvre.

In my discussion of lateness, it is not my intention to discuss Monet's late art as documentations of his life. Therefore I do not look upon

1 • This is what Monet said to the Department Prefect when he applied for a building permit. See Paul Hayes Tucker, *Monet in the '90s. The Series Paintings* (Boston: Museum of Fine Arts, 1989), 269.

his late style as a symptom of old age, reduced motor function or eyesight. Nor do I interpret his late works as expressions of mourning after the death of his second wife, Alice.[2] Thus, instead of regarding the pictures as symptoms of depression and instead of adapting a Freudian understanding of the paintings as expressions of melancholy, I shall take melancholy as an aesthetic-theoretical category as it is formulated by Karl-Heinz Bohrer in his book *Der Abschied. Theorie der Trauer*.[3] It is also lateness as an aesthetic-theoretical category that forms the point of departure in Adorno's article on Beethoven's late style, making him emphasize the importance of focusing on "the formation itself, rather than its psychological origins."[4] And as Adorno further emphasizes, "No interpretation of Beethoven's late style, or indeed any other, is adequate if it only explains the ruins of convention psychologically, with no attention to the actual appearance; for it is only in its appearance that art's substance lies" (BLS 15). In my approach to lateness, Adorno's aesthetic theory plays a central role.

As gesture, appearance is what is inscribed on the canvas and meets — or even hits — the eye. It is as gesture that the artwork, as Lyotard has formulated it, opens up a surplus of formal matter that exceeds its conceptual definition. Without that, the artwork would be nothing but an object for cognition.[5] To understand Monet's late works as more than expressions of Monet's psychology, this gestural aspect of form is important. Rather than an object, the artwork is an apparition and it is as an apparition that Adorno has compared art with the firework: it appears, only to disappear. At the same time the gestural essence of art is in itself melancholic. Melancholy both as leave-taking in Karl-Heinz Bohrer and Baudelaire's understanding, and in Adorno's, as a realization of the limit of form in its not being able to form what it forms: "Form inevitably limits what is formed, for otherwise its concept would lose its specific difference to what is formed."[6] Form preconditions and puts a limit to art: not everything is possible at each particular time, at the same time as form, as style, forms the actual artwork, is the artwork. Style implies the same constraints at the same time as style, just as form, is what art cannot avoid. "The concept of style refers as much to the inclusive element through which art becomes language — for style is the quintessence of all language in art — as to a constraining element that was somehow

2 • This forms a central argument in the interpretations of the late paintings made by Jeremy Lewison, *Turner, Monet, Twombly. Later Paintings*, exhibition catalogue, Moderna Museet, 2011.
3 • Karl Heinz Bohrer, *Der Abschied. Theorie der Trauer* (Frankurt am Main: Suhrkamp, 1997).
4 • Theodor W Adorno, "Beethoven's Late Style." In *Night Music: Essays on Music 1928–1962*, edited by Rolf Tiedemann and Wieland Hoban (London: Seagull Books, 2009), 12. Henceforth cited as BLS.
5 • Jean-Francois Lyotard, *Gestus* (Copenhagen: Det Kgl. Danske kunstakademi, 1992).
6 • Theodor W Adorno , *Ästhetische Theorie* (Frankfurt am Main: Suhrkamp, 1973), 144; *Aesthetic Theory*, trans. Robert Hullot-Kentor (Minneapolis, University of Minnesota, 1997).

compatible with particularization" (AT 205/ÄT 305). Therefore late style is different from lateness as a postulate: in art, as it unfolds in form through style, it allows for a materialization of an essential aspect of art. Therefore lateness as style also becomes an important aesthetic concept that surpasses the late works of artists, at the same as some artists in their late works qualitatively formulate what can be determined late style. One such artist is Monet.

But what is lateness? As is obvious, when looking at the paintings in the exhibition at Moderna Museet, to be late does not necessarily mean to be too late. It can also mean to be perfectly on time. Old age has a history, one that revolves around two incompatible views: one of physical, mental, and psychological decline; the other of a spiritual liberation from our corporeal limitations. "Old age style is usually seen as a German invention and hence first named German (*Alterstil*). Goethe is often cited as the progenitor of an old-age style as a positive phenomenon, one involving "a gradual withdrawal from appearances" and a consequent approach to the infinite and mystical."[7]

Late Style

In a classic article by Walter Friedlander on "Poussin's Old Age", he described and subscribed to the traditional view:

> It is a remarkable and often discussed phenomenon that great artists develop in the last years of their lives a sublime style which differs symptomatically from the style of their youth and maturity. The works of the late or "old age" of Titian, Rubens, Rembrandt and others display a deepening and broadening of imagination in form and idea that compensates for the natural uncertainty of vision caused by the decay of bodily forces.[8]

On the ontogenetic level of Adorno and his definition of Beethoven's last works as late style, there are some parallels to the way in which Hegel, polygenetically, looks upon the role of spirit in the period of romanticism, which is what Hegel calls late medieval art. In *Beethoven's Late Style* Adorno writes: "In fact... this subjectivity, existing mortally thus in the name of death, diappears from the work. The force of subjectivity in late works of art is the eruptive gesture with which it exits them. It breaks free of them — not to express itself but, rather, to discard expressionlessly the semblance (*Schein*) of art" (BLS 16). And in *Aesthetic Theory* Adorno writes, "If there is something like a common characteristic of great late works, it is to be sought in the breaking through of

7 • Philip Sohm, *The Artist Grows Old. The Aging of Art and Artists in Italy. 1500–1800* (London: Yale University Press, 2007), 8.
8 • W. Friedlander, "Poussin's Old Age." *Gazette des beaux-arts*, 60 (July-August 1962): 249; Sohm, *The Artist Grows Old*, 9.

form by spirit" (AT 90/ÄT 139). In Hegel's romantic period it is "die schöne Schein der Idee" that loses its relevance in art because spirit has progressed into religion. Just as Hegel does not consider romanticism a regression — on the opposite, this art has more truth than the previous period, i.e. antique sculpture, so Adorno in his definition of late style does not imply a degeneration of art. Instead he considered it a liberation of spirit, on the individual level, of form. This way, late style is qualitatively a different style, but not inferior. In Adorno's definition of late style the artist is confronted with death, in Hegel art is not confronting death, only another form in which the absolute, the idea, appears.

According to Adorno, what subjectivity leaves behind when it bursts through form and rids itself of the *Schein* that is art, is ruins. Therefore late works do not bear the marks of growth but of history. At the same time it is important, with Said, to emphasize that "Late style — and the term is Adorno's — can't be a direct result of aging or death, because style is not a mortal creature, and works of art have no organic life to lose. But the approaching death of the artist gets into the works all the same, and in many different ways."[9]

How the approaching death of Monet materializes as late style in his last works I shall now try to approach. Just as Adorno talks about Beethoven's middle and late period, I am going to differentiate between an early, middle and late period within Monet's oeuvre. And as Adorno emphasizes in relation to Beethoven, that only a technical analysis of the works in question could help to revise our view of late style, I shall go into an analysis of Monet's works based not on technique, as that is only possible in music, but on composition, color and gesture.

The early Monet was a Monet that composed his paintings carefully and harmoniously, adopting a harmonious color scheme. *Bridge at Bougival* was painted in 1869 when the artist was 29. In the picture we are looking across the bridge from Croissy Island towards Bougival. The raking light from the east tells us that it is early morning in the fall. The effect of color and light is one the most impressive elements of this picture. The angle of the autumn sun produces strongly lit edges on the left sides of the central tree trunks, the figures on the bridge, the houses at the end of the bridge, the bridge railing, and the tree trunks on the right. Effects of lights, in other words, are a metaphor of the paired relationship of river and bridge. The play of sun and shade continues in miniature on the quay in the left distance, where tiny figures walk among the trees. Beyond, morning mist and distance produce a bluish-grey haze in the hollow of the valley.

9 • Michael Wood, introduction to *On Late Style* by Edward W. Said (London: Bloomsbury, 2006), xii–xiii.

Monet's colors, laid down in brushstrokes which are carefully dragged over the surface and which take on a unifying role, have the relatively subdued intensities that suit autumn. The blues of the sky are repeated in the distant hills and are mixed with some red to form the grey-purples and grey-blues of the foreground (from left to right they shift progressively from ruddy to blue tones.) Together with the browns and dull greens of hillside, trees, and hedges, they act as a stable matrix for the brighter touches, the orange crowns of the plane trees, the orange and mustard yellows of bank and hedge, the brick red of the long roof to the right. The classical color opposites are embedded in the structure, although reduced in saturation to satisfy the artist's muted scheme: orange and blue, red and green, yellow and purple.

Color takes on the vital role of integrating a composition that has two nearly self-contained halves, one stretching from the left edge over to the line of the curbstones, the other, from the right edge over to the four trees. The left side of the canvas occupies less room than the right and its rush into space is slowed by the stasis of the figures and by the flattening effect of the four trees, whose trunks do not come closer together as they recede. The same is true of the three trees on the right side. This horizontal works with the central verticals to establish a rectangle that embraces the bridge's surface, flattening it despite its plunge into the distance. In its complicated network of geometric shapes, his pictures impose order and regular intervals over nature.

Almost the same strategy is seen in *Gare Saint Lazare* from 1877. Here a railway station is subjected to the same geometry, the same harmonious compositional scheme exemplified by the horizontal rails that are part of the roof construction. They do not recede into space, but hold the composition on the surface of the painting. The potential movement of the two trains is directly towards, or away from, the observer, with the result that neither seems to move. The sense of being held in a timeless moment is abetted by the puffs of steam that come from the undercarriage of the engine. They hide its wheels and further diminish its power to threaten us by making it float in an atmosphere of light, steam, and smoke. To further the effect of a hovering balance, of a delicate resolution of forces, Monet constructed a grid of symmetrical, measured composition. This balance of forces is emphasized by the same classical color opposites as in the previous picture: orange and blue, red and green, yellow and purple. Even the smoke is depicted as solid and decoratively colored matter.

In *Gare Saint Lazare* solid mass has overcome light and air, forming the moment of timeless harmony and balance. In

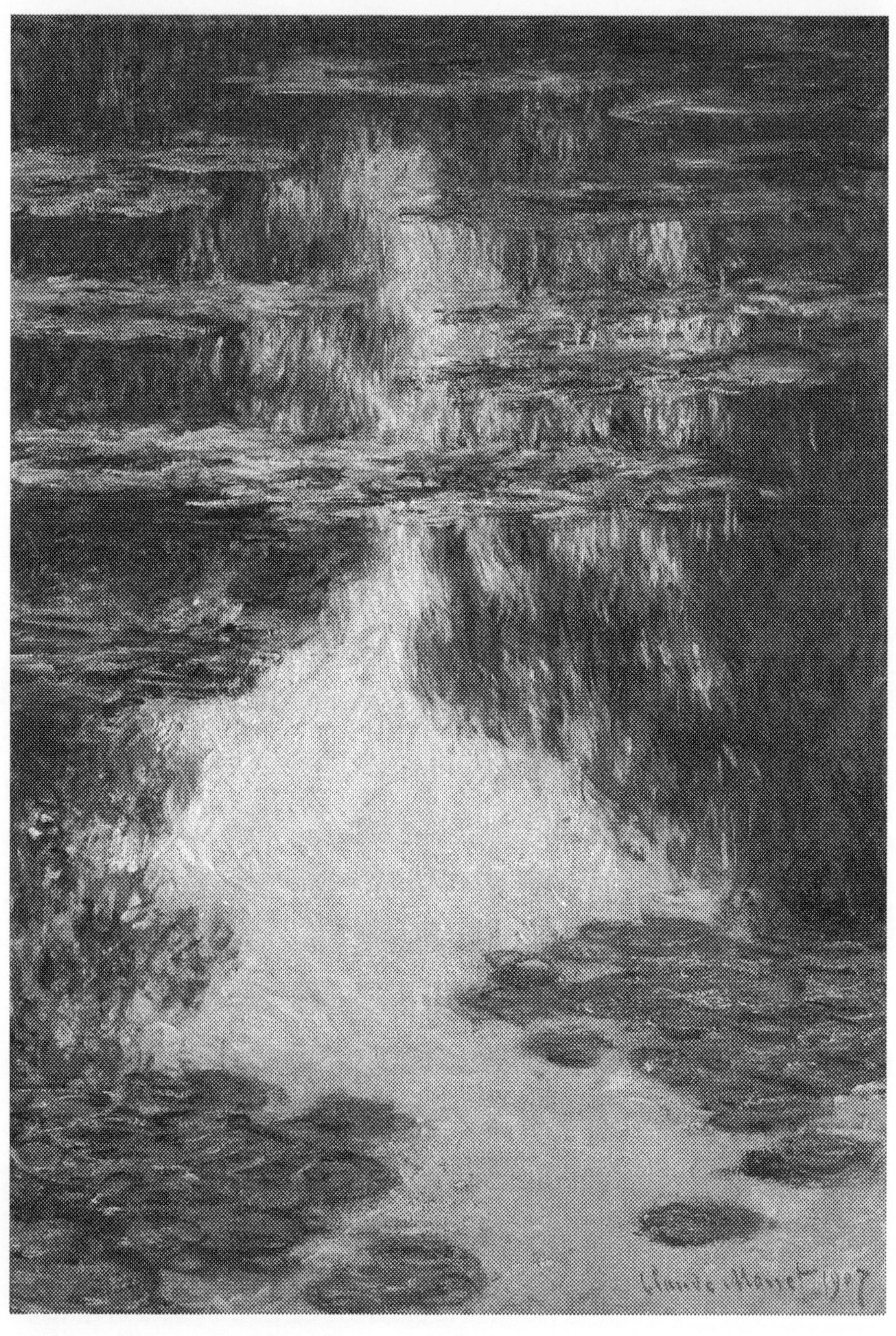

▲
Claude Monet, *Nymphéas*, 1907

what I determine as Monet's middle period, these qualities are purified in the serial paintings.

This can be illustrated by a comparison of two pictures of *Church at Vernon,* one from 1883 and the other from 1894. In the 1894 picture the object almost dissolves into the air, with Monet focusing on the depiction of the atmosphere, the air between his eyes and the object. The surface quality of the delicate balance of compositional forces that dominates the early paintings has been replaced by another balance of strokes of color dissolved into an almost abstract surface quality of timeless momentariness. The church seems to be about to dissolve, to disappear or reappear at any moment, by the stroke of sunlight or the fog becoming denser.

This ephemeral and at the same time timeless quality is essential to the serial paintings that Monet produced in the 1890s, what I call his middle period. Here Monet purifies what has become his pictorial language, a language in which any differentiation between color, object, light and atmosphere is without importance, the depiction of air being the focus. The ephemeral quality is emphasized by seriality: the unique, autonomous picture has been replaced by process, by depiction as an unceasing flow of changing sensations, radiation, magic and beauty. In his serial paintings Monet opens up a new conception of art and the artwork. Monet chooses different motifs for his serial painting, one being poplars. In this, Monet has chosen a motif of a high degree of decorative elegance, and with strict linearity that he could marshal to emphasize abstract qualities.

Another motif is the Rouen cathedral. In the facade one can actually read the passage of time, emphasizing the ephemeral at the same time as he allows for the monumentality of the facade to unfold through the change in light and atmosphere.

In the serial paintings, *The Ice Flows,* we can see how he makes time stop even when the motif is ice flowing on the Seine. These paintings are at once elegiac and soothing, appropriately familiar in their composition and handling, while striking in their coloring and their chilling atmospheric effects.

Around 1900 a fundamental change takes place in Monet's works. Withdrawn in his house in Giverny, Monet focuses on a completely different motif, the water lily, featuring at the same time as the Japanese bridge. These paintings all have the same essentially square formats. The atmospheric quality is diminished, as is the instantaneousness; instead there is a concentration on the pictorial elements, and an individualization of the strokes. Their surfaces are more activated and the scenes are filled with many more elements. The water has once again formed a wedge-like-shape that stretches across the entire foreground of the scenes. It leads the viewer into the distance, where billowing foliage cushions the eye on either side.

Why did Monet return to his pond, and why did he paint in what seems to be a less adventurous style that returns to the firmness and clarity of his former impressionist touch? By withdrawing into his world at Giverny, Monet appeared to be removing himself from contemporaneity and indulging in the unparalleled pleasure of painting his self-styled Eden.

Late Style

But Monet's focus on his garden in his late years did not imply a return to earlier impressionist style. From 1900 and on Monet's palette becomes bolder, it is less tied to naturalistic colors, with various shades of red, yellow, and orange mixed with the predominant blue-greens to create a much hotter, almost garish effect. In his production during the last twenty years of his life there is an increase in dissonant use of pictorial elements. In his obsessive concentration on this seemingly limited motif of the water lily, Monet carried his idea of serial painting to its logical extreme, culminating in the magisterial *Water Lily* canvases now in the Orangerie. At the same time the gesture of decomposition is radicalized.

These two pictorial strategies, the one dissolving the artwork as a closed unity, the other dissolving the delicate balance of forces and colors of his previous works into dissonant gestures, dominate Monet's late works. These paintings surpass any of Monet's earlier paintings: they are more touching and have more profound expressive qualities at the same time as they tend to withdraw into their own, enigmatic world. Their beauty is overwhelming, but it is a beauty that combines radical dissonant gestures with conventional decorative figures and motifs.

In the detail of *Water Lilies* from 1914–17 we can see how beautiful red water lilies are tossed on the clear blue water and surrounded by green leaves. The dominant color scheme is the one of primary and complementary colors, as we know it from Monet's earlier works. At the same time, dissonant circles of black pencil, muddy brown shadows cast by the flowers, breaks in. At several places the picture plane is left in a raw, sketchy, almost primitive manner that would be unthinkable in his earlier periods.

In another detail from *Nymphéas*, the water lilies assume a gloomy, threatening, almost animal-like character and in *Nymphéas Reflects the Willows* from 1916–19, the purple water lilies seem almost to struggle against being absorbed by the darkness of the trees, at the same time as they decoratively radiate together with the dark blue water and dark green leaves of the willow.

In *Water-Lily Pond and Weeping Willow* from 1916–19, the

small white water lilies are helplessly drawn into the unfathomable darkness under the willows, which are again decorative and sorrowful, and let their branches and leaves fall into the water at the same time as the same leaves participate in the absorption of the white water-lilies. Again the harmonious color scheme dominates. Here it protrudes decoratively from the gloomy darkness of the shadow. In the *Nymphéas* from 1915, the water assumes a solid blue shape, supported by the green, claw-like leaves. The abstract quality of these late works is emphasized by the lack of horizon. These late pictures do not have the firm structure of the pictures of the first period, nor do they have the momentary, ephemeral quality of the paintings of the second period; instead they withdraw into an immanent world of the calm intensity of a surface decorated on the one hand with beautiful flowers drifting on the calm water of the pond, and on the other with gloomy, almost aggressive, dissonant colors and shapes. This absence of time and atmosphere is emphasized by the fragmentary character of the water lily pictures.

On Beethoven's late works, Adorno writes: "in his entire formal language [...] one finds sprinklings of conventional formulae and phrases. They are full of decorative chains of thrills, cadenzas and fiorituras, and often the convention becomes visible in a stark, unconcealed, unaltered form" (BLS 14). And later about Beethoven's *Bagatelles*, Adorno points out how the last of them "presents introductory and concluding bars like the distraught prelude to an opera aria — and all this amid the hardest rock layers of the polyphonic landscape, the most restrained stirrings of isolated lyricism" (BLS 14–15). Like Beethoven, Monet sprinkles his paintings, if not with conventions as such, then with decorative pictorial elements that in Monet's own vocabulary have become conventions, such as the flower theme, here the water lily. The water lilies remain isolated as they appear with a frail, vulnerable beauty against the background of rough and primitive gesticulations (they transgress their own conventionality and acquire a new expressive quality). Similarly, Adorno says about Beethoven's final works that "conventions become expression in the act of their own naked self-representation. This is the purpose of the oft-noted abbreviation of his style: it seeks not to cleanse his musical language of formulas but, rather, to strip the formula of its semblance of subjective control" (BLS 17). In his late works Monet strips his pencil of its semblance of subjective control.

This is most clearly seen in pictures he did of his Japanese bridge and his rose path while he worked on the Nymphéas. These belongs to his most disturbing works.

Lateness is not the name of a single relation to time, but it always brings time in its wake. This way late style also brings with it melancholy. According to Said, Adorno's "fractured landscape" is only one of the ways in which late works quarrel with time and manage to represent death, as he puts it, "in a refracted mode, as allegory." And lateness becomes a form of exile. It is *in* but oddly *apart* from the present. For Adorno lateness includes the idea that one cannot really go beyond lateness at all, which gives rise to melancholy. Not melancholy understood as a mental condition, but melancholy as a leave-taking (*Abschied*), and as such it brings with it a consciousness of time as always lost. Melancholy becomes a style that remains subordinated to the reflection of the time of the subject. In his analysis of time in *Der Abschied: Therie der Trauer*, Karl Heinz Bohrer defines time as the irretrievably lost. In "leave-taking" as an aesthetic experience, and not a historical or psychological one, melancholy is radicalized. It is a leave-taking that is transformed into an act of consciousness: the present figure is a figure of reflection and as such it always already belongs to the past. In Baudelaire this has materialized in a poetics of grief, a grief that neither has historical nor autobiographic reasons. Instead it is a recognition of a poetic grief as a consciousness of leave-taking as phenomenal. As a gesture of melancholy, time as leave-taking has become spatial in Monet's works.

But style is conditioned by appearance, and appearance implies gesture. On the one hand, the work coincides with its appearance, on the other hand — and this is the enigma of art — this appearance does not coincide with the work, or its language. Gesture is the surplus of an action; gesture is the apparition of the artwork.

As is the case in late Beethoven, the conventions have become expressions in the act of naked self-representation. His style has become language stripped of formulas, or rather the formulas stripped of their "semblance of subjective control." But the subject, Adorno underlines, is still there: "Once released and lifted out of its dynamic context, the formula begins to speak for itself — yet only in the moment when subjectivity, escaping, rushes through it and suddenly illuminates it with its intention" (BLS 17). At the same time as the substance of art is only its appearance, intentions lurk, and this is where the motif of lateness, and of death, enters. "It is precisely in the thought of death [...] that the formal law manifests itself" (BLS 15), Adorno points out, but as death only is imposed on creatures and not on their creations, death appear in broken form, as allegory. In fact, however, this subjectivity, existing mortally and thus in the name of death, disappears from the work. The force of subjectivity in late works of art is the eruptive gesture with which it exits them. It breaks free of them — not to express itself but, rather, to discard expressionlessly the semblance of art. All it leaves

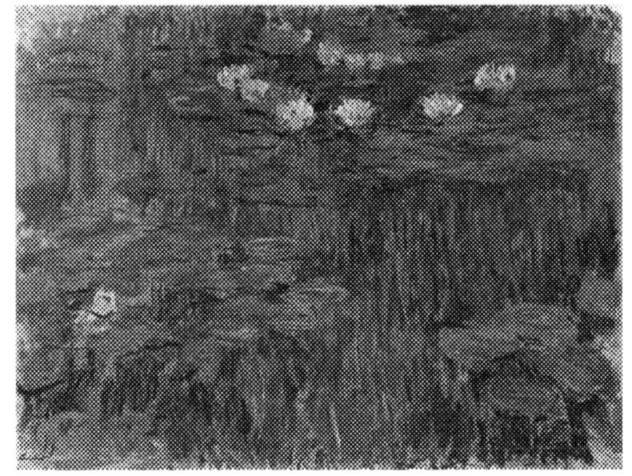

▸ **Claude Monet, *Nymphéas*, after 1916 © Musée Marmottan Monet, Paris / The Bridgeman Art Library.**

behind are the ruins of the works, and it communicates, as if in code, only through the hollows it erupts from. Touched by death, the master's hand releases the heaps and cracks in it, testimonies to the ultimate helplessness of the ego in the face of the existent, are its final work. In this way, in Beethoven's — and Monet's — final works conventions become expressions in the act of their own naked self-representation.

Let us move on to the most important works Monet did in his late years: the murals. In some ways these murals can be seen as logical continuations of the water lily paintings, in that they just seem to extend them infinitely. And as we see it in the water lily paintings, in the murals there is no perspective, no compositional beginning or ending, no atmosphere. But in the murals, and in particular in the *Nymphéas* at the Orangerie in Paris, something different takes place: a displacement between work and viewer.

In the catalogue, Lewinson points out that Monet was determined that the viewer of the decoration should be surrounded by paintings and even at one point thought that they should be displayed with the bottom edges resting at floor level.[10] But Monet has succeeded in this project of integrating audience and work by other means. The *Nymphéas* of the Orangerie comprise eight compositions divided between two rooms. In the two rooms one is plunged in a colored environment, which is situated at eye level, scarcely interrupted by two passageways, and occupies the entire visual field of an adult spectator looking straight ahead, neither raising nor lowering his gaze.

10 • Jeremy Lewison, "Turner Monet Twombly: Painting in Later Life," in *Turner, Monet, Twombly: Later Paintings*, ed. Jeremy Lewinson (Exhibition Catalogue, Moderna Museet, 2011), 49.

What reinforces this impression of a whole without beginning or an end, rather than a contrived succession, is the absence of definite details. There is nothing that catches the eye, no fragment calling attention to itself. One can barely distinguish here and there — and only by paying close attention — a drooping branch, flowers floating, and in the second look only, the trunks of willows.

The color-scheme is homogenous and not very varied, dominated by violet-blues and greens, highlighted by the bright spots of flowers. But neither the flowers, nor the banks, nor even the willows, completely stop the eye. The gaze wanders in a circle, passing from one panel to the other, focusing only when one approaches for a closer look at the brushwork.

There is little or no "drawing" as such. Often, it is impossible to say if such and such a part of the canvas represents the surface of the water, the bottom of the pond seen in transparency, the grass on the banks, a branch, or a cloud. As for the water lilies, they appear only in four or five places: they are rarely placed in a clearly "stepped" way, nor are their contours, which are scarcely indicated in perspective, nor does their decreasing size really help to suggest space. In the *Nymphéas* the choice of a format corresponding to the totality of the visual field, the defocalization, the asymmetry, the absence of points of reference and contours, and the absence of planes — all suggest an immersion in a timeless chaos. Volume and depth are completely absent. All of the pictorial elements have been placed on the same plane, devoid of thickness. Monet avoided any motif which could have suggested space: the water lilies are generally depicted in fairly similar sizes, regardless of their position on the canvas, so as to avoid all suggestion of a stepwise progression in depth. We are plunged into a substance which is both liquid and organic, and in which the light comes from nowhere.

In this work subjectivity is present, not through the artist, but through the viewer. Spirit has liberated itself from form. In *Nymphéas* Monet has liberated spirit from the constraints of form and replaced it with a gesture in which subjectivity has not only broken free of the constraints of art, the artwork itself has become silent. •

Bente Larsen is Professor of Art History at Oslo University. She is at present completing a book provisionally entitled *The Sensuous Gaze: On Presence and Distance in Ad Reinhardts "Abstract Paintings."*

Late Style

Adorno and the Problem of Late Style

Sven-Olov Wallenstein

The Question of Late Style

"Art's substance," Adorno writes in *Aesthetic Theory*, "could be its transitoriness. It is thinkable, and not merely an abstract possibility, that great music — a late development (*ein Spätes*) — was possible only during a limited phase of humanity."[1] The phrase appears in the beginning of the book, in the context of a discussion of Hegel's theory of art's historical nature, and of why Hegel's historicizing of art as a moment in the history of spirit may be insufficient. How should we understand such a claim? What is this *lateness* — here perhaps somewhat normalized by the translation "late development," which seems to place it within a linear chronology — if we understand it outside of the Hegelian theorem of art as a thing of the past with respect to philosophy, to which Adorno undoubtedly did not subscribe? Might this lateness, in a way that seems to contradict the obvious meaning of the term, in fact be something that belongs to the *present*, and even to the *future*, as a possibility?

Put in terms of a somewhat crude alternative, which will simply serve as a point of departure, and I will come back to it in the end in order to question its presuppositions, also outside of Adorno's own philosophy, the idea of lateness, or of a late style, seems to point in two directions.

The first is indicated by the passage just cited: great music, perhaps great art as

1 • Adorno, *Ästhetische Theorie* (Frankfurt am Main: Suhrkamp, 1973), 13; *Aesthetic Theory*, trans. Robert Hullot-Kentor (London: Continuum, 2004), 4. Henceforth: ÄT/AT.

such, and maybe also great philosophy, belong a unique historical moment that can never be retrieved. In this first version, the idea of lateness thus points to some historically singular event, an *Einmaligkeit* that condemns all that will follow to repeat, or more precisely, to unfold and radicalize a "logic of disintegration," as it is called in *Negative Dialectics*. For Adorno, this is one of the basic features of modernism in philosophy as well as the arts, although it is undoubtedly always in conflict with other tendencies.

The second direction is that of continually present possibility, which cannot be tied to any particular moment in time. In this version, lateness discloses a dimension that belongs to an individual oeuvre as such, it is a limit of art that is also its highest possibility, and although it is always instantiated in precise historical contexts, it cannot be identified with any one of them.

When Edward Said, in several of his writings, above all *Musical Elaborations* (1991) and the posthumous *On Late Style* (2006) picks up Adorno's idea, he opts for the second sense. Even though he follows Adorno in locating a decisive moment in Beethoven, and particularly in the reading of the *Missa Solemnis*, Said's principal idea is to extend the applicability of the idea to all historical periods. Just as there is an "unearthly serenity" in many last works (Sophocles, Shakespeare, Rembrandt, Matisse, Bach, and Wagner) that "crowns a lifetime of aesthetic endeavor," there is also a lateness, a condition characterized by "intransigence, difficulty, and unresolved contradiction," and a "bristling, difficult, and unyielding — perhaps even inhuman — challenge."[2] Late style, Said suggests, refuses to reconcile what is impossible to reconcile, and such a refusal is what he locates in the tragedies of Euripides, the music of Mozart, Richard Strauss, Arnold Schönberg, and Benjamin Britten, the literature of Thomas Mann, Jean Genet, and Constantine Cavafy, the cinema of Visconti, and even in the art of the performer, as in the case of Glenn Gould, who takes the condition of exile that Said discerns in lateness to the limit by exiling himself from art as such by ceasing to perform.[3]

2 • Edward Said, *On Late Style: Music and Literature Agains the Grain* (New York: Vintage Books, 2006), 6–7, 12.

3 • Said's theory of a late style obviously differs in many respects from Adorno's, and these brief remarks are only meant as an indication. For Said's relation to Adorno, see Lecia Rosenthal, "Between Humanism and Late Style," *Cultural Critique* 67 (Fall 2007): 107–40. There is also a musicological reception of the idea of lateness that draws as much on Said as on Adorno; see Margaret Anne Notley's *Lateness and Brahms: Music and Culture in the Twilight of Viennese Liberalism* (Oxford: Oxford University Press, 2006). For Notley, Brahms's chamber music testifies to the "alienation" inherent in late style, and to an artistic isolation resulting from a rejection of the monumentality of Beethoven's symphonic structures.

A similar idea of lateness is hinted at in the introduction to the final collaborative work by Deleuze and Guattari, *What is Philosophy?*, and interestingly enough they refer us both to Turner and Monet:

> There are times when old age produces not eternal youth but a sovereign freedom, a pure necessity in which one enjoys a moment of grace between life and death, and in which all the parts of the machine come together to send into the future a feature that cuts across all ages: Titian, Turner, Monet. In old age Turner acquired or won the right to take painting down a deserted path of no return that is indistinguishable from a final question. *Vie de Rancé* could be said to mark both Chateaubriand's old age and the start of modern literature. Cinema too sometimes offers us gifts of the third age, as when Ivens, for example, blends his laughter with the witch's laughter in the howling wind. Likewise in philosophy, Kant's *Critique of Judgement* is an unrestrained work of old age, which his successors still have not caught up with: all the mind's faculties overcome their limits, the very limits Kant had so carefully laid down in the works of his prime.[4]

Although Deleuze and Guattari as far as I know never make any substantial references to Adorno, who seems absent from the counter-history, or "minor history," of philosophy that they often evoke — he is undoubtedly too Hegelian, too historicist, too negative, for their taste — the idea of a certain limit is present here too. And already the reference to Kant's third Critique, and to the conflict of faculties that it instigates, which at once sets the idea of aesthetic autonomy on its path and indicates its limit, show that we should not too quickly seal these conceptions of lateness into two separate and non-communicating traditions. I will come back to this at the end, and attempt to discern what is at stake in the conflict between these positions, and to what extent the idea of "lateness" can serve to articulate this difference.

Beethoven's Lateness

Before moving on to Adorno's writings on late style, we must note that the idea of there being something particularly enigmatic, enticing, and challenging in Beethoven's late work is not a perception

4 • *What is Philosophy?*, trans. Hugh Tomlinson and Graham Burchill (London: Verso, 1994), 2–3.
5 • For a brief survey of earlier views of Beethoven's late style, see Christoph von Blumenröder, "Vom Wandel musikalischer Aktualität; Anmerkungen zum Spätstil Beethovens," *Archiv für Musikwissenschaft*, vol. I (1983): 24–37.
6 • Michael Spitzer, *Music as Philosophy: Adorno and Beethovens's Late Style* (Bloomington: Indiana University Press, 2006), 17.

unique to Adorno.[5] For many historians and musicologists of various creeds and theoretical persuasions, Beethoven's position in these pieces is a singular one; perhaps in an astral sense, so that it curves the very fabric of time and historical succession, as Michael Spitzer suggests in his rich study of the idea of late style in Adorno, when he says that Beethoven is "so heavy that he bends light."[6]

The question hinges upon Beethoven's position in relation to the "Classical Style," as Charles Rosen has called it.[7] For some, this classical style, which, as Rosen acknowledges, is less a set of rigid technical criteria and more like a general attitude, is malleable enough to encompass even the deviations of a late style like Beethoven's; for others, these late works disrupt the categories and structural models inherited from Mozart and Haydn (the two main protagonists of the classical style in Rosen's study), and late Beethoven becomes a proto-romantic, or even proto-modernist. Disunity, disintegration, fragmentation, and other such categories have established themselves as key concepts in the discussion of these works, although they are by no means uncontested, especially among formalist scholars for whom the analysis of pure musical structure seems to preclude all such themes as irrelevant to music proper.

Outside of musicology, the idea of a radical breakthrough in Beethoven's late work has become almost a literary trope or even cliché. The most prominent case is of course Thomas Mann, whose *Doktor Faustus*, published in 1947, drew heavily on discussions with Adorno, as Mann acknowledges in his companion book *Die Enstehung des Doktor Faustus*, published two years after the novel.[8] Mann was familiar with both the ideas of Adorno's *Philosophie der neuen Musik* (1949), as well as the 1934 essay on Beethoven's late style, and he builds them into his literary narrative in a way that has made them familiar to a large audience long before Adorno's own writings on the topic were published.

In the novel, the composer Wendell Kretzschmar explains why Beethoven's piano sonata op. 111 breaks off after the second movement. It is a "process of dissolution, estrangement, a step into the sphere of the foreign and no longer familiar," that finally loses itself in the "vertiginous height" that could be called "transcendent or abstract."[9] Unlike in his middle phase, Kretzschmar suggests, Beethoven here allows conventions to emerge in naked form, and subjectivity and convention enter into a new relation determined by death, which transcends the merely personal and moves into the

7 • Charles Rosen, *The Classical Style: Haydn, Mozart, Beethoven* (New York: Norton, rev. ed., 1997).
8 • See Mann, *Die Enstehung des Doktor Faustus*, in *Reden und Aufsätze* (Frankfurt am Main: Fischer, 1960), vol. III, 171–77.
9 • Thomas Mann, *Doktor Faustus* (Frankfurt am Main: Fischer, 1973), 73.
10 • *Ibid.*, 75.

realm of the mythical and the collective. This also puts an end to art, and the absence of the third movement is a farewell to art, to its *Schein*, in favor of "crystal spheres in which hot and cold, calm and ecstasy, are one and the same."[10]

It has often been noted that Mann, to the extent that we see his novel in the light of Adorno's idea of lateness (which obviously does not exhaust the novel as such, whose major concern is not the break-up of classical forms at the beginning of the nineteenth century, but the rise of fascism in Germany),[11] while picking up several motifs and concepts from Adorno, also misrepresents him. The breakthrough achieved in Beethoven, where music has to stop, in Mann's version opens onto a divine and transcendent sphere, whereas in Adorno this is only present as a faint glimpse. And the music produced by the composer Leverkühn in fact seems closer to romanticism than to the twelve-tone technique of Schönberg (in the novel, the analysis of Schönberg's dialectical ending of dialectics, which Mann borrowed from Adorno's *Philosophy of New Music*, is in fact proposed by the devil, whom Leverkühn encounters in a dream-like scene in Italy).[12] The popularity and presence of late style as a literary trope no doubt derives from Mann's novel, and the sublime, transcendent, and quasi-religious quality that was ascribed to Beethoven's late work, especially op. 111, for a long time made them sacrosanct. As Jost Hermand notes,[13] when included in piano recitals in Germany in the late 1940s and '50s, op. 111 was always placed last, and applause was forbidden, so as to underscore the work's wholly singular and unique position. But let us now turn to Adorno himself, and see what he has to say about the idea of a late style.

Adorno, Beethoven, and the Philosophy of Music

The first essay, "Spätstil Beethovens," was written in 1934 but published much later, in the 1964 collection of essays *Moments Musicaux*. It forms a part of a larger, systematic but unfinished work on Beethoven, which has been posthumously published as *Beethoven: Philosophie der Musik*.[14] Apart from 1934 essay and the much later essay from 1957, "*Missa Solemnnis*: Verfremdetes Haupterk," we here find notes and reflections on Beethoven, which Adorno was collecting with the view to a systematic work that never materialized. These are fragments, and yet they display a remarkable

11 • For a discussion of the role of Adorno in Mann's more encompassing vision in the novel, see Evelyn Cobley, "Avant-Garde Aesthetics and Fascist Politics: Thomas Mann's Doctor Faustus and Theodor W. Adorno's 'Philosophy of Modern Music,'" *New German Critique*, No. 86 (Spring–Summer, 2002): 43–70.

12 • As is wittily noted in the title of Jean-François Lyotard's essay "Adorno come diavolo," in Lyotard, *Des dispositifs pulsionnels* (Paris: Bourgois, 2nd ed. 1980).

13 • See Jost Hermand, "'Weitermachen' auch in 'wüsten Zeiten': Beethovens Klaviersonate op. 111," *Archiv für Musikwissenschaft*, vol. 2 (1999): 85–100.

14 • *Beethoven: Philosophie der Musik: Fragmente und Texte*, ed. Rolf Tiedemann (Frankfurt am Main: Suhrkamp, 2004). The text was first published in *Nachgelassene Schriften. Abt. 1, Fragment gebliebene Schriften*, vol. 1 (Frankfurt am Main: Suhrkamp, 1993). Henceforth: BPM, cited with fragment number.

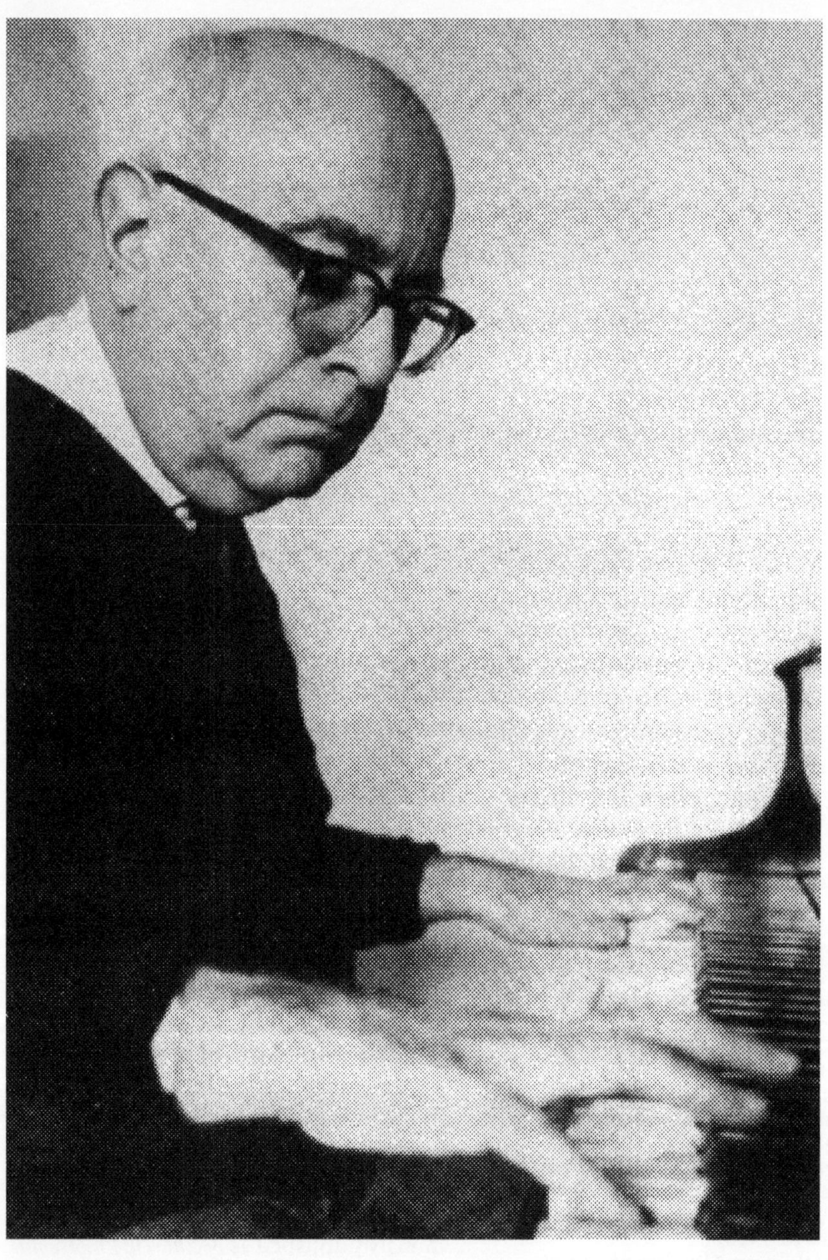

▲
Theodor W. Adorno at the piano in his apartment on Kettenhofweg, Frankfurt am Main, ca. 1967.

continuity; they cover virtually all facets of Beethoven's work, and give us a picture of a thought that is always underway and ready to question its own results, and even begins by retracing its steps back to the author's early childhood experiences.[15]

The material on late style has been assembled in two chapters (9 and 11), between which the tenth chapter presents us with the idea of "Spätwerk ohne Spätstil," i.e. the analysis of the *Missa Solemnis* that develops many themes from the first essay, while also subverting them — the inability to come to terms with the *Missa* was the key problem that prevented the book from taking on a definite shape, as Adorno notes in the preface to *Moments Musicaux*. A close reading of this material would no doubt detect a multiplicity of problems and interpretative angles, and perhaps it would be possible to here follow a thread that runs through Adorno's development up to the final major works, *Negative Dialectics* and *Aesthetic Theory*, and that would show the problem of lateness to be not just an aside, but in fact something like a nucleus or formative figure in his thought. Such a systematic reading obviously falls outside of my scope here, and I will mainly focus on outlining the basic ideas of the first essay in 1934, and only give a few hints as to how they may be aligned with Adorno's subsequent work.

Late style, Adorno suggests, is not like a fruit that becomes ripe; it resists being tasted, it is furrowed and ravaged, and in rejecting the unity demanded by classical aesthetics, it points to the power of history rather than to the idea of growth and maturing; it is a process, but not a development towards a completion, in a sense that leads these two terms into a profound antagonism.

This laceration is normally understood as a subjectivity that breaks through the crust of form and imbues harmony with passionate dissonance, which can then be related to the

15 • This is how the text opens: "Reconstruct how I heard Beethoven as a child" (1). The following three fragments develop the same theme. In a review essay on the Beethoven book Colin Sample even suggests that "Adorno's philosophy of music is essentially contained in his remembrance of the child who would give to nature the tongue to speak as it wished." Colin Sample, "Adorno on the Musical Language of Beethoven," *The Music Quarterly*, vol. 78, No. 2 (Summer, 1994): 378–93, here: 380. Given that late style seems to reopen the question of nature and subjectivity in a more tragic fashion, it is tempting to develop the question further and ask if there might be a link between lateness and childhood, perhaps in the sense of something that remained unmastered from the beginning, and propagates its effects over all later phases. This is the sense of childhood proposed by Lyotard, for instance in his essay on Hannah Arendt: childhood is "the condition of a soul inhabited by something to which no answer could ever be given. The activities of this childhood are guided by an arrogant fidelity to this unknown guest, whose hostage it feels itself to be. The childhood of Antigone. Childhood should here be understood in the sense of obedience towards a debt that could be called a debt to life, time, or the event — the debt of being there in spite of everything; and it is only the constant feeling of this debt, and the respect towards it, that can save the adult from being a mere survivor, from living under a postponed sentence of annihilation." "Le survivant," in Lyotard, *Lectures d'enfance* (Paris: Galilée, 1991), 66.

composer's biography, even a kind of abdication of mastery in the face of death. But for Adorno, the inverse is true: the law of form here resists being subsumed by expression, and instead we encounter forms that are distanced and seem devoid of expression, a form that is just as objective as it is subjective. Rather than an encounter with death, or something demonic, this music seems often enigmatically idyllic.

Subjectivity is indeed there, first in a Kantian fashion, not in order to disrupt form, but to create form; but then, in a second moment, there is a profound questioning of subjectivity, beginning in Hegel, but also going beyond Hegel, as we will see. These two gestures are played out against each other, in a process that is also at the center of Adorno's own philosophical development, which gives this analysis a paradigmatic value.

Late Style

Conventions are the center of late style, which is what distinguishes it from Beethoven's middle period, which was in fact more subjective, in the sense that it did not tolerate conventions that had not been broken down and integrated into the subjective dynamic. In the late style, they inversely appear almost as if naked, in a way that would have been unacceptable earlier. These are conventions in the state of ruin, although not in the sense of a psychological failure or trauma, rather they pose the question of subjectivity and convention in a new way.

It is true that the relation to death plays a role, but not as the theme of the work: it discloses the law of form, and deprives us of the right to art, which is why death cannot become a theme; it is only given in broken form, as allegory, otherwise it becomes a deceptive metaphysics (here one may probably detect a polemic against Heidegger). If subjectivity disrupts the works, it is not in order to express itself, but to shake off the appearance or semblance, the *Schein*, of art (the frequent translation "semblance," while not simply incorrect, makes it difficult to hear the positive quality of *Schein* as the process of appearing, i.e. the essential proximity between *Schein* and *Erscheinung*, which is essential to Adorno, whose concept is modeled on Hegel's "logic of essence").

In this destruction of *Schein*, the material is as it were emancipated from the process of forming, and there is a profusion and overabundance of material, just as the conventions are left standing, to the effect that they themselves become expressive. This, Adorno suggests, is the role of abbreviation in Beethoven: not to purify music of clichés, but to liberate them, in their disparity, while still projecting intentions onto them. For instance, the frequent crescendos and diminuendos that often appear independent of the musical construction, the fiorituras, the substitution of polyphony for thematic development, and the absence of modulations in favor of abrupt transitions, all testify to this coming-apart — or negative dialectic, to use one of Adorno's later terms — of intention and material.

If these later works can be taken as a kind of landscape, then Beethoven does not gather all of its details into a unified image, but instead, Adorno suggests, he lights it up it with a fire that ignites subjectivity, a spark transmitted between extremes that remain in a state of tension. Subjectivity is what forces these extremes together, but only so as to itself appear as petrified. The caesuras and breaks are moment of a breaking through or out, *Durchbruch*; the resulting parts are forced together through the command of subjectivity, but the secret, the enigma of late style, is that which occurs in between, it is the secret of their constellation, the figure formed by the discordant parts. In this way, Beethoven's late work is both subjective and objective: the ruinous landscape is the objective moment, the light cast over it is the subjective moment, and what the late style does is to dissociate them, to tear them apart in time — but maybe in order to finally preserve them in eternity (and here we can glimpse the utopian moment of redemption in Adorno, although in this early text, just as in the later, it is struck by the ban on images).[16] These late works are catastrophes, he concludes, but we should undoubtedly not hear this in the sense of failures, or simple disasters, but in the Greek sense: *katastrophe*, the sudden moment of reversal and overturning, when something is revealed, as in tragedy, the final part when we move towards the resolution of the plot.

There are two important extra-musical references, that take the idea of late style beyond the confines of an analysis of a single artist, no matter how dense and astronomically singular: Kant, but more profoundly Hegel, in particular his *Logic*; and, seemingly more incidentally, but in way that throws considerable light on the historical conjuncture of Beethoven, Hölderlin's late poetry. Let us begin with Hegel, who unquestionably remains the key philosophical reference throughout Adorno's entire work on Beethoven.

First of all, what is the relation between music and concept? Obviously music is not simply identical to concepts, and it has no direct reference — it is the "the logic of the judgment-less synthesis" (fr. 26), which is why the true synthesis occurs in the interplay between subjectivity and inherited forms; the "matter" of music is the history of accumulated conventions, as in Beethoven's treatment of the sonata form, with its theme and variations; there is both an internal and an external dialectic, both a development of a theme and a subjectivizing of a

16 • In fragment 363, dating from 1948, Adorno writes: "hope in Beethoven is decisive as a secularized and therefore not neutralized category [...]. The image of hope without the lie of religion. NB hope is one of the imageless images that specifically and immediately belongs to music, i.e., it belongs in general to music."

convention, so that they eventually are sublated, *aufgehoben*, on a higher level.

We noted that Adorno in Beethoven detects a move from a Kantian version of the concept, in which it generates form out of a fixed subjectivity that accounts for the unity of experience, to a Hegelian version, in which the concept has a movement of its own and inscribes the position of the earlier subject as a limited one, and where there rather is an experience *of* subjectivity as an object, as an appearance. The Kantian movement corresponds to Beethoven's move into the second phase of his work, where the system of tonality is brought back into subjectivity in the form of the musical subject that lets the formal structure develop organically out of the thematic material; the symphonies are a great testimony to this, as well as the sonatas. The subsequent Hegelian step, where a full mediation of particular and universal is achieved, crowns the second phase, but is then pursued in the third phase, in such a way that it goes beyond its own confines. This is the crucial critical move, and it is here that Beethoven's singularity comes to the fore. In a rather hyperbolic fragment that summarizes Beethoven's second phase, Adorno exclaims: "In a sense similar to that in which there is only Hegel's philosophy, there is in the history of Western music only Beethoven" (fr. 24); but to this we must also add the subsequent step, where Beethoven is "more Hegelian then Hegel" (fr. 320) — it is only through the late works that we see the limit of Hegel, and where the circular time of completion opens onto the reversal of catastrophe.

How should we understand this process, where totality is achieved only to be broken down? In Hegel, the objective forms first become historicized and are set in motion, they are understood both as points of departure and results, just as individual and particular musical elements mean something only in and through their contradiction and mediation through the whole. This is the outcome of the second phase, where "the sensuous, non-qualified and yet in itself mediated, and that which sets the whole in movement, is the motivistic-thematic," whereas "spirit, mediation, is the whole as form" (fr. 27). On the one hand, as Adorno suggests in a letter to Rudolf Kolisch, "the formal meaning essentially consists in disclosing the nothingness [of the particular] brought about by the whole" (appendix, p. 256); on the other hand, "the whole is never external to the particular, but only proceeds out of its movement, or rather, is this movement" (fr. 57). Tonality is thus both what is always *presupposed*, as well as what *results* from self-development and self-reflection, in the movement of a negation that returns to its point of departure. The analyses of the Waldstein sonata (fr. 131), would be the most clear-cut and pedagogical case, even to the point of displaying the kind of ternary thesis-antithesis-synthesis model that Adorno, and rightly so, in many other places rejects as a cartoon or "claptrap" version of Hegel; the third movement in the C-major sonata op. 101, he says later, is, "were one not ashamed to write it down — the synthesis" (fr. 265).[17]

But this fully worked out synthesis is also the moment of *untruth* in this music, which also, in a sense, points towards *truth*: the whole, the totality that seems to flow seamlessly from the movement of the particular and yet is violently forced onto it, reflects the emergence of an administered society, although not just as a static image, but already as an interpretation of it (for comments on the link between musical and social totality, see for instance fr. 87, 88, 92, 113). But beyond this, and as a latent consequence of this interpretation, the supreme greatness — or *lateness* — lies in the next step, where Beethoven unleashes the "mimetic" power inherent in the second phase and becomes "more Hegelian then Hegel," pursuing a negative dialectics, with *and* against Hegel.[18] This is not simply a critique of Hegel; as Adorno will say much later, rather than abandon metaphysics as a false theory, we must attempt to think systematicity in a fractured form, as "constellations" and "micrologies," i.e. develop a mode of thought that remains "in solidarity with metaphysics in the moment of its downfall," *im Augenblick ihres Sturzes*.[19] Thus, if Beethoven finally explodes the Hegelian model, he does not do so by opposing it to some other system, but from *within*, which is why his late style contains the seeds of an immanent critique that will become paradigmatic for modernism in the arts and in philosophy. If Hegel is the last moment of security, metaphysics thinking itself in the form of a system that would be able to ground itself, then this also

17 • See Spitzer's discussion of this in *Music as Philosophy*, 48ff. 18 • Here Spitzer's otherwise excellent analysis leads astray, when he claims that late Beethoven would be "anti-Hegelian, just as modern philosophy critiques metaphysics" (*Music as Philosophy*, 45). While Spitzer's book is the most systematic treatment so far, and superb in its command of musical detail, it must be noted that his characterization of Hegel's *Logic* is misleading. It is true that the Hegelian concept takes its cues from the subjectivity of the I (or rather: from the synthetic unity of transcendental apperception in Kant), but its goal can in no way be the "inwardness and self-sufficiency of the human subject" (ibid, 50). Even though the reading of the *Logic* as culminating in a theory of the human subject may seem as a philosophical technicality, it in fact produces a somewhat distorted reading not only of Adorno's relation to Hegel, but also of his entire philosophical project of negative dialectics.

19 • *Negative Dialektik, Gesammelte Schriften* (Frankfurt am Main: Suhrkamp, 1984), vol. 6, 396. Trans. Dennis Redmond, available online at: www.efn.org/~dredmond/ndtrans.html.

20 • "Its [philosophy's] critical self-reflection may not stop however before the highest achievements of its history. It needs to be asked if and whether, following the collapse of the Hegelian one, it would even be possible anymore, just as Kant investigated the possibility of metaphysics after the critique of rationalism. If the Hegelian doctrine of the dialectic represented the impossible goal of showing, with philosophical concepts, that it was equal to the task of what was ultimately heterogeneous to such, an account is long overdue of its relationship to dialectics, and why precisely his attempt failed." *Negative Dialektik*, 16. Trans. Redmond.

corresponds to the summit of a "classical style" that claims to derives particulars from form and form from particulars in a total mediation. Consequently, the downfall of the Hegelian system not only signals a crisis for the possibility of metaphysics,[20] but also an opening toward modernism in the arts, within which Beethoven's late style would be not only the initial envoi, but also that which already in advance anticipates the impossibility of ever again achieving something like the classical mediation and totality out of which it emerged.

The proximity to Hölderlin on the other hand only comes across in a few passages in the Beethoven book, and in a somewhat inconclusive fashion,[21] but it is no doubt possible to make a connection to the 1963 essay on Hölderlin, "Parataxis," where the poet's encounter with language in many respects seems similar to Beethoven's struggle with the inherited language of musical form. And beyond the exegesis of historical material, the idea of parataxis finally has profound implications for Adorno's understanding of his own philosophical discourse, as in the letters to Rolf Tiedemann cited in the latter's editorial postface to *Aesthetic Theory*, where he suggests that the architecture of the treatise, with its hierarchies and prescribed order of reading, which still organized *Negative Dialectics*, has finally become impossible, and that "the book must, so to speak, be written in equally weighted, paratactical parts that are arranged around a midpoint that they express through their constellation" (ÄT 541/462).

Parataxis, in philosophy as in poetry, points to a loosening of the joints, an unbinding of discourse, which is also a foregrounding of its materiality. We find such a "disjoint" at many levels in Hölderlin: theoretically, in his analysis of "caesura" in Greek tragedy; on the level of poetic content, in his vocations of the Greek gods precisely as departed and absent; textually, in the aberrant use of logical connectives (*dann, näm-*

21 • In fr. 152, Hölderlin's "calculable law of tragedy" is compared to the "symphonic exposition of Beethoven's type", and the "caesura" that Hölderlin famously locates in tragedy, and expounds in his "Remarks on Oedipus," is seen as an analogy to the "moment when subjectivity breaks into form," which seems to enclose the relation to Hölderlin squarely in Beethoven's second period. It is only in the radio lecture from 1966—sublimely enough broadcast under the title "avantgardism of old men" ("Avantgardismus der Greise")—that Adorno makes the connection explicit: "In these late works, the language of music or the material itself speaks, and the composing subject only properly speaks through the gaps in this language, perhaps not wholly dissimilarly to that which occurs with poetic language in the late style of Hölderlin." (BPM, appendix, text 9, 268). For a discussion of how to relate Beethoven and Hölderlin that systematizes Adorno's scattered remarks, see Spitzer, *Music as Philosophy*, chap. 7.

22 • "With parataxis, we should not only think of the transitions that juxtapose micrological shapes. Just as in music, the tendency takes hold of larger structures. [...] In a way similar to Hegel, mediations of a vulgar type, a middle outside of the moments, should be eliminated as external and unessential, as is often the case in Beethoven's late style." "Parataxis," in *Noten zur Literatur, Gesammelte Schriften* vol II, 473.

lich, also etc) that instead of binding his poems together cause them to fracture, destroy the hierarchical links of hypotaxis, and leave us with a paratactical landscape of ruins.[22] Here too, the ruinous landscape can be seen as the objective moment, the light cast over them as the subjective moment, and if the late style is what dissociates them, in Hölderlin it is even more the case that it tears them apart in time — the temporal and historical caesura, in tragedy, poetry, as well as in modernity's task of translating the ancients into our own language, is one of the great themes of Hölderlin — but perhaps then in order to preserve them in eternity.[23]

Lateness, Time, and the Virtual

In a certain sense it would be relatively easy to transpose Adorno's analysis of late style as a particular historical moment to the sphere of painting, even though, given the present context, we must note that his specific remarks on Turner and Monet are of little use.[24] Beethoven's lateness as the effect of a historical caesura or disintegration brought about by the downfall of something like a "classical style" would as its equivalent in painting have the crumbling of the authority of the Academy at the beginning of the nineteenth century, which is perhaps not just the beginning of a new style, but the beginning of a modern idea of style as such.[25] As such, this idea is obviously not specific to Adorno. In 1932, Paul Valéry writes, not about Turner or

23 • Many of Adorno's claims must here be understood as systematically opposed to Heidegger: the impossibility of retrieving an origin, Hölderlin's dialectical relation to German Idealism, the resistance of poetic language as *Schein* to translation into philosophical statements. As Philippe Lacoue-Labarthe notes, these differences notwithstanding, we should not overlook that Adorno and Heidegger share the problem of how to account for a philosophical truth of poetry that cannot be reduced to philological, biographical, and literary-historical categories; se Lacoue-Labarthe, *Heidegger: La politique du poème* (Paris: Galilée, 2002), 93ff. For a discussion of this relation that focuses on the idea of parataxis, see Sabine Wilke, "Kritische und ideologische Momente der Parataxis: Eine Lektüre von Adorno, Heidegger und Hölderlin," *Modern Language Notes*, vol. 102, No. 3 (April 1987): 627–647.

24 • Just as Gesualdo, El Greco, and Büchner, Turner, Adorno says (ÄT 68/52), belongs to those artists who may be revived because of a retroactive correspondence discovered through later work that breaks with the continuous tradition. While this complicates the idea of successive and cumulative history, it does not seem to be fundamentally connected to an idea of a late style. The comments on Monet's late work 252 wholly deny him any such quality, and Adorno (hesitantly, it is true) aligns him with Richard Strauss, casting both as artists whose work "diminished in quality when, seemingly happy with themselves and with what they have achieved, they forfeited the power for historical enervation and the appropriation of the most progressive materials" (287/252).

25 • In the modern concept of style there is a moment of contradiction as well as contingency, in the sense that a style on the one hand could be chosen at will, and that whoever chooses a particular style will himself merge with this style, so that it is understood as a natural expression, which now becomes a personal signature. The question posed by the architect Heinrich Hübsch in 1828: "In what style should we build?" could in this sense be taken as the beginning of a long debate on whether style could be reattached to a ground, a body, a solid center, or if it must be accepted as a free-floating entity determined by fashion. See the texts translated in Wolfgang Hermann (ed.) *In What Style Should We Build? The German Debate on Architectural Style* (Santa Monica: Getty Center, 1992).

26 • Valéry, "Autour de Corot," in *Pièces sur l'art, Oeuvres Complètes* (Paris: Gallimard-Pléiade, 1984), vol II, 1323.

Monet, but about Delacroix: "The transition from the earlier grandeur of Painting to its present state appears in the works and writings of Eugène Delacroix. Unrest and the sense of impotence is what tears apart this modern artist, so full of ideas, at each moment running up against the limits of his own means in his attempts to equal the masters of the past." Delacroix, Valéry continues, is "fighting with himself, and he engages feverishly in the last battle of the grand style in art."[26] Here the language of art falls apart, unleashing a multiplicity of styles and formal features that all claim to be the new language, although without ever succeeding in attaining the authority of the language of the Academy. This would in a sense come close to Adorno, although without the heavy Hegelian architecture that subtends his idea.

Late Style

But as we have noted, the most important facets of Adorno's theory point in the opposite direction: late style is not so much the emergence of a subjectivity that breaks free in order to upset an inherited, objectivized formal canon, rather it is the irruption of the objective, the force of the world, inside a subject whose former freedom now proves to have been an illusion and thus in fact unfreedom, and it registers the impact of history, or "the law of form" in the aesthetic register, on expressivity, in the sense that meditation no longer appears possible between them. It is not a sheer destruction of the subject, but a petrifying of its former capacities, an immobilization that at the same time lets them live on in the constellation of fragments that points, albeit in a veiled, obscure, oblique manner, towards eternity and a reconciliation between history and subject. The ruinous landscape of lateness emerges in the recognition of the *limit* of art, the boundaries set for its *Schein*, but precisely in order to preserve the imageless image of redemption beyond all empirical forms into which it might be prematurely sealed.

It is at this point, which constitutes the metaphysical horizon of Adorno's late style and is what finally allows it to break free from the limits of an empirical-historical moment by entering into its innermost contradiction, that I would like to conclude by coming back to Deleuze and Guattari, who would rather speak of such lateness as an irruption of the untimely, of that which resists historical narration, even in the negative-dialectical form envisaged by Adorno, and acts to dislodge the present from its axis in order to release different pasts and futures, or what they call the "virtual." Eternity is surely there for Deleuze and Guattari too (immanence does not simply mean the *eradication* of transcendence, but a different distribution between the two) in the sense of an outside that envelops time, the *Aion* that traverses *Chronos*, although not in the sense of a redemption, but of time as the Open, *l'Ouvert*, to use the

Bergsonian vocabulary from Deleuze's books in cinema (which, as he notes, is a point where Bergson's path crosses Heidegger's). Instead of a reconciliation that can only be glimpsed through a subjectivity that enters into the deepest estrangement, there is a dispersal of the subject in the Open, which in this case just as little means sheer destruction,

Are these two options wholly at odds? In both of them, there is on the most simple and straightforward level an emphatic distrust of cumulative time and narrative closure, and of a certain idea of subjectivity that would be able to give form and unity to experience. In Adorno, this becomes visible in the clash with historical conventions that refuse integration, and in a relation to death and finitude that divests art of its *Schein*; in Deleuze and Guattari, late style, which for them too is related to death as a limit, signifies that the mind's faculties begin to overcome their limits and enter into "the deregulation of all the senses" that Rimbaud once presaged as the basis for a poetry and music of the future.[27] As we saw in the introductory quote from *What is Philosophy?*, Deleuze links this deregulation to Kant's third Critique, and the possibility of a kind of discordant concord of the faculties,[28] once they are emancipated from the form the subject. The subject is not reified, not given over to an estrangement that is the other side of redemption and reconciliation, but becomes a field of experimentation and construction. Lateness, to the extent that it can be figured temporally, here becomes an opening toward the future.

At stake here are not only two versions of the modern work of art, but also two seemingly incompatible metaphysical options that both derive from opposed readings of Hegel. For Adorno, there is already an anticipation of the wholly administered society in Hegel's *Logic* — which only today, in late capitalism, has become true, he says somewhere — where all elements are defined by their interrelations. This is also the moment of untruth in Beethoven's middle period, since the subjectivity that claims to deduce all conventions is only a mirage; and it is by bringing this contradiction out in the open, and by allowing the force of historical necessity to strike back at the heart of the subject, that Beethoven's late style acquires its moment of truth, at once linking it even more closely to a precise historical moment and opening it up to a

27 • Here I have entirely left out what a positive Deleuzian contribution to the philosophy of music might look like, since this would take us far from the present context; for a discussion of Deleuze and music that focuses on the relation to Adorno, see Nick Nesbitt, "Deleuze, Adorno, and the Composition of Musical Multiplicity," in Ian Buchanan & Marcel Swiboda (eds.): *Deleuze and Music* (Edinburgh: Edinburgh University Press, 2004).

28 • See also the more developed comments in Deleuze, "Quatre formules qui pourraient résumer la philosophie kantienne," in Deleuze, *Critique et clinique* (Paris: Minuit, 1993). In *What is Philosophy?* Turner is later cited in passing as someone who experiences this deregulation and confronts chaos in order to extract a composes sensation, or a "chaoid variety" (205). Monet receives more attention, and his creation of a universe-house becomes a paradigm case of the balance between art's need to create permanence and stability in the composite of sensations that it extracts, and the opening towards an infinity of color; see 180 and 204.

redemption beyond time. For Deleuze too, the late style acquires its power by rejecting unity, but rather in order to let us discover that unity was never there, that the wholly administered society is in fact traversed by lines of flight, even that it is held in place only by the creation of momentary conduits for forces that always overflow it. Thus, the "sovereign freedom" that is also "a pure necessity", attained at the limit of time, does not belong to the order of the subject or history in Adorno's sense, but to the untimely.

Lateness, untimeliness, redemption, the virtual — do these concepts, drawn as they are from very different vocabularies, themselves form a kind of constellation, organized paractically around a midpoint that they express, but which cannot be given as such, to the effect that truth, as Adorno says, is what passes between them, as it does between the objective landscape and the subjective light in late Beethoven? •

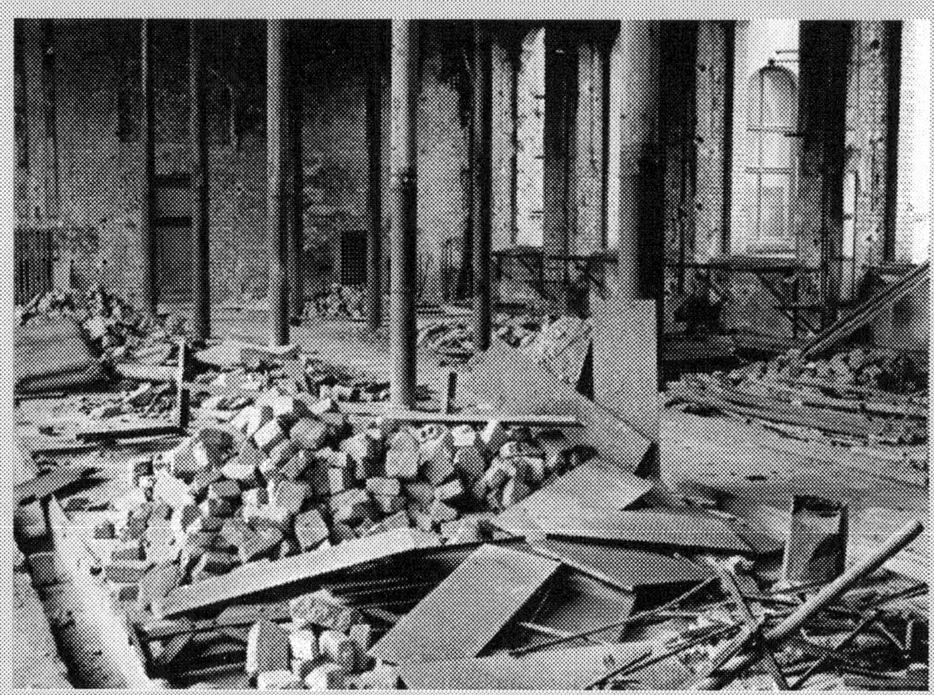

Quality Education

Karl Lydén
Kim West

> The question (overt or implied) now asked by the professionalist student, the State, or institutions of higher education is no longer "Is it true?" but "What use is it?" In the context of the mercantilization of knowledge, more often than not this question is equivalent to: "Is it saleable?" And in the context of power-growth: "Is it efficient?" —J-F. Lyotard

In recent years there has been a tremendous dismantling of higher education in many European countries. The university, particularly the humanities and social sciences, has come under attack in various ways in the UK, Italy, Austria, France, Germany, Greece, Spain, and in virtually every country of Europe where the Bologna

◂ **Humboldt University in ruins, December 1950. Bundesarchiv, Bild 183-08833-0003. Photo: Hans-Günther Quaschinsky.**

Process has produced a general quantification of higher learning along with restricted academic freedom and worsened labor conditions for professors, lecturers, and university employees at large.

There is a general trend, but there are also stark individual differences. In the UK, for example, downsized public funding has led to sharply raised tuition fees for students; while in Italy, an aggressive commodification of education has tilted the university's focus from the study of traditional disciplines of knowledge towards professional training for highly specialized commercial sectors.

In addition to these devastating reforms of the university, aggravating measures have also hit other educational structures. This should be emphasized, because these structures might have no direct connections to student movements, they might not be included in public or democratic decision making, or they might not be inscribed in the media-favored narrative of university struggle. In the Netherlands for example, the government that was elected in 2010 has simply decided to cut the funding for the country's renowned independent post-academic research institutes: de Ateliers, Jan van Eyck Academie, and Rijksakademie — institutes which will most likely be effaced after 2012. If the Bologna Process has been regarded as the final doing away with the independent university devoted

Quality Education

to *Bildung* and research as it was envisaged by Wilhelm von Humboldt,[1] the current Dutch policy also equals a destruction of that which, for Humboldt, "must be retained as the highest and last sanctuary of learning and as the body most independent of the state," namely the free academy.[2] Humboldt held the academies in high esteem not simply because he considered them places devoted purely to science (without any of the university's responsibilities to "guide the youth"), but also because they guaranteed a space of important independence from the university and its formal conditions. Similarly, another of those rare institutions in the periphery of the academia proper came under threat recently: the Warburg Institute in London. This unique library — Aby Warburg's own, classified according to the art historian's idiosyncratic system — was saved from the Nazi regime in 1933 when it was moved from Hamburg to London, and placed under the care of the University of London (UCL). Citing elevated costs, the UCL suddenly wanted to increase the Institute's rent dramatically, virtually forcing it to relocate to a storage space or be included and reclassified in the university's library.[3]

Finally, there are the events that occur on a more symbolic level, such as when the Copenhagen Free University received a letter from the Danish Ministry of Science, Technology and Innovation citing a new law prohibiting unauthorized use of the term "university" and establishing that any further educational activities would be illegal.[4] It is no coincidence that such legal monopolies appear in times of a vehement commodification of higher education, and it is certainly not without consequence to alternative, self-organized educational structures. The artist-run Free University, however, which more or less had ceased to exist some years ago, immediately proclaimed the existence of a new Free University in response to the decision.

Much has been written about this already and a lot remains to

1 • The extent to which the Humboldtian ideals were really applied in the German (or any) university can, however, be questioned. See for example: Mitchell G. Ash "Bachelor of What, Master of Whom? The Humboldt Myth and Historical Transformations of Higher Education in German-Speaking Europe and the US", *European Journal of Education*, Vol. 41, No. 2, 2006.
2 • Wilhelm von Humboldt, "Über die innere und äussere Organisation der höheren wissenschaftlichen Anstalten in Berlin", in *Gründungstexte: Johann Gottlieb Fichte, Friedrich Daniel, Ernst Schleiermacher, Wilhelm von Humboldt. Festgabe zum 200-jährigen Jubiläum der Humboldt-Universität zu Berlin*, ed. Engelbert Habekost (Berlin: Humboldt-Universität zu Berlin, 2010).
3 • For a description of the initial fears of a closing down of the library, see Anthony Grafton and Jeffrey Hamburger, "Save the Warburg Library!" *New York Review of Books*, September 30, 2010, and Bernard Schulz, "In Bildern versteckte Symbole waren seine Leidenschaft", *Die Zeit*, February 7, 2011. Currently, the threat seems to be momentarily staved off.
4 • See "All power to the free universities of the future!" copenhagenfreeuniversity.dk.

be understood, theorized, and investigated, but the basic problematic seems to have been captured very well already in Jean-François Lyotard's *The Post-Modern Condition*. Subtitled "A Report on Knowledge", this book was indeed written as a report to the Canadian government in 1979, and the conception was clear: "It is not hard to visualize learning circulating along the same lines as money, instead of for its 'educational' value or political (administrative, diplomatic, military) importance; the pertinent distinction would no longer be between knowledge and ignorance, but rather, as is the case with money, between 'payment knowledge' and 'investment knowledge' — in other words, between units of knowledge exchanged in a daily maintenance framework (the reconstitution of the work force, 'survival') versus funds of knowledge dedicated to optimizing the performance of a project."

To rehearse Lyotard's classic analysis, the grand narratives of legitimation of education have lost their credibility in contemporary, "post-industrial" society: both the narrative of knowledge as a means of emancipation, and the German Idealist narrative of a *Bildung* which "grounds the development of learning, of society, and of the State in the realization of the 'life' of a Subject, called 'divine Life' by Fichte and 'Life of the spirit' by Hegel." Therefore, legitimation must come through performativity, resulting in the "mercantilization" of higher learning.

Naturally this characterization of the current crisis before the fact is not sufficient to fully understand its contemporary workings. Limiting our selection to things published during our work with the current issue, we can mention the pirated reader *Dispatches from the Ruins*;[5] the anthology *Curating and the Educational Turn*,[6] a collection of essays by artists, curators, and critics; and the excellent first issue of *Edu-factory Journal*, which collects international experiences and reflections on the cuts. Here Mary Evans puts the current metamorphosis of the university in analogy with the process described in Marx's *Capital*, in which the instruments of labour come to employ the workman, instead of the reversed. That is, the university is no longer an instrument for labor, but that which instrumentalizes students for a constantly more specialized and shifting labor market.[7] And perhaps this thinking about the crisis of education in terms of labor issues can be very productive. In the same magazine issue, Brophy & Tucker-Abramson note that: "The most effective resistance to the roll-out of the neoliberal university

5 • Dispatches from the Ruins, 1,000 Little Hammers, May 2011: 1000littlehammers.wordpress.com.
6 • *Curating and the Educational Turn*, eds. Paul O'Neill & Mick Wilson (London and Amsterdam: Open Editions/de Appel, 2010).

has thus far come from the labor force which fuels it, although, as we have seen, new and potentially powerful combinations are being produced between labor, student, and community activists within this epochal transformation of the institution."[8]

In a similar vein, it is as a means of resistance that Sven-Eric Liedman and Mark Fisher — in their highly disparate accounts of the managerialization and bureacratization of the University — come to the same conclusion: disregard from all bureaucracy, all reporting, all measuring and all application *while* you are doing it. Minimize your attention, just send in the report.[9]

Quality Education

The texts in this section attempt to assess what has happened, what is happening, and to a certain extent what is to be done regarding the European crisis of higher education. In assembling these texts, our aim is simply to contribute to the ongoing critique of the double crisis[10] of finance and higher education that currently cripples cultural production in large parts of the world.

In her essay on the Italian university, Sara R. Farris discusses how neoliberal restructuring and commodification have gone hand in hand with a precarization of the university's workforce, all in the face of an apologetic Italian left.

Starting from his recollections from a seminar with the Swedish Minister of Education and members of the boards of trustees of all the country's universities and colleges, Hans Ruin discusses the effects of the implementation of new management structures in Swedish higher education, and considers the prospects for the university's age-old ideal of a common and democratic commitment to truth and dialogue.

From a French perspective, Stéphane Douailler in turn examines the contested notion of the university's "autonomy", analyzing the ways in which it has been appropriated by both state and corporate interests.

Danny Hayward recounts the events in the UK, starting in November 2010, when the Browne report suggested the cuts in public spending that led to the 300% increase in tuition fees. This was the starting point for the widespread student protests, riots and student struggles that in turn revealed a whole other class dynamics when these were

7 • Mary Evans, "The University of Barclays Bank", *Edu-factory Web Journal*, First issue, September 2011, 48. www.edu-factory.org.
8 • Enda Brophy and Myka Tucker-Abramson, "From Utopian Institution to Global University: Simon Fraser University and Crisis of Canadian Public Education", *Edu-factory Web Journal*, First issue, September 2011, 16. www.edu-factory.org.
9 • See Sven-Eric Liedman, *Hets!* (Stockholm: Bonniers 2011), and Mark Fisher, *Capitalist Realism: Is There No Alternative?* (London: Zero Books, 2009).
10 • For an investigation of the double nature of the crisis, see: Edu-factory Web Journal, Issue Zero, January 2010, www.edu-factory.org.

joined by the youth receiving Education Maintenance Allowance (EMA).

Finally, in conversation with Karl Lydén, Katja Diefenbach discusses the current events in the Netherlands and the possible destruction of the Jan van Eyck Academie in 2012. How do we resist the "austerity politics" of the current populist and plutocratic regimes? What are the possibilities of an autonomously organized knowledge production and circulation? •

Quality Education

Cogito Ergo Insurgo! The Italian University: Laboratory of Crisis and Critique

Sara R. Farris

Today, the metaphor "books as weapons" has become concrete, in a way that is unprecedented, through a multiplicity of references, dense with meanings. Seeing a cop hammer away at a classic… well… it's priceless!
— Wu Ming

Books are weapons, weapons for critique, that you must learn to use well: the target clear, the aim sure, a cold eye, a warm hand. — Mario Tronti

Between the end of 2010 and early 2011 there was a mobilisation of the world of higher education in Italy, Greece, the UK and Spain, involving both students and academics. Among the most important aspects of this mobilisation was not only the synchronisation at the European level — with demonstrations and occupations of university buildings across Europe occurring between November and December 2010, with new demonstrations planned for the end of March 2011 — but also the usage of common slogans and symbols (i.e., "We won't pay for your crisis" and the *Book Bloc*). In all cases, students and lecturers protested in order to resist laws that will deepen the commodification of higher education, extending processes of class selection and wreaking havoc upon the Humanities and Social Sciences.

Manifestations of dissent have increasingly demonstrated a European dimension, because the neoliberal assault against what remains of public education and of the idea of learning as self-improvement has been launched at this level (although it is part of a global venture). So-called agreements for the free exchange of commodities have already accustomed us to vivid acronyms such as NAFTA, CEFTA etc., which recall the geography of their application. In the same way, the creation of the area of free exchange of that special type of commodity called "knowledge" could not avoid adopting its own geo-political acronym. Thus, in 1999 — the year in which the Ministers of Higher Education of thirty European countries signed the so-called Bologna Declaration — the EHEA, the European Higher Education Area, was born. Today the EHEA comprises forty-seven countries, covering an area which reaches from Ireland to Russia. Correspondingly, as in a pure business lexicon, the governments of these countries have committed themselves to trade in knowledge, or, as they see it, "to strengthen the competitiveness and attractiveness of European higher education and to foster student mobility and employability through the introduction of a system based on undergraduate and postgraduate studies with easily readable programmes and degrees."[1]

In fact, the adhesion of the EHEA countries to the so-called Bologna Process has meant the increasing substitution of previously existing study programmes with the double cycle (BA+MA), the introduction of the credits system, and the increasing transformation of universities into companies with a commercial vocation. They are increasingly concerned with finding external sources of funding (both by raising student fees and by "selling" courses to private companies) and less and less supported by State budgets.

Although there are still many differences between higher education systems in the EHEA countries, certain common dynamics and problematics can already be discerned. In this regard, the Italian case is particularly emblematic. Since the approval of the Zecchino reform in 1999, the rapidity of the application of the guidelines determined in Bologna, the subsequent overturning almost *notte-tempo* of the previous educational system, the liquidation (sale) of many academic curricula — in particular many MA programmes (*lauree specialistiche*) — to private companies, the extreme precarisation of researchers and lecturers: all of these are aspects which have led to dramatic consequences both in the labour market and in the quality of research and teaching. The Italian version of the Bologna agreement has in reality achieved almost the exact opposite of the triumphalistic promises with which it was introduced.

Instead of increasing the number of students, especially of graduates, official data show that in the last two

1 • See the official website: www.ehea.info

years there has been a decrease in enrollments — particularly in public universities, in the South of the country (i.e., in the poorer regions), and in the Humanities and Social Sciences.[2] Instead of facilitating the employment of graduates by bringing the university closer to the requirements of the labour market — which constitutes the most insistent claim of the Bologna Process — today's statistics reveal a higher rate of unemployment and under-employment amongst new graduates.[3] Instead of promoting continuing or further education, students of the neo-liberal university system read much less and possess a much lower level of general "culture". Thus, as it stands, Italy can be seen as a laboratory in which the neo-liberal counter-revolutionary transformation of higher education is at an extremely advanced stage. Its perverse outcomes are already so conspicuous as to assign it to a seemingly inglorious vanguardist position in Europe. *De te fabula narratur!*

Quality Education

In a recent essay Giulio Calella duly noted that the "Italian road" to neo-liberalism in the context of higher education has not been marked by a process of privatisation, but rather by the commercialisation (managerialisation) of university institutions and by the complete commodification of its study programmes. As Calella puts it:

> It is not convenient for the ruling class to privatize the university, which is an institution full of micro-powers and petty interests that are difficult and expensive to manage — it is more than enough to use it for private ends as a disposable tool (...) Through the private trusts established by bill number 133, private companies will in fact be able to directly enter public institutions without being forced to fork out any money. This idea of private trusts, which comes from the Berlusconi government, is in fact the exact opposite of the kind of intervention devised to bail out big banks and save them from the crisis: Berlusconi — with Veltroni's support — is ready to give billions of euros to the banks without asking for any right over their management. Private companies, on the contrary, will be able to join universities' boards of directors and therefore decide which professional figures should be trained, what kinds of internships these trainees should take, or what kind of research universities should do — again, all without forking out a single euro. (...) This way, universities tend to become public labour precarization agencies. Moreover,

2 • See data made available by the National Council for Universities (CUN) in 2011.
3 • Cf. Andrea Cammelli, *XIII Rapporto Almalaurea sulla condizione occupazionale dei laureati*, 7 March 2011.

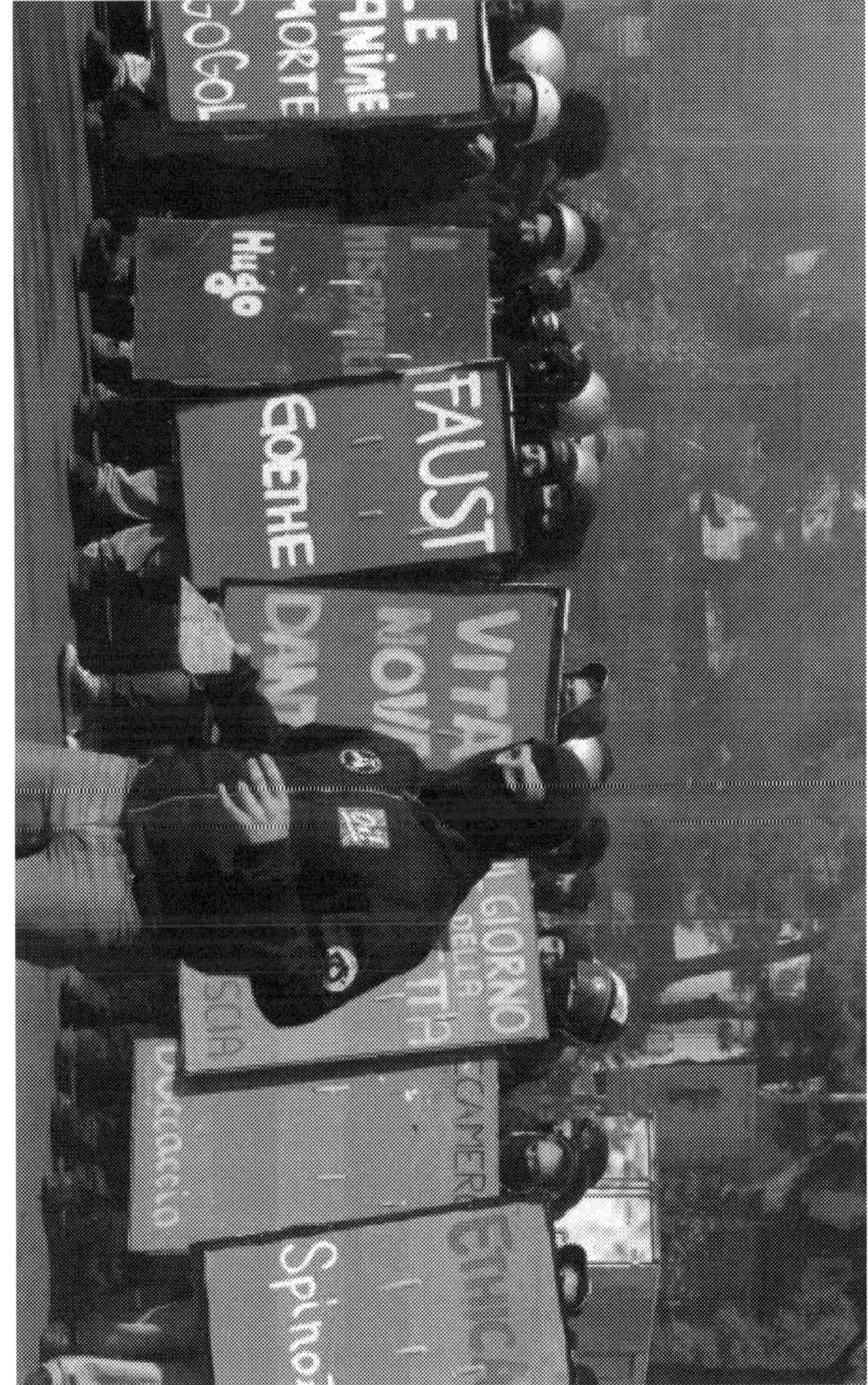

▲ Demonstrations against the Education Reform of the Berlusconi Government, Palermo 22 December 2010.

through the introduction of internships (which in many cases are considered a prerequisite to getting course credits) they have created a new permanent army of workers, who are not just precarious and poorly paid but completely 'cost-free'.[4]

Quality Education

Although it is increasingly less supported by public funds and is coming more and more to resemble an enterprise in the service of private interests, it would be inaccurate to argue that the Italian university has undergone a process of Americanisation. Though the US higher education system is certainly the inspiring muse of the Bologna Process, its translation into the Peninsula has little to do with the American model. In the latter case, the growth of federal and state funds for basic and applied research is much higher than in Europe — not to mention in Italy. The commodification of the American university is not in fact effected by means of the sale of its structures; rather, it is brought about through its full incorporation into the twin processes of the internationalisation of the economy and of the reorganisation of labour. With the proliferation of corporate universities, of life-long learning programmes and the multiplication of distance learning courses, the organisation of the American university is adapting to, reproducing, but also anticipating the tendencies of current economic globalisation: i.e., diversification of output, reduction of labour costs, outsourcing of services, competitiveness and technological innovation.

Scientific and professional skills, as well as qualified labour-power in general, are important commodities for a mode of production which increasingly conceives of education, not only as a passive resource to be shaped by the *hic et nunc* needs of market demands, but also as a pro-active, and even performative, type of commodity: namely, one which is able to produce technological innovation and thereby to increase the competitiveness of American capital on the international markets. Yet, the commodification of higher education that is now underway at the international level, and whose practical agenda is dictated by the US system, is not a "night in which all cows are black", an undistinguished whole without movement and internal contradictions. Contemporary capitalism has not transformed itself into a completely cognitive capitalism, and nor has knowledge become a "real commodity", the education system having undergone some mythical process of absolute real subsumption.

Indeed, if the current period is characterized by the growing application of knowledge to technological innovation, services- and commodity-production, one should not assume that "knowledge work

4 • Giulio Calella, "The Factory of Precarious Workers", in *Springtime. The New Student Rebellions*, edited by Clare Solomon and Tanial Palmieri (New York: Verso, 2011), 97.

has now usurped 'physical' or 'material' labour power in the creation of surplus value; and concomitantly that knowledge work forms a separate category of work from 'material' labour".[5] Even though knowledge as a collective human resource is commodified by separating intellectual labour from the means of production — by privatising and marketing knowledge output in the form of copyright royalties as well as in the form of payment for the purchase of knowledge-based commodities, or by using intellectual resources to produce knowledge in the process of development of the technical and social forces of production — "'knowledge' cannot create value in isolation. Rather, it can only do so as part of the totality of the living labour-power that is subject to valorization within the circuit of capital".[6]

Indeed, in Italy the commodification of the university system is being realized in terms of an extreme vampirisation of its apparatuses by entrepreneurs who are ready to suck out its intellectual energies but who do not invest money to support it. Universities are being mostly transformed into centres of professional training for small- and medium-sized companies, with a very small geographic area of activity and whose degree of technological innovation is often very low. Their opening to private interests, therefore, is of a very limited nature. Bachelor's and Master's programmes do not go beyond providing students with the elements strictly necessary for those professions that are most required in the area. Knowledge programmes, therefore, simply adhere to the economic demand of the territory as it is currently configured but without stimulating new possibilities within it. Moving from tragedy to farce, the Italian neo-liberal university thus offers degrees in "Management of Urban Greenery", "Sciences for the Raising, Hygiene and Well-being of Cats and Dogs", "Sciences and Technologies of Fitness", "Sciences of Alpine Tourism"... It is difficult to imagine how indoctrination into such narrow-minded fields of expertise could enable students to face the challenges of a world of labour which is characterized by continuous transformation.

5 • Peter Kennedy, "The Knowledge Economy and Labour Power in Late Capitalism, in *Critical Sociology*, 36.6, 2010, 822

6 • Peter Kennedy, 2011, ibid. Likewise, though students can be regarded as workers, albeit precarious ones — as when they undertake internships which are nothing but unpaid labour, or when they need to take precarious jobs to allow them to pay increasingly higher fees — *qua* students they constitute a special type of commodity under training which is skilled labour power. Within the education cycle itself, in fact, they are not yet fully exploited workers but rather "precarious workers in becoming". As Calella notes, "with the new laurea degrees that offer fragmented knowledge for a precarious future, with the fast-paced study paths imposed by the 3+2, which train students to lose control of their lives and to be ready to accept any job (...) the student is turned from customer into commodity. So that, if he is unsatisfied with his study path, he 'can still rejoice at being considered a 'product' to be released just-in-time to the local productive fabric'". (Giulio Calella, ibid., 99).

Yet the price of the neo-liberal university kickshaw is being paid not only by students — who are increasingly reduced to passive receptors of disarticulated notions and a-systematic knowledge, thereby rendered into extremely "precarious workers in the making"[7] with no intellectual resources for critique — but also by researchers and lecturers. Due to the disinvestment in the university system and research — which the recent decree of Minister Gelmini has worsened — and, at the same time, because of the multiplication of courses and sub-courses, the burden of teaching falls to Ph.D. students and extremely precarious lecturers. They are not only under-paid but very often not paid at all. As a feudal system grounded on personal relations with the Baron-Professor, the recruitment process in Italy does not even follow basic meritocratic or market criteria.

Quality Education

Ph.D. students and recent doctoral graduates know very well that their only hope for future employment is to be submissive and to work for free for the Baron-Professors who will express their gratitude by inserting graduates' names in the waiting list. The recent drastic reduction of university funding, however, will leave many young researchers with promises and nothing more, something resembling a more general international trend, as a recent dossier by *The Economist* revealed.[8] When the possibility of a stable position depends on the recognition and gratitude of the master, the slave is forced to serve and be obsequious. Consequently, it is unlikely that such a situation will produce original and critical research, since this requires intellectual as well as economic independence and autonomy. Furthermore, one of the most depressing aspects of the Italian situation is represented by the fact that the destruction of public higher education, which Berlusconi's government wants to bring to completion, was initiated by centre-left governments. The devastation of Italian universities, therefore, takes place in a scenario without parliamentary opposition (since the radical Left was swept out of parliament in the 2008 elections).

In this context it is worth noting that the thesis advanced by Perry Anderson on the reasons for the defeat of the Italian Left requires some emendations. According to Anderson, the Italian "invertebrate left" — as he effectively labelled the inheritors of the PCI — favoured the advent of the Berlusconi era mainly thanks to its snobbish attitude towards popular culture.[9] It was thus unable to understand the "anthropological mutation" facilitated by the continuous exposure of the population to the vulgarity of the Prime Minister's television. However, such an account needs to be revised. The Italian invertebrate left contributed to

7 • Cf. Giulio Calella, ibid., 2011.
8 • Cf. "The Disposable Academic. Why doing a PhD is Often a Waste of Time", in *The Economist*, 16th December 2010.
9 • Cf. Perry Anderson, "An Invertebrate Left", in *London Review of Books*, Vol. 31, n. 5, 2009.

the hegemony of Berlusconi, not so much because it remained in the ivory tower, contemplating the peaks of its own culture, but rather because it did everything it could to remove all memory of the culture of the Left from the political lexicon. Particularly after the fall of the Soviet Union, the successors of the PCI aimed at nothing but accrediting themselves as trustworthy (i.e., anti-communist) leaders and thus as legitimate candidates for government. In the context of university institutions, the once-communist *intelligentsia* rushed to banish terms now considered *demodé* — "social class" or "capitalism", for instance. It preferred to employ more neutral categories and *passepartout* concepts — like "stratification" or "globalisation" — while reducing, when not entirely eliminating, the inclusion of important texts of the Marxist tradition from the curricula.

One of the reasons which makes the commodification of the university intolerable for its critics is the fact that such a process runs against the idea of higher education as a set of institutions which guarantee universal access, serve the public good, educate individuals in an independent and critical manner and shape scholars and professionals such that they are able to advance the state of knowledge and welfare of a society. Yet, it is an idea that only gained currency in relatively recent times. The admittance into the university of women, students of working-class and ethnic minority backgrounds, for instance, was a quite contemporary achievement obtained at the price of long struggles and mobilisations on the part of the excluded subjects.

On the one hand, since historically it has had the role of the formation and reproduction of society's leaders, the university has always been a terrain of contention due to the will of the dominant classes to preserve its elitist status. On the other hand, the university's disciplinary structure is itself the product of the bourgeois economic revolutions. The division between disciplines mirrors the division of labour, namely, what Marx in the *1844 Manuscripts* called "the economic expression of the *social character of labour* within the estrangement." The criteria and modalities of the partition between humanities, social sciences and natural sciences, as well as their internal subsections, reflect the pedagogical model of a society which is dominated by the need to separate producers from the means of production, intellectual from manual labour.

Likewise, the present rearrangement of subjects of study that goes under the name of multi- or inter-disciplinary programmes arguably matches the changes that have occurred in the last twenty years in the organisation of labour and of the economy more generally. The neo-liberal reshaping of universities has thus been able to turn an idea which is potentially revolutionary — since multidisciplinarity could potentially challenge that division of knowledge which "allows the body politic to divide and rule"[10] — into a tool for the reproduction of the *status quo*.

In the Anglophone world, the term inter-disciplinarity is increasingly used to designate an approach and a modality of producing knowledge that challenges the traditional ways of conceiving the barriers between disciplines. In the United States and in the UK, schools and departments of inter-disciplinary studies are multiplying, while in France and Germany conferences and research institutes are being organized which promise to go in the direction of a simplification which is in line with international tendencies. But what does the new valorisation of inter-disciplinarity mean? What does the present crisis of traditional disciplines, which were once the institutional pillars of the organisation of knowledge in modern times, amount to? One possible answer comes from one of the sanctuaries of inter-disciplinary research, the Centre for the Study of Inter-Disciplinarity (CSID) of North Texas University. The term "interdisciplinarity", we are told, has first of all to be decoded: "What the academy calls interdisciplinarity, the world at large calls accountability." University research, in other words, must be accountable; it has to be subjectable to accounting criteria and responsible for the value of its output by submitting itself to a logic of "relevance". The old disciplinary borders are considered incapable of facing the new challenges as they reproduce fields of knowledge which are no longer productive. It thus becomes apparent that interdisciplinarity is nothing but the new belief of the disciples of *problem solving*. Rather than the old Enlightenment dream of the unity of knowledge, the proposals put forth by interdisciplinary programmes in reality display the deepening of the process of the capitalist marketisation of knowledge. Interdisciplinary programmes aim to transform universities into centres of counseling in which research projects are focused on practical problems of immediate utility. Given the process of marketisation of higher education, however, utility itself is defined in terms of the needs of private interests and not in terms of the needs of a broader social collectivity which is, instead, entirely excluded from the discussion about — and especially from the decisions over — these processes.

If the neo-liberal version of inter-disciplinarity thus entrenches the commodification of knowledge and its submission to private profits, little space is left for unproductive disciplinary contexts like the humanities and the social sciences. They do not produce outputs which can be easily sold or that can be profitably applied to the

10 • Cf. David Harvey, *Social Justice and the City*, Blackwell Publishers, 1988.

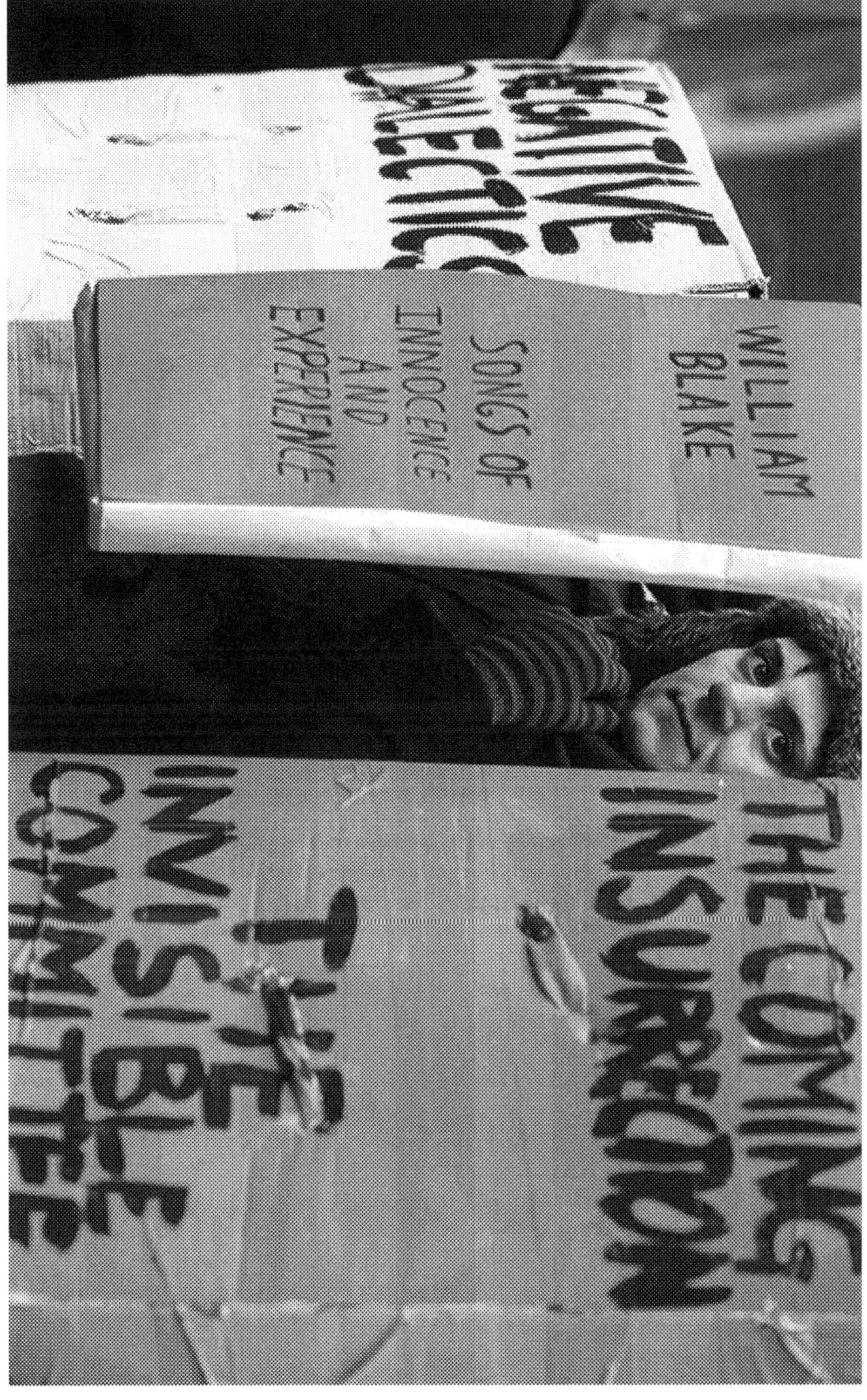

▸ London, 9 December 2010.

production of further knowledge to be put at the service of technological innovation and the accumulation of capital. Furthermore, the precarious workers-in-becoming that these fields of knowledge churn out can mostly be employed only by those institutions which are reducing their capacity, particularly due to States' increasing lack of subsidies (schools and universities above all). In addition, humanities and social sciences students of the neo-liberal age are often at the forefront of protests and critical perspectives. This is not due to the intrinsic vocation to critique of the humanist, the philosopher or of the social or political analyst, whose historically distinctive role has rather been that of the "counsellor of the prince". In the current period, they are bearing the brunt of the attack as degree courses in philosophy and social sciences, in Europe as well as in the US, are closed or drastically diminished; the corresponding faculties receive increasingly less financially support and due to the lack of immediate profitability of the knowledge they produce, they are less able to attract external funds that could guarantee their survival. In this context, it is as if their very existence is symbolic of the current situation, for they demonstrate the increasing incompatibility between an idea of knowledge as a goal in itself and an idea of knowledge as merely utilitarian. In light of their uncomfortable positioning in the present conjuncture, then, they have almost become monuments *in se* against the neo-liberal conception of higher education, since they are fields of knowledge whose outputs are much harder to turn into marketable goods.

Quality Education

Faithful to their common etymology, therefore, *crisis* and *critique* come together at the meeting point of the humanities and social-political sciences. As the latter are riven by a crisis which is the discernible effect of capitalist logic, the seeds for its critique spring up. *A new revolution is possible only in the wake of a new crisis. But the one is as certain as the other.*[11]

As a modality of representation and act of protest adopted by the recent student demonstrations against the privatistic restructuring of the university, it is this potential of unmarketable knowledge represented by the humanities and the social sciences to which the *Book Bloc* referred. From Rome to Madrid to London, the chosen "Books" were classics of literature, of philosophy, of sociology and political theory, ones well-known in every corner of the so-called Western world. *Book Blocs* are a *Manifesti* of protest but also shields to stave off the destruction of higher education and its pure reduction to a commodity; they are invitations to subversion and weapons of critique. Thus, the student movements in Europe

11 • Karl Marx and Friedrich Engels, "Revue. Mai bis October" (1850), MEW, vol. 7 (1960), 440.

show that education and knowledge are qualitative and collective resources which increase individual and collective consciousness, and that they are very effective fuel for igniting the fire of protest.

Against the commodification of higher education which promises to turn them into nothing but exploited workers and limited individuals, the young people who have been involved in the insurgent protests of the last few months have demonstrated that critical thought is still the motor of action. *Cogito, ergo insurgo!* •

Sara R Farris is a sociologist and Research Fellow at the Institute for Advanced Studies in Konstanz, Germany.

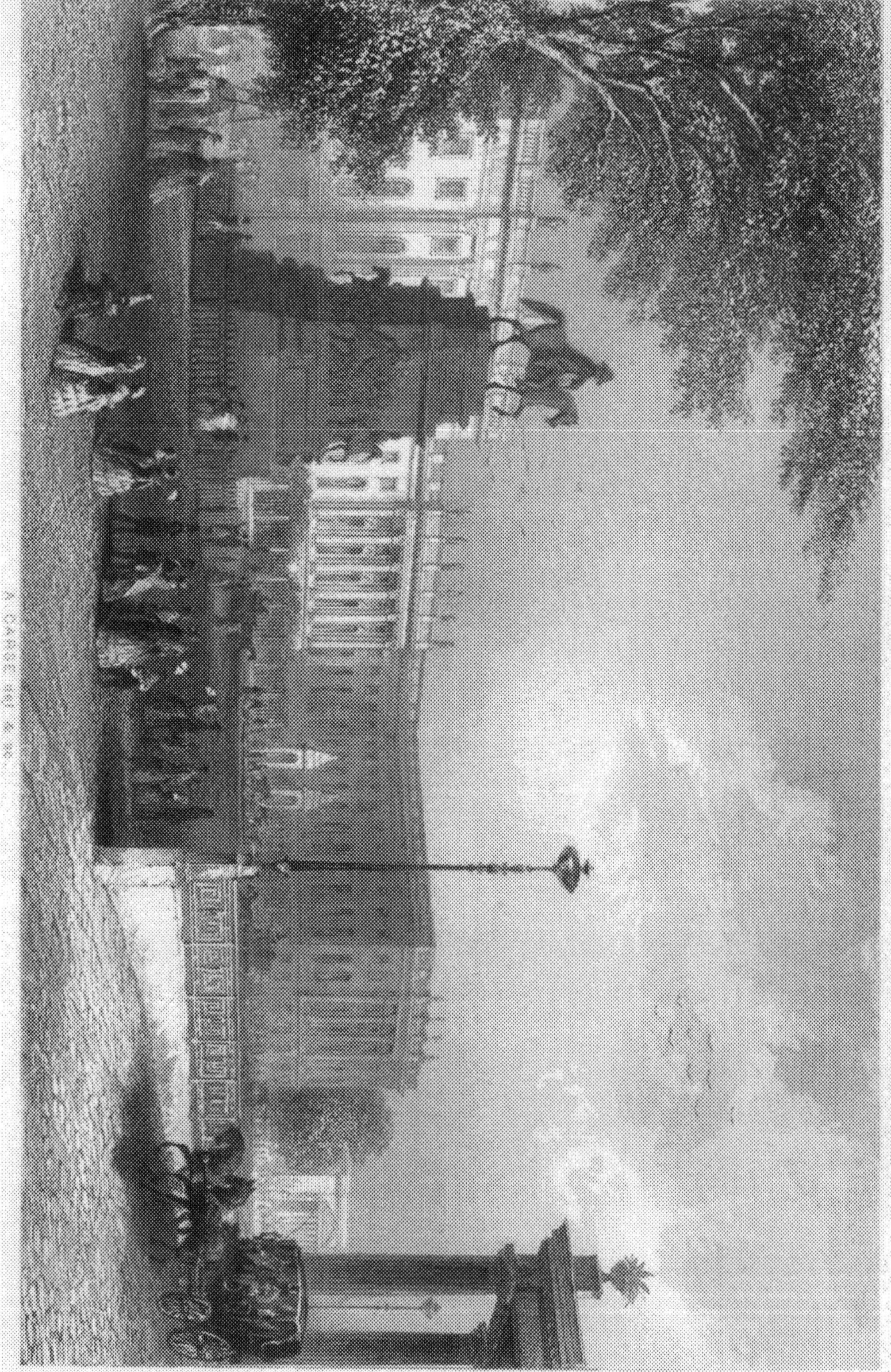

Quality Education

On the Role of the University in the Age of Management Politics

Hans Ruin

◂
Berlin University around 1850, in 1949 renamed Humboldt University.

A while ago I attended a seminar where the Swedish Minister of Education Jan Björklund gave a long policy speech to the members of all the boards of trustees of the universities and colleges in Sweden. He was thus speaking to the entire group of people responsible for running higher education in the country over the next couple of years, providing them with the basic outlook of the present government. The way in which he chose to frame his discourse reflects certain tendencies in European higher education policy that deserve to be carefully analyzed and critically discussed. In this speech he began by saying that in his youth (born 1963) he experienced how money was collected by the Swedish Lutheran organizations to alleviate the poverty and suffering in Asia. Nowadays, however, some of the same countries that we supported with our little donations show the highest economic growth rates on the planet. To this he added an anecdote from an international high school somewhere in Southeast Asia, where they had organized a meeting for the parents. The European parents were complaining that the children were getting too much homework. The Asian parents, however, were complaining that the children were not getting enough homework. In combination with a remark on the embarrassing fact that Ericsson had just lost a contract to a new Chinese competitor, the moral of this introduction was clear: that the Asian economies and educational facilities are working harder than we are, and that it is time to realize that we are competing on a global market.

In Björklund's conception, the multilayered phenomenon of "globalization" thus boiled down to the fact that there is a growing global market with intensified global competition. Against the background of this new reality the principal task of the Swedish university system was already implied, namely that we must become "best" through knowledge, research, science and innovation. This is today a general framework within which many senior European administrators think and conceptualize the present. What used to be the sibling rivalry with the United States, and the ideologically framed struggle against Communist Russia and its satellite states, has gradually developed after the fall of the Iron curtain into a competition between the West and the growing market economies of the East. The competition is no longer with military means and it no longer has an ideological content. Now it is fought with measures of economic performance, and thus with technical skills and knowledge. In the so called "knowledge economy", knowledge performance is both the means and the goal. And this knowledge is to an important extent generated — or is expected to be generated — within the academy.

The universities themselves are also understood and described as competing among themselves on a global education market, where their relative position on the ranking lists determines their success, a success which is at once a symbolic success — recognized for its merit — and an actual or potential economic success, since it can generate paying students. The latter situation has been the basic condition for a long time in countries that have a large private education sector, with universities competing on a national education market, but for the European university, this way of conceptualizing its role and function is something fairly recent. In short, we can see how the university today is increasingly being integrated in a discourse of power, influence, and economic success. This is also an explanation for why the European universities have been, and continue to be, exposed to an intensified organizational reform agenda.

There was a growing sense among many politicians and senior administrators that the universities had outdated organizational structures that needed to be reworked in order to make them perform better. Many of the reforms undertaken were also described as innovations that should enhance the performance of these institutions. From the perspective of many of the practitioners within the academy, this avalanche of politically orchestrated reforms over the last two decades has been experienced as a mostly destructive enterprise and one that has led to an increasing sense of disenchantment and alienation, and a general growing sense of discontent among many academics in Europe.

In a conference I took part in organizing two years ago at Södertörn University, on "The Future of the Humanities", Simon Critchley described this development as he experienced it from the British horizon, working at the University of Essex in the early nineties, when this really picked up momentum.[1] "What began under Thatcher as an ideological attack on the liberal intelligentsia in the universities, particularly those left-wing experimental universities like Essex, was perfected in a Blairilite bureaucratization of universities obsessed with three concepts: transparency, accountability, and quality." These concepts, in addition to that of "excellence", have then spread throughout Europe and become a guiding matrix for how bureaucratic reforms have been carried out. Instead of focusing on how best to train individuals for intellectual maturity and good judgment, the reforms have often led to a culture of excessive control and internal rivalry. In Critchley's somber conclusion this is not only an external event that has taken hold over the university. For, as he writes, the academics have mostly "conspired with this process and are completely culpable." It has led to a process of Foucauldian self-disciplining, where previously oppositional individuals in a common fight for their sphere of autonomy are now mostly cooperating with the managerial decisions handed down to them, while complaining in private, in what he even calls a contemporary "culture of depression" where people experience themselves losing influence and initiative.

Quality Education

For everyone working within the current academic system it is important to understand the inner logic of this development. From a philosophical viewpoint it is tempting to interpret it in the context of a larger narrative of a society of increasing control and self-control, from Heideggerian analyses of the *Ge-stell*, or the critical theorists' conception of increasingly coercive forms of rationality, to the power-analyses of Foucault. But in order to properly understand what is happening to the European university we also need to step down from this level of philosophical abstraction, and learn from the research that is being done concerning this transformation. It is important not least to really take in the ambiguity of the situation, in order to orient oneself more freely within a paradoxical ideological landscape. For whereas many practicing academics see the current development more and less as the gradual destruction

1 • Simon Critchley, "What is the future for the humanities?", in *En annan humaniora en annan tid / Another Humanities, Another Time*, eds. C. Cederberg & H. Ruin (Södertörn University: Stockholm, 2010).

of the European university, we are at the same time witnessing an increasing political emphasis on the role of the university, with politicians overbidding one another to increase budgets for research and development, within the overall paradigm of "knowledge economies".

The implementation of the new management structures is an interesting story in itself that is now being excavated by researchers into public administration.[2] The starting point of the present reorganization can be dated back to the mid-1980s, when the entrepreneurial model for public administration really took hold, eventually recognized as "New Public Management" (NPM). It grew out of economic models elaborated in the US and UK, and was depoliticized and adopted as the guiding doctrine of the increasingly influential Organization for Economic Co-operation and Development (OECD). The British example is especially important, since the English political elites were the originators of many of these reforms. As noted in the quotation from Critchley, the process of getting managerial control over the universities was partly colored by the political agenda of Thatcher, whose liberal market policies were combined with making the universities more into state run companies. Yet, the New Management Policies can not simply be reduced to a libertarian-conservative political agenda, since it was taken over and even extended by the Blair administration, and from there it also spread into European university policy at large. Its guiding concepts of transparency and accountability are not the concepts of a tyrannical impulse, as some of their critics would have it. They reflect a certain ideal of a liberal, democratic, well-managed, and well-performing society. In themselves the concepts originate from classical intellectual virtues, but when implemented in practical policies they often produce awkward procedures and disruptive practices, with bonuses and benefits that transform every academic into a competitor with every other on an artificially created internal marketplace.

For the universities this new form of management first meant that they were geared towards a market model for handling resources. Overall the idea was to create more business-like conditions and incentives for higher education, where resources were distributed on the basis of production results. Organization theories developed for business efficiency entered the domain of universities, including the creation of more hierarchical decision-making and the cultivation of a "leadership" culture.

This business paradigm stood against, on the one hand, an older culture

2 • A good recent summary of the situation is provided in an article by Kerstin Sahlin, professor in business economy and vice chancellor of Uppsala university, "Att leda universitet och högskolor – en balansakt I den högre skolan" In *Från högskolan i Borås till Humboldt* (Borås, 2010), 37–56.

of state management, but more importantly the ideal of "collegial" rule, associated in particular with universities. Collegiality was not only important within universities, it was also the traditional way of organizing, for example, health care, where the doctors would have a similar role in the hospitals as the professors in the older university system. With New Public Management this collegiality was challenged by a very different paradigm that made the senior professionals more into employees under a common business-like administration. One of the key issues to reflect on today is the future role of this "collegiality", and of collegial rule generally for the university. It is easy to find examples of inefficiency and petty rivalry within an academy run by collegial decision-making, which is one reason it was often also discredited. But collegiality has to do not only with administrational efficiency, but with legitimacy and ultimately with the ethos of the university as a unique type of public space.

A university is — ideally — a unique space within a society where people do not meet simply to compete for power and success, but where the center of activity is a common commitment to truth, not the one and only eternal truth, but an always preliminary truth that can only be reached through dialogue, discussion and mutual critique. To be exposed to such an environment is to train oneself in democratic virtues, such as tolerance and rationality. When collegial rule is today challenged by the New Management Culture, it is important to remember that its role can not be reduced to what is most efficient: it must also be placed in the context of what kind of public space the university is.

Collegial rule has always belonged to a culture where people within an institution function as each other's evaluators. In the academy, researchers are constantly engaged in assessing each other's work. It is a culture of both training and evaluating, first of students, but also of one's peers. The culture of peer-review, in this respect, is at the center of the academic ethos. However, in their search for clear standards of measurement, the administrators of the new management culture, with their stress on accountability and rational and transparent allocation of resources, have adopted standardized matrixes for the evaluation of research performance. This is the effect of what is nowadays also often referred to by social scientists as the new so-called "audit society". Since the quality of research cannot be evaluated outside the space of the qualified judgment of one's peers, the model of peer-reviewing and publication in peer-reviewed journals has now been adopted as a world standard for research performance.

In adopting this standard, the administrators of higher education have in a certain sense followed the ideal of collegial rule, yet at the same time they have also produced a grotesque perversion of this standard. Since resources have to be allocated according to some objective and transparent standard, one has adopted the only standard that the system can generate, namely peer-review. But precisely in picking up this standard, not ultimately with the purpose of securing quality and truth, but for resource allocation, one is also undermining the very ethos that lies at its heart. When researchers learn that their funding is dependent on peer recognition, they will behave rationally not in a long-term sense, but for short-term gains, which means that the system will also generate more of the same, like-mindedness, and cynical cartels of knowledge production, where researchers are quoting one another for short-term gains. This is a both sad and — depending on from what perspective one looks at it — ironic development.

In his commentary on the future of the humanities, Critchley is led to the conclusion that in the end the universities, and in particular the humanities, must reconsider their role in this new situation, and reflect again on their core purpose: namely to practice and develop good intellectual skills, which means teaching people how to think, how to search for the true, how to experience the joy of realizing how it is. In its obsessive desire to produce and deliver good management, the new management culture is currently risking the corruption of precisely that very public institution that it claims to foster.

In his speech to all the members of the boards of trustees in Sweden, the Minister of Education recalled the rising challenge of the Asian schools and universities. There is no doubt that the global competition to build and maintain high-ranking educational institutions will also generate an increased ambition among politicians to guide and control this process. Once the Chinese researchers start getting the Nobel prizes that they so fervently seek, we will hear more about the Asian way of doing business. But we must not forget that the first Chinese to get a Nobel Prize was the incarcerated literary scholar, Liu Xiaobo. It is also no coincidence that the universities were at the center of the events of the Arab Spring. The university, ideally, is a public space within the larger context of society that comes with certain abilities and responsibilities. What is troubling with the new managerial paradigm is that the increasingly business-like structure of these institutions will gradually undermine their ability precisely to serve as such a free, rational and dialogue-based public space that can also generate critical reflection of society within society.

If the students and researchers begin to identify with the idea that the overall purpose of the institution is to produce results, there is a risk that the very ethos of the academy is gradually dismantled. We should therefore be suspicious when the ambition is articulated that it is our primary task to compete on the global world market. This competition may well turn out to become an adaption to standards of human performance that the university, again ideally, should guard us against. Still, one should not give way to dystopic thinking, what in the end often comes down to a kind of passive nihilism. There are certainly also openings in the present situation, but they need to be cultivated carefully. To some extent, however, this will require a continued resistance from within against giving way to the business and market ethos that has guided public policy for the last decades. This is especially important in the face of an encouraged competition with the hierarchical and non-democratic Chinese state capitalism.

If the worn down and long misused concept of an "open society" should be given a new meaning, we should perhaps reconsider the importance of the university for this idea. With its collegially organized, common commitment to the search of the truth, in the spirit of an incalculable quest for a common good — not just the good of oneself or even the good of one's own community — it could still prove to contain a radical potential in the face of the current trends toward standardized models of performance and success. •

Hans Ruin is Professor of Philosophy at Södertörn University

Quality Education

The Multiple University and the Heroism of Forms: Variations on an Infinite Autonomy

Stéphane Douailler

In the context of a series of remarks published in a collective volume entitled *Démocratie, dans quel état?*,[1] and in his introduction to *Les scènes du peuple*,[2] Jacques Rancière points out that the reality of democracy is particularly tied to practices that subjects attach to certain words. Perhaps it is to these kinds of stakes that the word *autonomy* is attributed. Autonomy is in effect one of those terms that economic and political forces which have nothing to do with democracy and are exercised on the regional and global levels, have retained in order to mobilize it against the university's existence in various forms, in order to gain control over its development, and to realize a set of aims, both intended and otherwise.

This gesture no doubt surpasses the question of the university as such. Everything indicates that it, in various forms, also bears on the hospital, on justice, on culture, etc. For example, we can look back forty years at the dismantling of the Office de Radio Télévision Française (ORTF) and see many similarities with the current struggles around the university. In France, we have seen initiatives from within the universities, in a manner reminiscent to protests forty years ago at the ORTF complex, to organize human chains around particular buildings, like the one that

1 • Giorgio Agamben et al., *Démocratie, dans quel état?* (Paris: La Fabrique, 2009).

2 • Jacques Rancière, *Les scènes du* people (Bourg en Bresse: Horlieu, 2003).

in 2009 lasted for a thousand hours at the Place de l'Hôtel de Ville in Paris — and there are examples in other cities.[3] The point of application and of resistance has fundamentally remained the same: it concerns the word *autonomy*, when it serves to designate the seizing of power over an institution connected to the state in order to hand it over to forces closely aligned with the movement of capital, and to describe this institution as an immobile and costly body. And in this respect it is surely insufficient to respond to these politicians that the body in question is active and alive, and that it, in relation to what everyone who knows the university recognizes are in reality miserably low costs, is in fact extremely productive. What is important is to give these terms, and the term "autonomy" in particular, different meanings.

If one looks at the context of those proposals within which arguments are made to derail the word autonomy and engage the universities in a more than doubtful transformation, one finds in principle a double-faced discourse. In its first version, which gives rise to a kind of distinguished knowledge, this type of discourse always addresses the question from the same angle. The university would have become "democratized." It would have become a "mass university." And it would be on the basis of this event, occurring in recent history, that everything can be explained — no matter what has determined its history, which extends over centuries, or what complexities that characterize its past and present. This idea, which is terribly hackneyed, and aligned with the well-intentioned studies that at the same time are devoted to constantly rediscovering the social inequalities in higher education, serves as background for all kinds of denunciations of those real ways in which students and families appropriate the university.

In the second version, the youth and student population is accused of making the university institution into an object of irresponsible or blind consumption, by entering into universities in too large numbers, rather than opting for shorter programs and vocational training, and for being guided only by their own pleasure, which turns into pure whim when they privilege non-profitable programs. If we were to believe those who describe the university in this way, and who attempt to direct the consumption they have identified to a competitive field controlled by other forces, it would be in all respects insane to allow everyone to enter university programs, above all in the humanities and social sciences.[4] If we were to

3 • See rondeinfinie.canalblog.com

4 • In 2010, the French government, following what was one of the largest student protest movements that France has seen, had a strange dream: that young students would have abstained as much as possible from entering those universities that were most engaged in the struggles, in order to punish them. There was no reality corresponding to this dream, but it expressed precisely the degree of violence attained by government attitudes toward the universities at this moment.

borrow an image of knowledge suggested in the sixth century by the philosopher Boethius in his *Consolatio philosophiae*, we could say that for those who under the pretext of economic and administrative common sense express this desire to control entrance to the university, the universities have become like this "clothing ripped by brutal hands, and from which all would take the shreds that they could."[5]

The idea of an irresponsible and partly blind consumption of the university must be opposed by the real *autonomy* of the ways in which the students who go the university make use of it. These practices have nothing in common with the idea of a consumption guided by pleasure or of a sociological illusion other than their effective multiplicity. And one must just as quickly make distinctions inside this multiplicity. To understand the university as a mass university is to grasp it from the point of view of a general and vague idea, limited to the reactions of whoever has this idea. To understand that the university has become less a mass university than a multiple university, means to instead turn towards the ideas elaborated by the student population. They calculate with social, institutional, and subjective realities. They connect this to projects, strategies, and reflections that have a tenor emancipated from those immature pleasures that one ascribes to them. This could be called a real and not fantasmatic appropriation of the universities, the *uses* that are made of it, if we give to the word "use" the force to finally show the illusory character of the will to mastery, which, in taking part in the existence of something also strives to limit it. Use fundamentally breaks up autonomy. In those moments when Plato did not content himself with thinking the limitlessness of the many by recourse to the idea of a grand animal body subjected to blind and unbridled passions — for instance in the *Phaedrus*, when he came upon such limitlessness in the case of the literary body of thought — he made visible, while attempting to conjure it, that with the arrival of writing an emancipation of written things occurs that causes them to escape from what Plato calls their fathers, and who believed it possible to remain at the origin. These things would go off in any direction they wanted. Everyone could in the end bend them to his own wishes. Seen from the point of view of this multiplicity, and since it is in many respects constituted precisely by written things, the university presents us with continually reemerging *innumerable autonomies*.

This implies a second proposition: it is generally illusory, or futile, to oppose a form to its uses. There is no doubt a permanent tendency to do this. Like all forms, the university needs to distinguish the form that it recognizes to be its own

5 • Boethius, *Consolatio philosophiae*, I, 5.

from a set of other forms. It requires an auto-affirmation, for instance in the form of science, of a rationally and encyclopedically organized institution of all types of knowledge, of an industrially dynamic complex of types of knowledge, of a transcultural network of collective truths. The form of the university certainly does not exist outside of these or other forms, which it knows how to give itself. When it comes to exist without any support from such forms, it easily becomes moral rhetoric, dilettante talk, or empty technicality. But the forms of the university that can be called its erudite forms and that possess an irreducible history and tradition, are not the forms of its existence. The latter are the forms that it creates in relation to the uses that are made of its erudite forms, and if the university is to be thought in the integrality of its scope, they must be taken into account in their retroactive impact on the very meaning of the university. In this sense, the uses that are made of the erudite forms of the university create an innumerable multiplicity of university-forms. They define as university-form forms of existence that, for instance in Antiquity, did not limit it to Plato's Academy, Aristotle's School, or the Library in Alexandra, but, if seen on a Mediterranean scale, included various invented communities and the errant preaching of sects. It is these uses that over the centuries have integrated such proliferating forms as, for instance, the prison writings of Boethius, Thomas More or Toni Negri, Descartes' correspondence with Princess Elisabeth, the seminars at Tübingen and the Untimely Mediations of Nietzsche, the experimental university in Vincennes and Julian Coupat's lectures at Tarnac. It is this excessive proliferation that finally determines both the erudite form and the life-form of the university, and it is impossible to see these forms as simply competing with each other. They are rivals, competitors, fighting with each other with varying levels of ferocity. This struggle takes place on different political levels, and it also invents them. In other words, they mobilize other forms of social and collective existence. They support certain forms against others, produce impure configurations and obscure symbolisms.

In the encyclopedia of proliferating uses of written things, we might linger on Walter Benjamin. He is not only an example of the creator of erudite work with a long posterity in the university, which the university-form began by rejecting. But the conflicts that opposed him to Theodor Adorno and the Institut für Sozialforschung, where he was employed, also shed light on several of the issues introduced by the institution of a form and the question of its autonomy. One of the orientations defended by Institute, and particularly by Adorno, as we can see from the work done by Bruno Tackels on the successive versions of the essay on "The Work of Art in the Age of its Mechanical

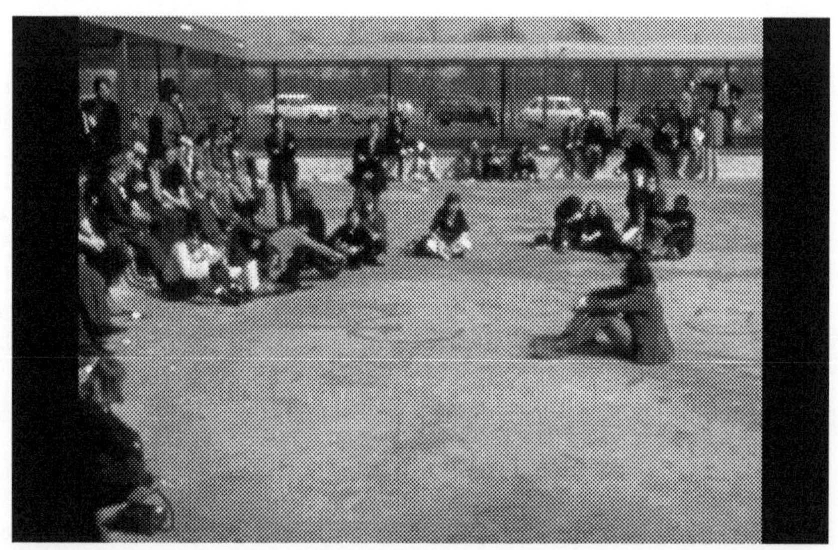

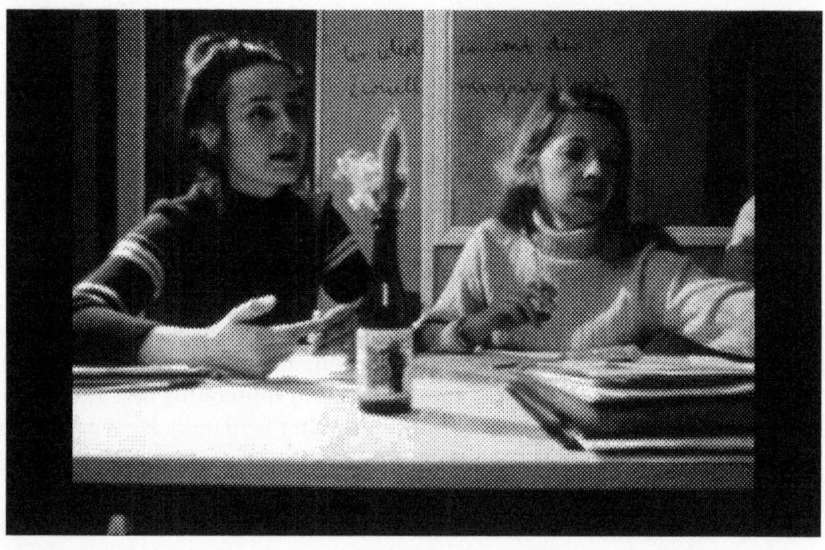

University of Paris VIII, Vincennes, early 1970s.

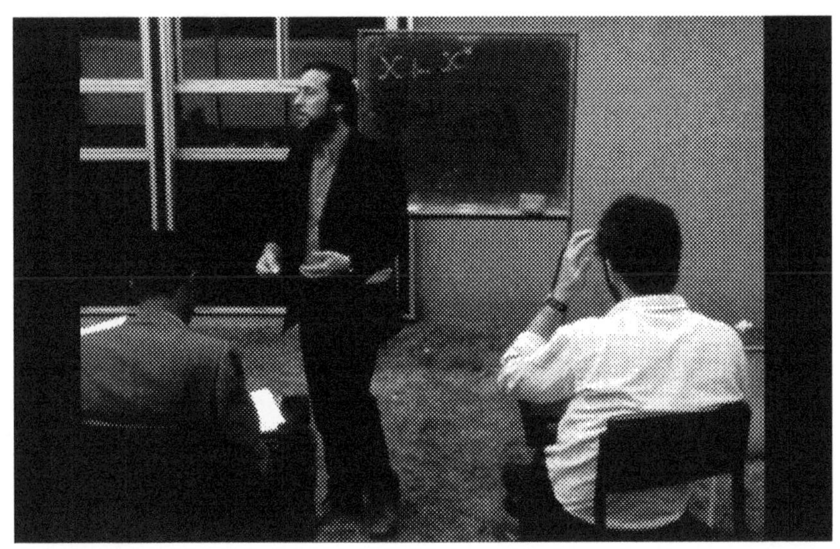

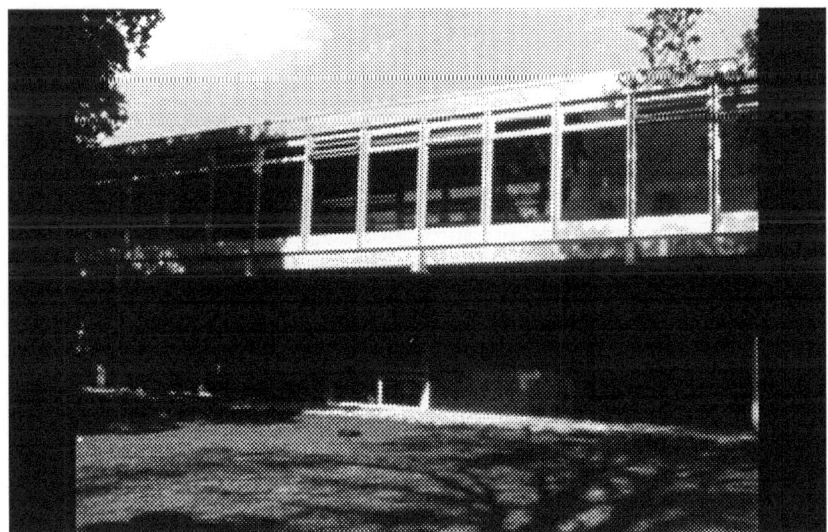

Quality Education

Reproduction,"[6] was surely to entrust a radical artistic autonomy with the task of preserving a higher culture and freer social relations. The power of this position was also that of its concomitant critical orientation. While formulating elevated expectations with respect to the works, it managed to stay away from a nostalgic discourse deploring the loss of the aura of the classical work. It took part in the revolt against appearance, whereby modernity attempted to denounce the false reconciliation with things of nature, and the true domination of men carried out in classic art. It made the diremption required for a liberated life its own, and in the autonomy of the work of art, it identified the promise of all those subtractions that must be made from those causal orders that are operative within the technologically and ideologically formed order of the world. In this task, the forms proper to autonomous art were attributed the double function of resisting mass consumption, whose alienating magic imprisoned the subjects in a reified and enchanted reality, and of showing the future revolutions the road toward emancipation.

This version of Adorno's aesthetic theory, to which its author arrived in 1936, at the moment when Benjamin was composing his essay, has as its visible limit the fact that it abstains from making distinctions inside the idea of the masses. On the contrary it draws on a uniform idea of a subjugated mass, alternately subjected to the energy of ideologies of fusion, and to the pleasures of private consumption. By way of contrast, the hypothesis of a subjugated mass confirms the claim to heroism of autonomous form. It makes legitimate the authority with which the latter is presented. It promises dialectically the most complete reversal of the state of things. By looking forward to this moment it makes it appear highly reasonable to save something of the separation that preserves the form and protects it from social pressures and determinations. But Walter Benjamin seems to have explored another path in his "The Work of Art in the Age of its Mechanical Reproduction," one of whose decisive traits is perhaps to show a possible displacement of the problem in relation to a paradigm modeled on the tensions presumed to exist between artworks and the masses, between the greatness of the works and the infinite banality of the masses. This displacement seems to allow for a different type of authority than the one that in autonomy identifies a resistance to the heteronomy of the masses by multiplying the formal features of separation.

Form makes visible both itself and its manners of forming, seeing, saying, and thinking. It exposes itself at the same time that it exposes the play that inhabits it. To understand this form is to understand the play at work within it, but also

6 • Bruno Tackels, *L'œuvre d'art à l'époque de W. Benjamin. Histoire d'aura* (Paris: L'Harmattan, 1999); see also Tackels, *Walter Benjamin. Une vie dans les textes* (Arles: Actes Sud, 2009), appendix 8.

all those rules already in play, or invisible rules, that it authorizes. To play, autonomously, the game of these forms — and this seems valid for all forms, also for those of the university — does not only mean to accept a demand for autonomy, such as can be realized in an exemplary fashion in the artwork or some other mode of separation, but also to create a diversity of connections prescribed by the form, according to the variable properties of all the possible subjects that puts the form to work. The properties of these subjects form a veritable cosmopolitan crowd. The adventures to which they subject the form are innumerable. They give rise to a multiplicity of games, uses, specific communities and associations. Finally, they imbue authority, in which the form sustains and keeps itself apart from inconsistent uses, with multiplicity. This form is no longer only distributed among the powers that attempt to constrain it and its intrinsic autonomy, but rather reveals itself to be the authority that any subject can give it while it is being used, in deciding to make it into a support for its own formation. In these games, the university is at once itself, in its form, and outside of itself, in a space of infinite autonomies. •

Translation: Jeff Kinkle and Sven-Olov Wallenstein.

Stéphane Douallier is Professor of Philosophy at University of Paris 8, Saint-Denis.

Quality Education

Adventures in the Sausage Factory: A Cursory Overview of UK University Struggles, November 2010–2011

Danny Hayward

Decomposing Higher Education: Stage One

During the 1990s, as the transition of the British economy to a giant services station continued apace, and as British manufacturing shrivelled into a kind of nostalgic mantelpiece ornament, British politicians and "independent observers" cast about in search of a new "driver" for long-term British economic growth.[1] In their quixotic quest for a saviour, or at least for a convenient footstool for the financial services sector, the politicians turned to the universities. And the British universities seemed the perfect solution to Britain's long-term macro-economic discontents. Their mix of dreamy spires and robust benchmarking in international league tables offered the kind of synergy that management consultants are willing to die for. On the one hand, cutting-edge global competitiveness; on the other, feudal nostalgia. The state had found what it needed. Quicker than an unforeseen stock-market crash, a thousand thousand-page reports were commissioned on how best to exploit this invaluable national resource. The future seemed golden. A "high-skill economy" would revolutionise domestic production. In the tiny but overheated imaginations of public policy planners, it seemed inevitable that the "stream" of British university graduates would meet a stream of capital credit from the booming financial services industry,

1 • Thanks are owed to JBR for György Kurtág and other critical inputs.

and that these together would make up a river which would fertilise the fields of national capital accumulation. Dynamic entrepreneurs would live in harmony in this bucolic post-industrial paradise. And then the dotcom bubble burst. And then growth failed to accelerate during the upturn in the business cycle. And then the credit crisis happened.

The slow death of this particular accumulation fantasy concluded on 12 October 2010 with the publication of a report on university "sustainability". The Browne Report — named after the ex- BP Chief Executive who chaired the review leading to its publication — advised that the state withdraw almost all of its financial subsidy to university teaching. The report advocated a new system of financing in which the degree-holder rather than the state would be liable for the costs of his or her education. English students, who since 1998 had been required to pay a "top-up" fee to complement the state's inadequate student subsidy per capita, were now to acknowledge that, as the "primary beneficiaries" of their degree in view of projected future earnings, it was their responsibility to bear the majority of the costs.[2] Exploiting the crisis rhetoric which had echoed and re-echoed in the bourgeois media since 2007, this moral argument was immediately de-sublimated into an argument about economic necessity. As Browne wrote in his Executive Summary,

> a degree is of benefit both to the holder, through higher levels of social contribution and higher lifetime earnings, and to the nation, through higher economic growth rates and the improved health of society. Getting the balance of funding appropriate to reflect these benefits is essential if funding is to be sustainable.[3]

The new "balance" which Browne proposed would involve the removal of the cap on university fees, set in 2010 at £3,290 per annum. The cap would be raised to £9,000 p/a on the understanding that state subsidies for teaching in English universities — still £4.4 billion in 2011–2012 — would be scaled down to near zero, with a continuing (though in absolute terms equally reduced) subsidy only for those students in disciplines where education is more capital intensive. These were the so-called "STEM" subjects: Sciences, Technology, Engineering and Mathematics. Because even the one time Chief Executive of BP is aware that most students cannot afford to pay £9,000 p/a plus monies for

2 • It's important to note that the reforms did *not* apply to Scottish students, where Higher Education continues to be 'free' in the limited sense that the State covers student fees.
3 • www.bis.gov.uk/assets/biscore/corporate/docs/s/10-1208-securing-sustainable-higher-education-browne-report.pdf, 2.

accommodation and maintenance, Browne's proposal was that the new fees would be financed in the first instance by an expanded system of state loan provision. Education would be "free at point of access" in the sense that students would be guaranteed access to credit both for their fees and for their living costs. These students once graduated and earning more than £21,000 per annum would repay their loans at either rates of interest fixed to inflation or at the rate of inflation plus 2.2%, depending on how far above the repayment threshold their wages fell. On the specifics, Browne's report adopted a kind of studious evasiveness: it was not clear (nor is it now) what level of earnings would constitute a high earner, and readers of the report were expected to accept its myriad bullet-points and graphs as a comforting proxy for detail as yet plainly undecided.

One month later, after a march organised by the National Union of Students (NUS), and while several thousand students celebrated in the courtyard, the windows of the Tory HQ— now referred to, after the area in Westminster in which it was situated, as "Millbank" — were kicked in. While police looked more or less helplessly on, the building was trashed. It was the riotous opening ceremony for several months of unusually intense domestic education struggle. The following account and analysis, focusing on the period from late-2010 to mid-2011, will dwell at length on what one gentleman correspondent in the London Review of Books called, in reference to the Browne Review and the state policy which it partially inspired, "the tired debate on class". It will do so because

1. the possibility for effective linkage between a narrowly "education-based" and a broader class struggle seems to me to derive from the failure of the process of domestic capital re-composition which growth in the university sector was intended to "drive". This includes the signal failure of university expansion to produce an *extensive* "high-skill" service sector, or, in other words, its failure to assure anything other than highly-policed jobless or at best "casualised" misery for most of its graduates; and
2. because I'm unconvinced that there is much of interest to be said about the function or structure of British Higher Education *or about the Humanities* without reference to class-organisation and class values; and
3. because with the benefit of a half-inch of hindsight it is easier to itemise the class-foundations of many of the most widely canvassed arguments *against* increased fees and university "marketisation".

And so the following will attempt an anatomy. Since I assume that the majority of its readers will not be working class teenagers but will instead be the "kind" (the class) of person who might be apt to make a case for Higher Education as a "social good" or for the value of academic "autonomy", its objective (insofar as it has one) is to call for a materialist re-evaluation of those categories.

The Timid ("Anti-Market") Battle Cry of the Professoriat
Much indecorous intellectual mud-wrestling followed the publication of Browne's Report. Disgruntled academics jostled in their in-house organs (the Times Higher Education, the London Review of Books) to complain about the declension from social democratic principle. The official complaints of the liberal academics were several. Their arguments were initially provided with a great deal of airtime. For that reason they might be worth summarising right away. Firstly, Higher Education is a "social" and not as Lord Browne's report implies a "private" good. Secondly, higher education is a noble practice, requiring time for reflection and contemplation and unable to thrive where academics are required frenziedly to assess their own benchmarking against ever proliferating new standards of measure, devised by dubiously "independent" monitoring agencies. Thirdly, students and lecturers ought to possess a collaborative relationship in which each party is entitled to challenge the other, and this relationship cannot survive after student-consumers have been raised onto a throne made of cheap beer and unfinished essays and declared sovereign. Fourthly, the state's genuflexion before the God of "market-discipline" is asinine, because closer inspection reveals that it is forced to build into its new funding system checks and safeguards to prevent student choice from perverting the supply of labour-commodities to employers. In short, quoth the professors, human calculators like Lord Browne were welcome to perform their tricks in the private sector kennel assigned to them — and the Orphic journalists of the Financial Times were welcome to sing their praiseful rhapsodies — but the wholesale supervention of market logic on the sweet cloisters of English Higher Education was a gross imposition not to be tolerated. There are, the professors argued, values which cannot survive in the spirit-vacuum of a market, and whether those markets are "natural" or "artificial", these high values must be preserved against the "consumer relativism" to which state politicians like David "two brains" Willetts, Minister for Universities and Science, are likely to defer.

Some of these complaints were borne out by later developments (to be dicussed below); but in any case these were popular arguments, aired in well-circulated journals and often dressed up with close textual reference to the relevant state policy documents. The documents were routinely sneered at for their febrile adherence to basic standards in business speak, ripped off from superannuated management textbooks now patiently gathering dust in the Sale sections of university bookshops. The cool and careful periods of state paternalists of the distant past — i.e., of the mid-nineteen sixties, from an era before Thatcherism, the destruction of the coal mining industry and the wholesale degeneration of the educated English of the enlightened bourgeoisie — were reconstructed and elegised.

Nevertheless the arguments suffer from an obvious explanatory deficit. Accounting for the changes in Higher Education, Stefan Collini writes that

> British society has been subject to a deliberate campaign, initiated in free-market think tanks in the 1960s and 1970s and pushed strongly by business leaders and right-wing commentators ever since, to elevate the status of business and commerce and to make "contributing to economic growth" the overriding goal of a whole swathe of social, cultural and intellectual activities which had previously been understood and valued in other terms. Such a campaign would not have been successful, of course, had it not been working with the grain of other changes in British society and the wider world. Very broadly speaking, the extension of democratic and egalitarian social attitudes has been accompanied by the growth of a kind of consumerist relativism.[4]

It is surely necessary to resist this account. On its terms, a business ideology, supported by a heterodox or confused alliance of free-market think tanks and "democratic and egalitarian social attitudes", has marched its rag-tag banner into the heart of the British state. The enemy and victim of this alliance is the University, which relies on a strict hierarchy of values and on the "educational judgment" which (it is implied) is exclusively competent to arbitrate between them. It is the characteristic feature of this kind of argument that it demands the restitution of a paternalist social democratic system whose internal decline was what accelerated the "privatisation" of formerly public institutions in the first place: the argument takes a prurient interest in the inability of markets to assure their own self-reproduction not, as it might at first appear, in order to demonstrate the deep relationship between UK Higher Education and the full market system in its crisis, but in order to

4 • www.lrb.co.uk/v33/n16/stefan-collini/from-robbins-to-mckinsey

convince markets that its contradictions are amenable to resolution *if only academic counsel is heeded*. The real relationship of English Higher Education to the wider British "business climate" — in whose toxic environs new graduates are currently expected to suffocate — and the relationship of the wider British business climate to the global economy as a whole — is therefore perfectly obfuscated. This is not surprising, since academics have not until now been the principal victims of large-scale economic crisis.

Student Struggle: November 2010 — March 2011

The 2010–2011 cycle of UK student protest began with the smashed windows of the Conservative Party HQ in Millbank; accelerated into a long sequence of occupations alternately (and often simultaneously) serious and farcical; dwindled into the introspective political manoeuvrings of an activist core during the long sequence of marches and demonstrations which culminated in late February; and, at last, sublated itself in the black bloc which formed at the Trades Union Congress demonstration on 26 March.[5] During that time its composition underwent a sharp expansion and contraction, as its initial — pre-eminently white and middle class — formation expanded to incorporate black and Asian inner-city youths, only then to contract again.

For those whose last recollection of a domestic popular protest was the anti-war march in 2003, the spontaneous re-design of conservative party HQ was, if nothing else, refreshing. All those chairs forever doomed to be used as *seating*, how tedious — why not hurl them through this window. The riot also put a swift end to the ideological hegemony of the National Union of Students (NUS) — which, stocked as it was (and is and will forever be) with vapid centre left aspirants with hopes for a parliamentary career — proved unwilling to endorse any campaign demand that might get up the noses of the politicians whose endorsement could enhance the aspirants' prospects at future party political meet and greets. At the beginning of the academic year in October 2010 the NUS was conducting a gloriously lacklustre campaign to "freeze" the fees, i.e., to maintain 2010 fee levels for all future students, beating its chest and demanding a reversion to Labour Party endorsed social misery. This was a compromise oddly inconsonant with the destruction of the Tory Party headquarters. The NUS's (then) president Aaron Porter, who, whatever his failings, was just about cunning enough to know when he might be stepping on the toes of his future benefactors, instantly squirmed into the arms of the national media to denounce the actions of the 2000–4000 participants in the "splinter demo" at Millbank. The

5 • For an account of the 26 March demonstration see "Marching for Whose Alternative?" at escalatecollective.net

splinter demo, Porter declared, was "despicable". The NUS was committed to peaceful protest and orderliness and the rapid introduction into students of diversified repertoires of soft skills; interested viewers could read its policy documents online.

All this had occurred by 12 or 13 November. The ideology of what might distastefully be called the *organising core* of the student movement was not as visibly reactionary as the NUS's, though, as the above ought to suggest, it would be hard to be more prodigiously reactionary than Aaron Porter. The germane features of that ideology (and allowing of course for significant individual departures from it) can be worked out of a narrative of events running from aftermath of the Millbank demonstration until the protest planned for the day of the Commons vote on 9 December.

The standard metaphorical vocabulary for the emerging student movement is now as fixed as the new fee regime: during the weeks of November, a "wave" of university occupations "spread" or "swept" across the country. Already this phraseology is very boring. The occupations were of course in fact *waves*, big and small, long and short, depending to a large extent on the class profile and region of the institution in which an occupation took place; its physical infrastructure; and the quasi-autonomous ideological commitments of the most active participants. There were long occupations at UCL, Cambridge, SOAS, Bradford and the Slade, a short, strategic occupation at London Met, abortive occupations in Camberwell and Birmingham, a Deleuzian occupation at Edinburgh.[6] The list could continue. There were, nonetheless, enough marked continuities in the statements issued by occupying students to attempt a brief sketch.

First, University occupations tended to demand that their managements resist cuts to state provision for British Higher Education.[7] The argument was often framed in terms of imprescriptable rights, in this respect — *pace* the endless avowals to the contrary in the commemorative headstones quickly erected by radical publishers — less 1968 than 1789.[8] As one of the more imperiously insipid student slogans ran, *Education is a right, is a right, is a right, education is a right, not a privilege*. Most students in the English university system have of

6 • occupations.org.uk lists the first occupations: a rough count gives eight ex-polytechnics to fourteen "post-1992" universities, which provides in turn some (extremely rough) suggestion of the class bias within the student movement in its first pulse of activity. Edinburgh's occupation was the most energetic in disseminating propaganda about the "swarm" quality of the student movement.

7 • Therefore the first demand of most student occupiers was that senior management issue on behalf of the institution "a statement condemning all cuts to higher education and the rise in tuition fees." blog.ucloccupation.com/demands The second demand — more general — demand was often that "[t]hat the University use its influence to fight for free education for all." www.defendeducation.co.uk/old-schools-occupation/our-demands

8 • cf. the already very dusty looking Verso anthology *Springtime*, which in accordance with party political principles selected as its textual "flashbacks" to '68 texts by Eric Hobsbawm and Ernest Mandel, doyens of the CPGB and the Fourth International respectively (Mandel, the younger of the two, was forty-five at the time, but as a social critic he was thoroughly superannuated).

course always *had* most of the things which they have a right to (which isn't to say that life is sweet) — but it is this which above all and unstoppably invests the word "rights" with its magic aura. In their "Education is a Duty" — which includes in its footnotes its own representative smattering of quotation from student occupation communiqués — The Wine and Cheese Society of Greater London suggested that the *materialism* of the student movement was "a strangely mediated and submissive materialism", which is to say that it tended to accept that the principal function of "UK HE" was and is to generate economic growth; and also to agree that finding yourself stuck between the contracting mandibles of the "labour market" after the "free" champagne at the graduation party has run dry was not, after all, so bad.

In the months following the occupations, large numbers of student "activists" generated whole data nests of thrilling online gossip about the availability of new "horizontal" organisational media, at last superseding such inherently totalitarian technologies as the telephone and the human mouth. This particular circle of indulgent introspection was squared by enthusiastic nothings about "generational" divides, including especially polemics against the elder "generations", living it up with their totalitarian landlines and cars and their plunging private sector pensions, in a position invidiously contrasted to the impecunious underfunded British student of 2011, whose part-time call centre job and 1/267 prospects of graduate employment were the result of insufficient abstemiousness by "babyboomers" in — one assumes; the argument was always vague — the 1980s. Like most transiently appealing forms of social analysis, this one was obviously generalised from the social circumstances of whichever student chose to voice it. Few students with access to column inches — and this itself is often if not always a function of social privilege — said much about the closure of elderly people's day centres and other state-resourced institutions then being retrenched from under the feet of the *proleterian* retiree, but then the users of elderly people's days centres cannot often be fruitfully accused of implicit totalitarianism (nor, for that matter, do they often appear to *boom*).[9]

All this first person plural posturing about "networked resistance" would have been more laughable had it not had a social guarantor. This is to say that, unlike the liberal "anti-market"

9 • For a rich mine of student activist consciousness, see *Fightback!: A Reader on the Winter of Protest*, ed. Dan Hancox et al., (London: OpenDemocracy, 2011). Other favourite themes included "information", unions, policing, and kettles. "Kettling" — the tactic of containment used so regularly (and so effectively) by the Metropolitan police during the student demonstrations — was a particular favourite: the Fightback! reader asserts pointedly that all eight of its editors had been 'kettled' in the course of the student protests. These themes describe social objects which middle class protestors had had occasion to experience at first hand. The class basis of the topics of preference was not generally acknowledged.

professors, the students did pay attention to some basic facts of social exclusion. At about the same time as the Browne Report was thumping onto the desk of every education journalist in the country, the Schools Minister Michael Gove announced that the state would be cutting the so-called "Education Maintenance Allowance" (EMA). This was a derisory grant paid out to students over the age of sixteen conditional on attendance. The grant was means tested and set to between £10 — 30 per week. (A note: since the maximum pay out was set around £20 per week *below* the monies paid out to British unemployed benefits claimants of comparable age, EMA would be better known as Education Below Subsistence Allowance, but we'll stick with the recognised designation in what follows.) Student activists regarded the cuts to EMA as a means of forging cross-class solidarity with expropriated college students. In this respect they were not *exactly* incorrect.

If you type "We're From The Slums Of London" into the search bar on YouTube you can watch a video from 9 December. It's very short. In it an Asian teenager, hat on and masked up, makes his case: "We're from the slums of London, yeah? How do they expect us to pay £9,000 for uni fees? And EMA, the only thing that's keeping us in college — what's stopping us from doing drug deals on the street anymore? *Nothing.*" He doesn't look like one of the "youths" that left parties like to use as props to invest their campaigns with some local colour. Nor does the transcription do justice to the statement, which is not muttered from a crib sheet but spat out in hot disgust. This might in part be because the speaker is addressing a camera held by a white bourgeois journalist. The footage is not untypical. When I arrived late for a demonstration at Westminster Bridge at the end of November, a kettle had been put in place. Those who had travelled south from the University of London Union building in Bloomsbury were safely "contained". The first group of people I noticed on my side of the police lines were about a dozen black and Asian teenagers, male and female, and all in school uniform. One of the kids, standing about five yards from the police line, leaned down to pick up a discarded Socialist Workers Party placard. The police watched him as he placed the sign under his foot and, nonchalantly enough, snapped off the stick. This was not the way that most students used placards.

At the demonstration on 9 December this kind of low-level readiness for confrontation was put to work. Fighting between "protestors" and police was ferocious: temporary fencing was ripped up and used as barricades or as shields as appropriate; groups of teenagers masked and hooded then used the bent and torn remnants of this fencing to smash out the windows of the Treasury; and in the square where the main kettle had been fixed in place, police lines were broken repeatedly. A friend providing legal observer functions in the kettle in Parliament Square spoke to a kid who had somehow acquired one of the larger police-issue riot shields. He advised the kid that if he was going to carry the shield then he should *for fuck's sake cover his face*. The kid replied that he'd rather go to prison than spend £9,000 a year going to uni.

This sort of anecdotalism is obviously pressingly limited as social analysis, but without the self-willed and emphatic arrival of working class teenagers in "the movement", the student discourse would have degenerated into polite badinage about the emancipatory potential of open-sourcing and web 2.0. Explaining the relative quiescence of the majority of the students who subscribed to this discourse is not difficult. They were the new fee regime's *beneficiaries*, since one of that regime's effects would likely be a long-term reduction in the uptake of Higher Education degree-commodities, and therefore a (statistical if not perceptible) easing of competitive pressures in the graduate labour market. Because working class teenagers *did*, fleetingly, "enter the movement", i.e., burst out into the streets, the demonstrations from late November onwards were more defiantly and generally disruptive than the demonstration in early November, despite Millbank and despite much more enthusiastic brutality on the part of the Metropolitan police and its specialist public order units.[10] Wanton press releases from the Met confirmed this fact, as the authoritarian PR service pumped out anxious declarations about how "extremely disappointed" the service was "with the actions of many protestors", who were evidently becoming more confrontational, quicker and more spirited, more prepared to abandon routes and disregard "advice" issued by frantic "organisers" wherever the balance of forces on the ground demanded it.

Rapid diversification in class composition also meant (for a moment at least) an expansion in the geography of confrontation. Out in the provinces, college students began to mobilise, and their actions were often taut with energy, in some respects more akin to the Bristol riots which flared up in April than the banner-waving exercises which comprise the most wildly transgressive fantasies that fill the minds of NUS Executive officers as they vegetate at their desks. A report from the Brighton demonstration gives a good feel for the pulse of a mob intelligence acting without any prompt from a student vanguard:

10 • None of this should be taken to imply that there were no working class students in the student movement. The point is only that the ideological production of the "student movement" was overwhelmingly "middle-class" in its structure of interests. A large student campaign did take place at London Metropolitan, which has a large working class intake, but not until after their senior managements began to announce heavy cuts in late June 2011. In consequence London Met was not a focus of the earliest upsurge of contestation.

> 2000 people, 90% school- and college-students, marched: they ignored the designated end-point for the demo and set off on a volatile and cheerful meander, with periodical attempts to block roads. When the police attempted a kettle it was broken: of those who broke the kettle and didn't disperse, 200 went to take refuge in the new occupation at the other, less "political" university [Brighton], where they were refused entry — then went into the bobo shopping streets and got kettled. 400 (school and college kids mainly, with a few, cheerful homeless guys) went off mob-form to attack Vodafone, then looted Poundland ("I got three Toblerone"), before arriving cheerfully at the other, kettled group. The police crumpled under the *strategic* pressure — they were outnumbered and uncertain — and released the group they were holding. The 400 then set off *expressly to block roads and cause maximum disruption*, launching an attempted attack on the police station before heading to the roundabout at the pier to block it. There, the momentum failed and the police successfully kettled 100 of the slowest.[11]

Students who urged "EMA kids" to join their demonstrations and whose political organisations printed placards that said "defend EMA" did understand that it was working class teenagers who would suffer in *truth* from the imposition of fees, much like the youngest of them would suffer in truth from the retraction of exiguous below subsistence bursaries for impoverished college students. But what the students in their descants on cross-class solidarity didn't much mention was that it was working class kids who were likely to suffer in truth from the whole exercise in the conversion of "stagnant" state welfare into "dynamic" private sector policing; and from the imperious drudgery of wage labour which it is no longer accurate to say is "on offer", when increasingly it is compelled on threat of starvation; and from the long convulsive contraction of British capitalism in general. Drifting right through the discourse on "building the movement" was the odour of class contempt. Its principal form was the assumption that "deprived" working-class college students wanted nothing more than to be like "us". It assumed that they wanted to be like us in a particular sense. Working class students might be strung up on a different (lower) rung of the labour market, but we would delegate to them our own snuff of social aspiration. Did we not have a universal right to it?

11 • Report taken from "10 Days in a Satellite Town" in Sous Les Pavés III, available at souslespavesonline.wordpress.com. The magazine contains a heterogeneous and useful selection of essays and poems written in response to the early stages of the student protests.

Such a view of social aspiration is inherently appealing to bourgeois students, because the contradiction in its ideal of universal bourgeoisification is always resolved in their favour. The formal right of access to degrees — in this respect like the formal right of access to citizenship or to legal representation — makes no specification of what the content of a degree is or ought to be: but training can be dire and suffocating whether it goes on in a call centre or the University of Sussex or an asylum.[12] But the bourgeois conception of educational justice is not only ineffectual in resolving the contradictions of class, soothingly renamed "relations of exclusion" as per the official lexicon of top-down social management. The conception generates another limitation. By imputing to working class teenagers the desire to "protest" *up to the point where they resemble us* in the cracked mirror of our own (bourgeois) sociological concepts (i.e., up to the point when they possess the minimal resources required to compete with us — at a safe disadvantage — in education and labour markets), the conception tells us nothing about the real complexity of class-based impulses or aversions or about how they might be put to work "on the ground" in the production of a real movement against capital and its servant-institutions. I'll come back to this point in conclusion.

Decomposing Higher Education: Stage Two

While the student movement stumbled into exam season and expired, the state attempted to problem-shoot its malfunctioning reforms. Its first error was almost amusing. The Browne report had assumed that, once "freed" to set their own fee level, smaller and less prestigious institutions would scale down their prices in order to remain competitive. Instead, desperate not to smudge or tar their pristine brand equity, almost all of the universities set their fees at the £9,000 p/a maximum. This act of herd insubordination compelled the state to revise its forecasts for the cost of loan provision, with the result that it could no longer afford to remove the "supply side" recruitment caps whose removal had been one of the principal justifications for fee "flexibility" in the first place.

As the academic year drew to a close, the government published its White Paper on Higher Education, which, among other exercises in side-tracking and obfuscation, proposed a convoluted quick fix to the above "supply side" problem. The quick fix operates a "core/margin" model which "allows" (i.e., forces) universities to compete for students above the state imposed quota. These are drawn from "pools" of students of a certain type

12 • Despite their passion for "networking" their resistance, no students included in their occupation statements a demand for the equalisation of conditions across institutions within the Higher Education system. But then this might have seemed like incipient authoritarianism.

—for example, high ranking school-leavers. Evidently this model has little to do with the creation of a free market without supply side restrictions and much to do with stuffing yet more competitive pressure into the Higher Education turkey.

Quality Education

But the most important role of the White Paper was to open the UK HE field to "new providers". Describing this process in detail would be exhausting, so the following will offer a stylised sketch.[13] The state proposes to withdraw from the sullen and corporate universities their monopoly on degree issuing powers, distributing this faculty to dynamic, thrusting "independent" institutions promising step-changes in efficiency on the intensification/pile-em-high model. These changes in tandem with a steady decline in the resourcing of now existing institutitions are likely to lead to the collapse of at least some traditional universities, who, once stranded in administration, can be swept up into the steroidal bosom of private-providers like the US Apollo Group, whose market leadership in IT solutions allows them to drive down costs by dispensing with previously "sticky" overheads like (e.g.) wages for lecturers. As the CEOs mount their white horses and descend from the sky to bestow the blessings of market efficiency on "underperforming" working class institutions like London Metropolitan and Liverpool John Moores, research in the humanities will be increasingly concentrated in a handful of elite institutions, each with a handful of "elite" (i.e., bourgeois) students.[14] The "practical" vocationalisation of all other institutions will work itself out on a model similar to the one currently "operating" (i.e., churning profit) in the US, where capital-intensive advertising campaigns lure working class students into programmes of study which issue in devalued degrees, sub-zero job prospects and an insupportable debt burden which bulges further with each passing year until like a monstrous paunch it fills the whole horizon. It is a fact well enough known that almost half of "propriety" students at Apollo Group institutions ultimately default.[15]

But these are not new processes. What Andrew McGettigan calls the "deliberate underresourcing" of UK Universities began perhaps as early as the late 1970s and has accelerated up until now. By a war of attrition, the senior managers of English

13 • This section is indebted to Andrew McGettigan's work on Higher Education reform. For a more detailed account of the levelling of the HE "playing field" in the interests of for-profit enterprises, see his "New Providers". The Creation of a Market in Higher Education. RP 167 (May/Jun 2011), and also the work made available on his blog, andrewmcgettigan.org.

14 • No one ever speaks about "underperforming" private education providers: the moralistic tongue-clucking is reserved for working class educations institutions which benchmark poorly against those bourgeois institutions which exist for no other reason than to reproduce a class hierarchy (i.e., to reproduce exactly the disparity that the benchmark indicates). It would of course be inane to say that the class system is "underperforming".

15 • www.time.com/time/business/article/0,8599,2000160,00.html

Higher Education institutions have been reduced to pathological (if fabulously well remunerated) brand custodians, dreaming of founding new campuses in the growth-sectors of the Middle East which until now have provided Britain with oil commodities and which today in consequence of that export industry offer up a new resource, i.e., untapped fields of undereducated bourgeois teenagers, ripe for harvesting. This global context is significant. The decline in per capita funding for English university students might be lamentable, and it might even be *ideological* in the contemporary sense of that word, i.e., voluntary and not fiscally exigent; but it isn't clear that maintaining levels of student funding would mean better lives for students. As British capital has ferociously restructured itself there has been a precipitous decline in the number of "good" jobs for which qualified students might apply. This may in part be due to "the destruction of manufacturing" (and most readers will know intimately this caricature of the rise of "neoliberalism") but it is also attributable to the increase in global competition in the upper-echelons of the value chain, in the misty realms where university graduates with bulky flexible skill sets are expected to thrive most emphatically. This is to say that it isn't clear that the production of "more skills" by the maintenance of high levels of university resourcing are at all likely to lead to more or better jobs. Between 1995 and 2003 the global supply of university enrolments doubled to 63 million. As a report by the state-financed Economic and Social Research Council put it in 2007 — note: in 2007, i.e., before the crisis had caused investors to become doubtful of their own omnipotence– "Many... companies were increasing the proportion of university graduates within the workforce. But it was difficult to assess whether this reflected an increase in the proportion of jobs involving technically difficult roles or 'over-qualification'... because 'anyone half decent has now got a degree.'"[16] Though employers continue to yammer about a "skills gap", the skills which are referred to are not "hard" (i.e., technical) skills but "soft" skills, which include competencies which could well be programmed into students at secondary school level — IT skills is the primary example — but which are defined above all by repressive pseudo-categories like "self-management", "customer-facing skills" and (best of all) "high-end empathy". In other words, *what British capitalism lacks is not educated students but obeisant employees*. The employer's tribal dance to the gods of skill acquisition are nothing more than a prayer that their human resources will acquiesce voluntarily to intensified degradation, and, what is more offensive, recognise in that degradation the

16 • The quote comes from a Human Resources automaton and is cited in the Economic & Social Research Council report "Education, Globalisation and the Knowledge Economy" (2007), 16, available at www.tlrp.org/pub/documents/globalisationcomm.pdf

continued acquisition of "skills". Skill acquisition along these lines is just virtualised accumulation for the exploited.[17]

In 2008, the then Prime Minister Gordon Brown gave a speech on the skills race. Jetting as he then was around the globe to "co-ordinate" and "problem solve" the global credit crisis, it is perhaps unsurprising that Brown was nurturing some high fantasies. "A generation ago," Brown said, "a British prime minister had to worry about the global arms race." But no longer. "Today", he continued "a British prime minister has to worry about *the global skills race*".[18] Brown's comparison was both accurate and inaccurate. It was accurate because like commodities produced during the arms race, the commodities which a British skills race is fated to produce are *non-productive*, by which I mean in economic terms a waste; but the comparison was inaccurate also, because unlike (say) the commodity called a Thales lightweight multirole missile, a highly skilled student is likely to become infuriated if he or she isn't "used". "Used" in this instance of course means "paid".[19] This was not, perhaps, the point that Gordon Brown believed himself to be making, which is only all the more telling.

The Future: What Not to Do and How Not to Not Do It

The point of this sketch is to carry us back to what I called above the liberal "anti-market" ideology. I have argued that that ideology appears by virtue of its enlightened sneering to oppose "markets" and to resist their undesirable "social outcomes"; but that in fact the ideology does not oppose markets but instead contents itself with a polite request that the university be cordoned off from their operations. This doesn't work. The ideology does not deserve to be repudiated because it is "reformist" but because it has a class basis. That is to say, it assumes that the "values" which it wishes to protect ought to be protected only *within* the University and therefore (if implicitly) only on behalf of those who have access to it. And there is a second problem. Conducting a reified tirade against the stupefactions of interested exchange and the idiot grunting of its public policy slaves is surely all well and good, and it might well be a noble thing to prevent the market from encroaching too far into Higher Education, where, who knows, it might wreak all sorts

17 • In March 2011 the NUS and the Confederation of British Industry (Britain's largest business lobby group) co-published a report aimed at "informing" prospective students of exactly what "soft skills" in self-mortification and passionate servility employers would expect of them. www.cbi.org.uk/pdf/cbi-nus-employability-report.pdf].

18 • news.bbc.co.uk/1/hi/education/7213127.stm

19 • The best and most provocative recent writing on the jobless dead-end is Endnotes, #2, though the articles in that volume deal chiefly (and understandably) with global tendencies in the production of consolidated surplus populations rather than with the tribulations of accumulation at the national level.

of havoc on the *life of the mind*, but the limitation of this safeguard is that however much money might in principle be canalised into the swag-bags and current account of the UK University Research Councils — *students will continue to graduate.*[20] (Professors, of course, do not.) And while it might seem somewhat impertinent to conclude an analysis of UK student struggle in 2010–11 with a discussion of life *outside of the university*, or to slough off to the footnotes and margins all discussion of the good things that do go on in UK Higher Education institutions, the exercise of analytic tact is misguided. The market decrees that students will be thrown out of the university (with or without their certification) even if "analysis" of student struggle remains fixed there, in ascetic restraint, paring its fingernails and hoping vainly for a research grant. What is the future of Humanities Education in the UK? There isn't any point in asking this question in this forum: if humanities education is worth anything then it will not die after "students" and other members of the proletariat new and old fight for the life-resources which provide the precondition for that education. And yet the riposte swells up: doesn't "higher" education (as in education finer and more spiritual) require independence from the "social"? Doesn't it require autonomy? But this doesn't mean very much. There must be better forms of autonomy than the type required for the production of "basic" research which — we learn from a University lobby group — contributes vastly more to the value of HE licensing and spin-outs (the sector-specific jargon for commercial enterprise) than so-called "applied" research.[21] These forms would be better worked out spontaneously in the process of collective action than "in principle" at the end of an article. While it might be true that contemplative reflection can in certain respects contribute to the cultivation of social antagonisms, the moment that the struggle for "autonomy" lapses into demands for "blue-sky thinking" it becomes

20 • I've assumed for the purpose of this argument that money could easily be transferred back into Higher Education by means of taxation, but given that it is widely recognised that per capita funding for students has been wretchedly inadequate for a couple of decades for all students excepting those at Oxford and Cambridge, and also that the sensibly realistic sounding centre-left proposals for tax levies to fund undergraduate teaching would frighten the capricious banking and financial services sector on which the economy is so reliant, it isn't clear that an adequately resourced HE sector would do anything to promote growth. What would it do? On the one hand it would produce more "skills" in a market already saturated with them; and on the other hand it might drive away some (presumably small) fraction of the demand for "skilled" labour which currently obtains. This is just to suggest one more internal tension in the social democratic defence of free University education which shares all of its terms with free marketeer's intellectual case for its demolition.

21 • The lobby group in question is the Russell Group, the consortium of the twenty or so richest and most powerful universities. The group spends most of its time lamenting the inefficiency of smaller and poorer institutions in the hope that the closure of the same might earn them (i.e., the constituents of the Russell Group) an extra buck in concentrated funding. www.ft.com/cms/s/0/274db410-3204-11df-a8d1-00144feabdc0.html#axzz1WbHcp9Ja

the inalienable possession of the official management theory which invented that category and which is stabilised by its propagation.

Quality Education

It is now 31 August. Two or three minutes ago I received an email which states that 87 departments in Greek universities are now under occupation. The Greek students are acting in protest against a recent education bill, part of the imposing edifice of "austerity" (the word is in this case infinitely euphemistic) now being hammered through the country's fine and democratic parliament. In the last week, two Chilean students have been murdered by state police; both were participants in a much older and more mature student struggle than the one currently in remission in the UK. In other words, the UK student struggle from 2010–2011, with all of its smashed glass and all of its waves and networks, is already very much old news, as indeed are all of the associated acronyms — NCAFC, NUS, EMA, EAN.[22] Even in the national context the domestic spokespersons of capital are much more hotly concerned with the riots which took place between 6 and 10 August. On the "left" those riots are still treated with a stunned confusion: who among the hordes of those who looted during those five days can be selected as a spokesperson? And how can we communicate our *ideas* to a political subject who has about as much interest in being the "new" 1968 as Guy Debord had in being the new Walt Disney? In response to this quandary, and in conclusion, one lesson of late 2010 stands out. As was argued above, students repudiated the suggestion that their "rebellion" was no more than a paroxysm of middle-class discontent by pointing to the working class teenagers who attended the street demonstrations which they organised. These teenagers were the "EMA kids". The label did more than *stick*: it implied an analysis. The analysis in turn implied that what the "kids" had to protest against was the withdrawal of their below-subsistence grant. This was of course in part a claim of convenience, necessary for a practical politics structured around "inclusive" demands. It was, in other words, the sort of thing that could be crammed into a press release and floated out into the media ether to fuel the enmity of proto-fascist newspaper columnists. But it was also an honest assumption. What the "middle class" students had to offer the "working class" college kids was an organisational framework in which those college kids could protest against a particular act of state-led resource-withdrawal. And in fact when the college kids acted "disruptively" or violently the middle-class students often became perturbed and spoke in wounded tones of

22 • National Campaign Against Fees and Cuts(NCAFC), National Union of Students (NUS), Education Maitenance Allowance (EMA), Education Activist Network (EAN).
23 • For gratuitous evidence of the just-mentioned, see www.guardian.co.uk/education/video/2010/dec/10/student-fees-protest-london-video

their beautiful pacifism and their high ideals, and tugged dolorously at their keffiyehs.[23] That EMA was a pathetic band-aid tossed by the state to "lower income" teenagers in compensation for a lifetime spent being churned through an underresourced and overcrowded state education sector (and for a thousand other iniquities better known to EMA recipients than to their bourgeois comrades) was not on the collective bargaining cards.

But what student demonstrations offered to the working class teenagers *in fact* was not an "organisational framework". What the demonstrations offered was a material setting in which working class students could partake in aggressive and confrontational collective action *in conditions of relative security*. It is difficult to make this point without sounding as if one is speaking through a mouthful of Habermasian ideal speech situation. The students did not offer to the working class college kids an ideal speech situation (more than this: all the execrable sign-waving and sloganeering at the demos ensured that the students didn't offer even a passable one): but in spite of the assumption that working class kids just wanted to keep their EMA, it is nevertheless true that the student demonstrations and the middle-class demonstrators did offer to working class college kids something for which they had a use. This was not the rhetorical straitjacket of a sensible demand politics, and nor was it thirty quid a week and the promise, sometimes in the future, of a worthless certificate, or in any case it was not *just these*, because the "student" demonstrations also offered to the college protestors the material suspension of the balance of forces whose permanent imparity is active in determining the results of working class struggle. What that material suspension provided for a lot of kids, in other words, was the opportunity for an intense collective expression of social agency whose object was not peremptorily confined to an inadequate programme of state provision but which could outstrip the limits defined by everyday (isolated) struggle against repressive authority, and which moreover could know each time that it clattered against a riot shield *exactly who was on its side*. And as the left toils to imagine what ideas it could "offer" to the inscrutable young men and women who went rioting in early august, and as the job market continues to stagnate, and the profits of McDonalds and Tesco to rise, and as the academics continue to bid for a role on the market steering committee and to dream, not of *1968*, but of *1965*, and as the EMA scheme ends and the housing benefits plunge, and as new students begin to arrive on bright autumn mornings at the campuses of their chosen training camps — this is something which might yet be worth learning.

For as long as the material conditions in the universities have not been equalised, "access" to university, whether or not it is universal, and whether it costs £9,000 per year or nothing, will continue to mean access to educational commodities of wildly discrepant value, distributed across institutions whose "diversity of missions" at last promotes nothing besides a diversity of class positions. Shall we ask then, access to what? And access to what with what exit onto what? These are questions, in good Beckettian prosody, which will have to be asked in Beckettian fashion, which is to say, again and again. Middle class students might piously hope that working class teenagers will be allowed to "access" universities and become more like them; but in fact the similarity is more likely to become visible not at the "point of access" to universities, but, instead, at their exits. And it's the view from the exit, from which can be seen the greatest expanse of nothing at all, which will perhaps suggest most provocatively how universities might be "reformed". •

Danny Hayward is a writer based in London.

Quality Education

Dutch Austerity and Free Academies: An Interview With Katja Diefenbach

Karl Lydén

KARL LYDÉN: The Jan van Eyck Academie is one of three post-academic institutions in the Netherlands — along with de Ateliers and the Rijksakademie — to lose its funding after 2012. You are running the open research project *After 1968. On the Notion of the Political in Post-Marxist Theory*, with guest lecturers such as Michael Löwy, Roberto Esposito, and Jacques Rancière to mention a few: given the critical insights of such a project, it didn't perhaps come as a surprise that the current government would launch these cuts?

KATJA DIEFENBACH: To give a precise explanation for the Netherland's swing to the populist right, whose most recent aggravation we witnessed with the constitution of a minority government built in late 2010 by right-Liberals (VVD) and Christian-Democrats (CDA) with support from Geert Wilders's Islamophobic *Partij voor de Vrijheid* (PVV), is not so easy. What one can immediately detect is the well-known political model the new government defends: it stands for a combination of workfare and austerity politics with fear-mongering security rhetoric and the enforcement of anti-migrant, in particular Islamophobic measures. Geert Wilders's party represents in this combination a radical right of a new type: it is highlighting Europe's Judeo-Christian heritage; it avoids contacts with the traditional currents of the radical right including their anti-Semitism;

it presents itself explicitly as non-extremist and democratic; it focuses on an anti-Islam mobilization of society's center. So it's no wonder that Geert Wilders is quite a figure in the Islamophobic populist Right; he has been invited to speak at Ground Zero by the SIOA network, *Stop Islamization of America*; he has been key speaker at an event organized by the former Berlin Christian Democrat René Stadtkewitz, who recently built a party after PVV's model, etc.

The drastic cutbacks in culture that passed the Dutch parliament in the summer have for quite a while been accompanied by an anti-elitist and anti-establishment campaign, in which the image of the *Jan met de pet*, the average Joe, was pitted against the image of a left-wing elite and their splurging cultural apparatuses. Briefly speaking, the strategy is: cultural projects or institutions — except the key traditional houses — have to finance themselves through market forces and private funding. However, the cutbacks in culture, which the new State Secretary Halbe Zijlstra (VVD) so happily supported, are just one part of a huge austerity package; the 200 millions that are supposed to be saved there are outdone by 1,5 billion in the social budget, 2,5 billion in homecare, and further cuts in the support of disabled people, people with mental illness, youth, etc. The campaigns and petitions that called for a defense of the cultural sector rarely addressed the broader logic of austerity politics and their connection to anti-migrant politics, which are particularly strong in the Netherlands. In the new integration guidelines, the Dutch Minister of the Interior, Piet Hein Donner (CDA), offered the entire canon of racist populism: abandonment of multiculturalism, primacy of "the values of the Dutch society", obligatory integration courses, deportation if one does not pass the course, ban on burqas, cut of subsidies for migrant institutions, etc.

The real question of the Dutch condition, however, seems still to lie somewhere else. What is at stake, I think, is to understand the conjuncture: Why did it happen that the Netherlands early on turned to neoliberal and workfare politics? How did, from a certain moment onwards, the technocratic and culturalist elements of the preceding liberal model of consensus and multiculturalism transform into elements of populist aggression and a swing to the right? Why and when did the radical Dutch Left — the Provo movement of the 1960s, the squatters of the 1980s and 1990s, the radio-pirates and net-activists — lose their momentum? What role did the transgressive mode of right-wing populism play that Theo van Gogh represented, which articulated a rather avant-gardist narrative belonging to an urban bohemia swung to the right? I think it is not without importance that we have experienced a rising right bohemia, which supplements the dumb discourse of Wilders and his ilk with a more sophisticated discourse advocating gay and women's rights, drug or alcohol use, the right to excessiveness and urban life, to which the stereotype of migrant insular conservatism is opposed.

KL: The "dumbness" is certainly evident. Previous Jan van Eyck director Koen Brams characterized it well in relation to a cultural symposium organized by government: "But who did Monique Vogelzang, Director for the Arts, and Judith van Kranendonk, Director General for Culture and Media at the Ministry of Education, Culture and Science, invite to keep us directors [of the post-academic institutes] on our toes? The following four speakers: Gerlach Cerfontaine, chairman of the Supervisory Board of the Onze Lieve Vrouwe Hospital in

Quality Education

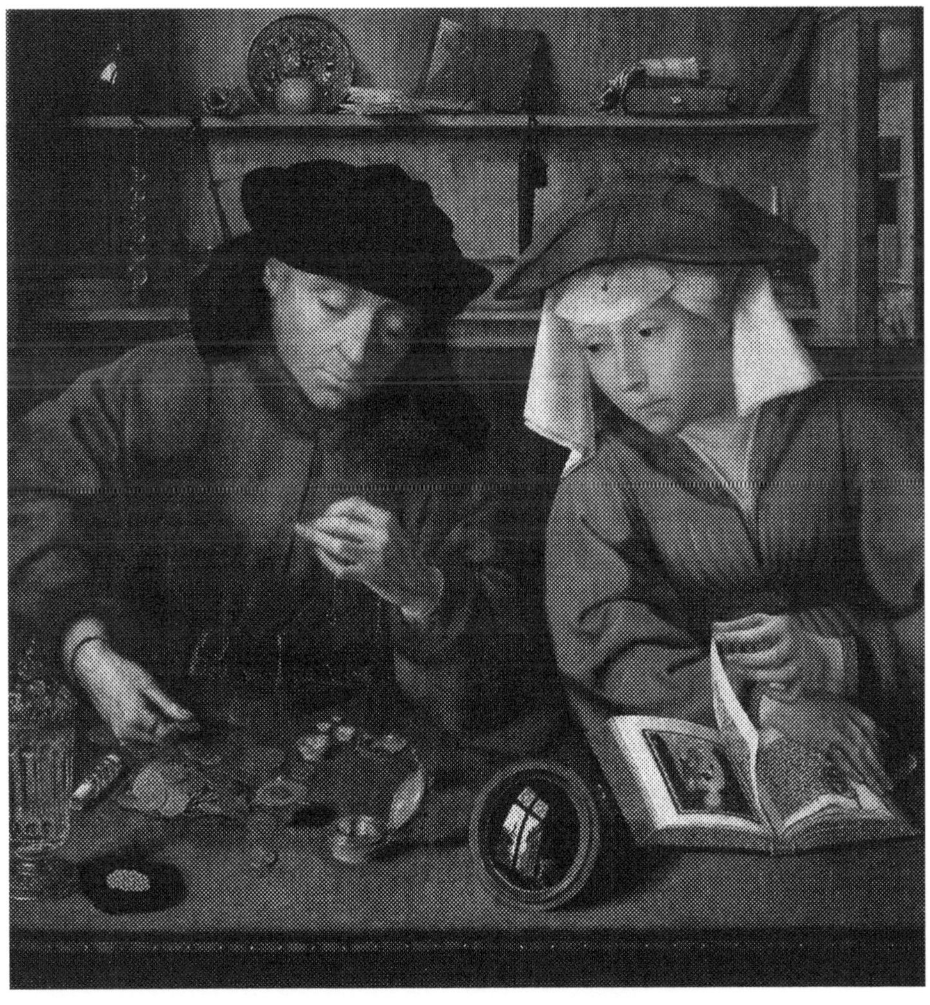

Amsterdam, Johan Wakkie, director of the Royal Dutch Hockey Association, Jildou van der Bijl, chief editor of *Linda* magazine, and Bart de Boer, chairman of the board of directors of the Efteling theme park. [...] Judith van Kranendonk sat in on the proceedings and was visibly delighted to hear the brilliant suggestions from the head of the Efteling, when he boasted how he had managed to entice more people to his theme park by building a higher and bigger roller coaster."

But isn't the Dutch situation remarkable also in *how* neoliberal it is? In State Secretary Halbe Zijlstra's policy letter *Beyond quality: a new vision of cultural policy*, he states that rather than attending research institutes, artists should buy their post-academic educations as "services in the field of in-depth practice or further training", which of course seems more than unlikely. This extreme belief in a free market could be described by Michel Foucault's *Security, Territory, Population*, where he analyzes the liberal idea of the market as a place of "veridiction": the market will not only set prices, but also determine the true and correct form of government.

KD: What we can learn from Foucault is a strong theory of the conjuncture. What does he emphasize at the beginning of his 1978 lecture series, *Security, Territory, Population*? He pinpoints that the governmental mechanisms having emerged with the capitalist mode of production cannot be grasped in the development of a historical law — the unfolding of one contradiction — but in terms of an immanent causality without inner sense, telos or subject. Governmental mechanisms, he stresses, are applied in an open space: they regulate the social milieu through probability techniques. In comparison to disciplinary techniques — applied in a confined space, capacitating bodies through prescribing their movements and productions — they are not prescriptive but preemptive. They manage a social problem through the administration of the effects generated by domination and exploitation. Two aspects are key here. First, as you said, modern governmentality presupposes a certain mode of freedom, a freedom immanent to the techniques of power guaranteeing the permanent possibility to change, convert and adjust the composition of social regulations: freedom of circulation, if you will, a freedom that requires a mobilized subject that has a couple of options and choices at its disposal. If we have to define this mode of freedom, we have to say it's an optional speculation integrating the future into the reproduction of the present. Neoliberal governmentality radicalizes this preemptive, anticipatory and cybernetic aspect of regulation. A second aspect comes into play here. Neoliberal politics of security are not eliminating disciplinary or juridical mechanisms; they arrange them anew. Disparate mechanisms are combined and the conjuncture

◂ **Quentin Massys, The Money Changer and his Wife, Oil on panel, 71 × 68 cm (28 × 26.8 in), 1514.**

is marked by multi-axial or multi-polar developments: hard exclusions and rigid disciplinatory techniques are combined with flexible integrations. Truth then is nothing but the process through which these combinations reproduce themselves by reacting on their effects. However, it would obviously be a big error to think post-Fordist mechanisms of global valorization and preemptive security politics would not coexist with ideological productions. The Netherlands is one of many examples to show how self-regulatory processes do combine with religious, racist and neo-conservative narratives of supremacy.

KL: Could we then, alongside this re-disciplinarization, describe the Dutch context in terms of a biopolitics? Don't we here have a complete downscaling of public services — higher education, healthcare, social benefits — producing a sort of extreme liberal subject, which would amount to little more than a biological entity, one which is already an asset in itself, something like living labor, or even naked life?

KL: I would be careful to use one single philosopheme or principle to define the logic of the given situation, its mode of production and type of regulation. There is a remarkable disagreement between Agamben and Negri about the notion of naked life and the meaning of biopolitics. Agamben insists on analyzing biopolitics in exceptionalist terms, by a mechanism of excluding inclusion that grasps life, in order to abandon it, to expose it to measurements of an exception-law. Negri, in contrast, puts forward that naked life is nothing but sheer human potentiality — the mere capacity of attention, improvisation, coordination — that he considers to be the key productive forces of today's imperial capitalism. Despite this disagreement, Negri and Agamben alike presuppose that there is an ontological or existential foundation of biopolitics. Both think that potentiality — be it the capacity to act or the capacity to tarry with the inactive — is the power that fuels the capitalist and governmental machine. Hence, both positions are characterized by a striking reductionism that shortcuts the heterogeneity of the conjuncture in terms of a single ontological instance that articulates the principle of the historical development. Foucault and also Althusser insisted that there is no such principle, but always only provisional tendencies that are expressed through complex and even disparate mechanisms. With the hypothesis of a neoliberalism of naked life, one could not think the differences existing between the flexible mechanisms applied in the economization of education and the rigid mechanisms applied in the regulation of migration, between the flexible precarization of the creative class and the rigid precarization of the low service sector — janitors, security guards or call center workers. As for the Dutch situation, one would have to analyze the internal differential of the current austerity politics that combines cutbacks in culture with the tightening of prosecution (three strikes law), new workfare measures and rigid anti-migration rules.

KL: If the Bologna Process is considered by some as a final disavowal of the Humboldtian university (and its principles of knowledge before skills, independent research, *Einsamkeit* and *Freiheit* and so on), do you think we can consider the current events — the current dismantling of higher education all over Europe — as a kind of revoking of the universal access to higher education that was being initiated in the sixties, when working class youth for the first time entered into the university?

KD: The universities of the 1960s were a laboratory in which two developments encountered each other and were intertwined. On one hand, the universities were remodeled along the Fordist type of regulation implying mass access to higher education. On the other hand, the universities, in particular the institutes of *Geisteswissenschaften* and the Humanities, became an intellectual laboratory of the 1960s radical Left. What the militant students experimented in the 1960s and 1970s was not Humboldt's vision. What was at stake, was the attempt to apply to the university itself the debates of the day that stretched from non-dogmatic Marxism to critical theory, feminism, anti-imperialism and the new post-structuralist currents in philosophy. The key was the critique of the authority of knowledge itself, its functionality in a scientific and technological system of production and the continuation of the division between manual and intellectual labor. The university became a place at which the disciplinatory and productive effectivity of knowledge and education was questioned and new currents of radical thought produced. For a couple of years, the universities transformed into places of struggle, in which one could experience an existentialist dissidence that at its best moments opened up decentered, expending and anomalous forms of life. When the reform university at Paris Vincennes was established, the militant students discussed the extent to which its left-liberal model institutionalized and normalized the radical spirit of 1968.

However, since the 1980s we witness the vanishing of both aspects, the Fordist model of mass education and the university as intellectual laboratory of the radical left. For thirty years now we are entering into a tightening process of an economization of university education. The challenge we are facing is not only to analyze the passage from a Fordist to a post-Fordist model of education, but also to problematize the struggles of the 1960s, the militant energy which dissipated into the society and helped to induce a gigantic wave of modernization. The creative class that populates the humanities institutes and the cultural sector, embodying a new type of normalized dissidence that constantly strives to combine social subversion with social success, presents a figure of passage between the militant students of the 1960s and a new figure of intellectual radicality still to come.

KL: So, what to do? How do we formulate a critique? Isn't there a risk of either producing a mere conservative critique — a critique striving to keep things the way they are, one which might attain a certain support, but which fails to recognize the systemic character of the crisis — or, on the other hand, producing a critique so systemic that it fails to see the differences and specificities at hand?

KD: This is a difficult question. If one is objecting to austerity measures, one tends to defend one's position, one tries to keep the level one has, to save the institution at which one works. I have no problem with the conservative character of this first mode of reaction, when one simply says "No!" to a certain change that removes the social rights one has. However, in the case of the Jan van Eyck Academy, which happens to have been for quite a time an intellectual laboratory of contemporary radical thought and neo-avant-garde practices in fine arts and design, we quickly realized that the protest against the social and cultural cutbacks is far too weak to change the course of the new government. In the given situation, the new director of the Jan van Eyck Academy attempts to save the institution under the conditions set by the cultural policy of the new government. The probable effect will be that the institution might be maintained but at the price of losing its singular features: its international quality, its aesthetic and intellectual radicality, its programmatic consistency. Though the members of staff and the research fellows initially agreed on defending the academy's Bauhaus model, its combined education in theory, design and fine arts and its internationality, it looks as if the Jan van Eyck will turn into a fifty percent Dutch institution that highlights its program in fine arts. In November we organized a roundtable on austerity politics and right-wing populism at the Academy, in order to open up at least a minimal space of intellectual disagreement with the Dutch swing to the right.

KL: Could our response to this dismantling of higher education all over Europe also take other forms? I'm specifically thinking of your work with b_books, the collective Berlin book shop that also functions as a publisher of queer theory, political theory, and critical urbanism, as well as a venue for talks and debates, and even as a pirate cinema.

KD: What people find interesting about b_books, I assume, is the practice of building an autonomous space of

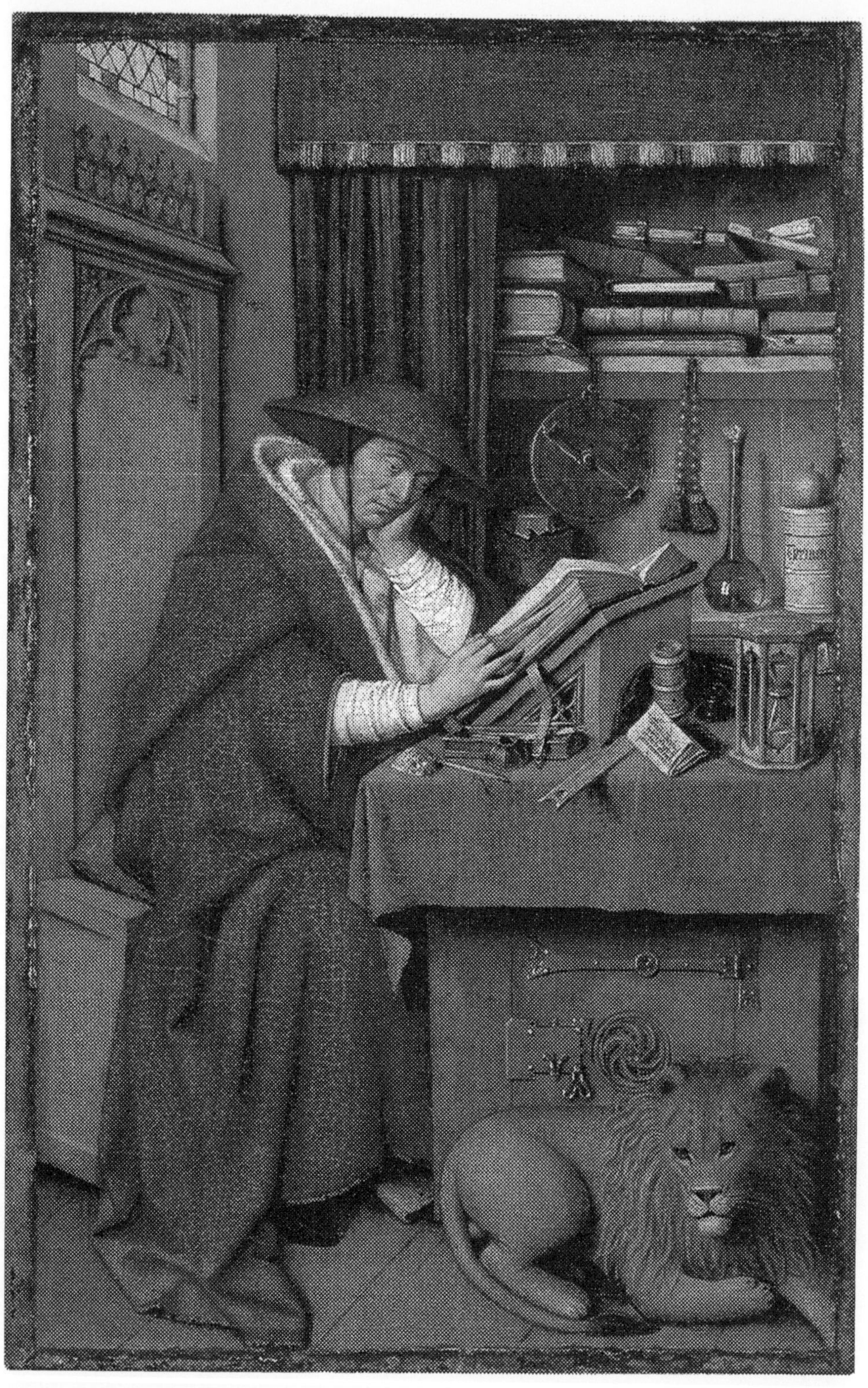

◂
Jan van Eyck, *St Jerome in His Study*, Oil on panel, 20.6 × 13.3 cm (8.1 × 5.2 in), 1442.

Quality Education

aesthetic and intellectual production that enables a certain political interventionism. To me, it is also important that we attempt to establish a non-conventional model of micro-economics, in which one does not get paid according to the time and intensity of labor one spends, but jobs and activities are circulating and gains are shared. However, as so often with alternative collectives, the economic reality is also determined by self-exploitation and the re-occurrence of divisions of labor and unequal payment. You have to take into account that b_books stems from a very specific political sequence of Berlin in the 1990s, in which parts of the (post)autonomous movement, the music and arts scene joined forces to attack the increasing racism and nationalism in Germany after the fall of the Wall. But can we see b_books as a general model of alternative education? I don't think so. You can't simply repeat this gesture in today's conjuncture: this particular non-university, non-shop, non-gallery and non-club, which simultaneously was all of these things at once. b_books's radical momentum has for quite some time exhausted itself in a situation in which everyone opens a bar, a shop or a project space, and DIY is multiplied on a commercial level in a city, in which creative micro-companies are an explicit part of its economical and image production. There seems to be a constant growth of critical and experimental events happening in Berlin, but they relate less and less to political activism and are more integrated into the professional apparatuses of academia and culture. So, no, I don't really see b_books as a model of alternative education. Today's questions rather seem to be how to dissociate critical intellectual and cultural production from the apparatuses of normality, and how to build radical political coalitions that bridge the huge gaps between the different positions of precarity and domination. And — it is surely at stake on an existential level — how to lead a life that is not terrorized by the production of sense in the form of one's activities and occupations, but one that opens up to non-sense, self-loss, expenditure and inactivity. •

Katja Diefenbach is advising researcher at the theory department of the Jan van Eyck Academy in Maastricht and member of the publishing house and bookshop collective b_books in Berlin.

www.ingramcontent.com/pod-product-compliance
Ingram Content Group UK Ltd.
Pitfield, Milton Keynes, MK11 3LW, UK
UKHW041829200726
13854UKWH00002BA/888

9 789186 883072